THE APPROAC

FIRST PART

THE APPROACH TO ROME—THE VIA APPIA,
most famous of the Roman roads

THE APPROACH
TO LATIN

BY
JAMES PATERSON, M.A.
FORMERLY HEADMASTER, HILLHEAD HIGH SCHOOL, GLASGOW

AND

EDWIN G. MACNAUGHTON, M.A.
FORMERLY RECTOR, HAMILTON ACADEMY

FIRST PART

OLIVER AND BOYD

OLIVER & BOYD
Robert Stevenson House, 1—3 Baxter's Place
Leith Walk, Edinburgh EH1 3BB

A Division of Longman Group UK Ltd

ISBN 0 05 000292 9

First Published   1938
Twenty-fourth Impression (revised)   1968
Thirty-ninth Impression   1987

Produced by Longman Group (FE) Ltd
Printed in Hong Kong

PREFACE

IN preparing this Primer we have kept two ends in view—first, the provision of a sound grammatical foundation; second, the maintenance of interest by a fresh, lively and many-sided application of the formal elements.

In the 51 lessons of the book a selected minimum of grammar is gradually unfolded, set out clearly, and grouped in a natural way. While aiming generally at conciseness, we have not avoided repetition or fullness of expression where warranted by the requirements of the pupil.

Special vocabularies are provided, one for each lesson. These vary in length with the exigencies of the A exercises. The longest, however, should not prove too much for the acquisitive memory of the eleven-to-twelve-year-olds; and essential words are kept " alive " by repetition in subsequent exercises. The total vocabulary slightly exceeds 600 words.

In the exercises the A sections regularly consist of connected passages dealing with Roman life and legend, and presently giving a skeleton history of the Republic. Each passage is written specially for the place it occupies. No grammar, vocabulary or syntax is anticipated; there is the maximum repetition of words and phrases. Given thorough preparation of grammar and vocabulary, the pupil can acquire a facility in translation which will enable him to advance to the unusually lengthy passages later in the book with a speed, zest and confidence which are of incalculable value in maintaining interest and banishing the sense of frustration and boredom.

The B sections and the Revision exercises are intended to secure the formal accuracy which was—and is—the justification of the traditional approach to the subject.

Due account has been taken of the varying requirements of schools and pupils. For an able class devoting five or six periods per week to Latin the A and B exercises constitute a complete course ; where time is less or pace is slower an adequate course will consist of the A, *plus* a selection from the B, sections, or *vice versa*, according as translation or composition is stressed. A generous supply of C exercises provides extra *pabulum* for selected classes or individual pupils of special aptitude.

Whichever of these courses be followed, it is hoped that time will be found for part, at least, of the word-studies and other interest-material. Here our aim has been suggestion rather than exhaustive treatment. Thus, in the Word Studies, attention has been confined to more difficult or less obvious derivatives, leaving discussion of easier words to teacher and class.

It remains to express obligations. We have to thank Dr. McGlynn for the Latin of the Songs. May pupils find delight as well as profit in his work ! To Mr. E. I. Denoon, of Daniel Stewart's College, Edinburgh, who read the work in proof, and to others who scrutinised the book at one stage or another, we are indebted for correction and criticism. Finally, thanks are due to the artists who have so admirably rendered the spirit of the book in their illustrations.

J. P.
E. G. M.

PREFACE TO THE SECOND EDITION

THE favourable reception accorded to the book has fortunately provided us with this early opportunity of making some minor corrections and supplying a few omissions.

J. P.
E. G. M.

CONTENTS

AN INTRODUCTION FOR THE BEGINNER

BEFORE you begin your first Latin lesson here are a few facts about the language and about methods of study which you should read over carefully and keep constantly in mind.

In the first place, what of the Latin alphabet and the pronunciation of Latin ? Well, in these matters you should not find much difficulty. The Latin alphabet is the same as that of English, except that it does not possess the letters *j* and *w*. Pronunciation is very straightforward, too. Attend closely to your teacher's pronunciation, say words exactly as he says them, constantly practise saying Latin words aloud and ask the teacher whenever you are in doubt as to how a word should be sounded. Regarding consonants, here are two points to remember. First, the letters *c, g, t* have always a hard sound in Latin—precisely the sound you have in the English words *c*aw, *g*o and *t*oe. Secondly, when the letter *i* comes immediately in front of a vowel in the same syllable, it has the sound of the English *y* in a word like *y*es. Hence we must pronounce the Latin word " **iam** " as if it were "*yam.*" The five vowels *a, e, i, o, u* call for a little more care. Notice how your teacher gives each of these sometimes a long sound, sometimes a short, quick sound. The length of a vowel is called its " quantity." In learning Latin make it a matter of personal pride to be absolutely exact with your quantities. Here again the golden rule is—listen carefully to your teacher

1

and imitate his pronunciation. To help you further, we have indicated long vowels in this book by putting the sign above them, e.g. ī. Sometimes, also, where a mistake is very likely to occur, we have marked a short vowel by putting the sign above it, e.g. ĕ. One last remark about pronunciation. As you listen to Latin words being said you will soon realise that they have a stress accent. *Now, the stress never falls on the last syllable of a Latin word.* Hence, in two-syllable words be careful to put the stress on the first syllable. As regards bigger words, begin by imitating your teacher; you will soon find yourself accenting them quite correctly by instinct.

We must now say a little about the most striking feature of Latin. That is certainly its great wealth of inflections. An inflection is a change in the form of a word. Inflections may be made for various purposes. For instance, a noun may be inflected to indicate number, e.g. singular *boy*, but plural *boys*; or to indicate case, e.g. nominative *boy*, but possessive *boy's*. We may inflect a verb to indicate person, e.g. *I run*, but *he runs*; or to indicate number, e.g. *he runs*, but *they run*; or again to indicate tense, e.g. *I run, I ran*. You see then that English has several inflections. Latin, however, possesses infinitely more. Indeed, the greatest difference between English and Latin is that while English has lost most of its inflections Latin is a highly inflected language.

You will find that Latin verbs in particular are rich in inflections. They use inflections to indicate all kinds of differences—like difference in person, difference in number, difference in tense, and even in voice and mood. According to the inflections which they use Latin verbs fall into four great classes called conjugations. The class or conjugation to which a verb belongs is shown us by the ending of its present infinitive active. For example, the present infinitive active of all verbs of the first conjugation ends in -āre, e.g. ămāre, to love.

Bearing in mind what we have said about pronunciation and inflections, you are now ready to start your Latin lessons proper. You will find that in this book a lesson consists of a piece of grammar, a special vocabulary (given at the back of the book), and then sets of exercises on the grammar and the vocabulary. Always begin by learning the grammar and the vocabulary. And notice that nothing will do but the most thorough learning. You must know your grammar just as thoroughly and as well as you know your multiplication table. Thus, before ever you begin Exercise 1, you must know, and be able to give, the Latin for " he loves," " we love," " they love," and so on, without a moment's hesitation and without needing to think at all. Remember that the very first step you take in Latin is the foundation for the second step, and so on all through the subject. The whole secret of success lies in absolutely mastering one step before you take the next.

And success in Latin is well worth while. It means that you possess and can use powers of memory, observation and reasoning ; it means that you become familiar with the language, literature and history—in fact with the very mind—of one of the most wonderful nations that ever lived ; it means that you acquire a deeper and wider understanding of English literature and of the English language ; it means that you secure a great aid to the learning and real understanding of many modern languages ; it means that you can tackle any hard, worth-while job honestly and well.

Now you are eager to get to Lesson 1 and what lies beyond. Good luck to you—and, *be thorough!*

II

FIRST CONJUGATION

§ 1. Present Indicative Active of **amāre**, to love.

PERSON	SINGULAR.	PLURAL.
1	**ám-ō** I love	**amā-mus** we love
2	**ámā-s** you love	**amā-tis** you love
3	**áma-t** he, she, it loves	**áma-nt** they love

Notes.—(1) The person-endings **-ō, -s, -t, -mus, -tis, -nt** indicate differences of person ; pronouns are not required.

(2) The present tense of **amāre** may also mean :
I am loving, you are loving, etc.
I do love, you do love, etc.

EXERCISE 1

A

1. Amās.
2. Superant.
3. Amātis.
4. Laudant.
5. Superātis.
6. Laudat.
7. Laudō.
8. Superāmus.
9. Laudāmus.
10. Amat.

B

1. We praise.
2. They love.
3. You (*pl.*) praise.
4. She praises.
5. You (*pl.*) love.

6. He overcomes.
7. You (*s.*) overcome.
8. It overcomes.
9. You (*s.*) are loving.
10. She is overcoming.

ROMAN GREETINGS AND FAREWELLS

Salvē, Good morning! Good day! (*when speaking to one person*).

Salvēte,   ,,   ,,   (*when speaking to more than one person*).

Valē, Good-bye! (*when speaking to one person*).

Valēte,   ,,   (*when speaking to more than one person*).

III

FIRST CONJUGATION—*continued*

§ **2.** Future Indicative Active of **amāre,** to love.

Person	Singular	Plural
1	**amā-bō** I shall love	**amā-bimus** we shall love
2	**amā-bis** you will love	**amā-bitis** you will love
3	**amā-bit** he, she, it will love	**amā-bunt** they will love

EXERCISE 2

A

1. Salvēte !
2. Amābunt.
3. Parābitis.
4. Portābunt.
5. Superābimus.
6. Festīnābit.
7. Ubi habitās ?
8. Festīnābimus.
9. Laudābimus.
10. Ubi habitātis ?

B

1. You (s.) will carry.
2. They will hasten.
3. I shall overcome.
4. Where does he live ?
5. They are carrying.
6. He will prepare.
7. You (pl.) will love.
8. You (pl.) will hasten.
9. You (s.) will praise.
10. They will carry.

C

1. Where do you (s.) live ?
2. I am overcoming.
3. They are preparing.
4. He will carry.
5. He praises.
6. We hasten.
7. You (s.) will hasten.
8. They will prepare.
9. You (pl.) will praise.
10. Good morning ! (s.).

LATIN PROVERBS

The Romans were an intensely practical people, shrewd and full of common sense. Therefore, as you might expect, their language abounds in proverbs and pithy expressions in which much experience of life is condensed. Here are a few such sayings :

Festīnā lentē, Hasten slowly (i.e. *The more hurry the less speed*).

Labor omnia vincit, Work overcomes all difficulties.

Nōn sine pulvere palma, The prize cannot be won without effort.

IV

FIRST CONJUGATION—*continued*

§ 3. Imperfect Indicative Active of **amāre**, to love.

PERSON	SINGULAR	PLURAL
1	**amā-bam** I was loving	**amā-bāmus** we were loving
2	**amā-bās** you were loving	**amā-bātis** you were loving
3	**amā-bat** he, she, it was loving	**amā-bant** they were loving

Note.—The Imperfect Indicative Active of **amāre** may also mean :
I used to love, you used to love, etc.
I loved, you loved, etc.

EXERCISE 3

A

1. Nārrābat.
2. Ubi habitābant ?
3. Vulnerābāmus.
4. Amābimus.
5. Vāstās.

6. Vulnerābās.
7. Amābātis.
8. Nārrābam.
9. Quō festīnābimus ?
10. Vāstābis.

B

1. We were laying waste.
2. I was telling.
3. They used to tell.
4. Where did you (*s.*) live ?
5. He will wound.

6. He was wounding.
7. You (*pl.*) were loving.
8. You (*s.*) were telling.
9. We used to tell.
10. I was laying waste.

C

1. Whither is he hastening ?
2. You (*pl.*) are overcoming.
3. I am preparing.
4. You (*s.*) will lay waste.
5. He will wound.
6. He is wounding.
7. You (*s.*) were hastening.
8. We were praising.
9. She will relate.
10. They used to praise.

WORD STUDY

One very important reason for the study of Latin is that so many English words are of Latin origin. Of course it is quite possible to look up these words in an English dictionary, and so find their meaning. But just as a radio set is a much more interesting thing if you have built it yourself, and your cycle is a far more intimate friend if you can assemble it from a heap of bolts and screws and pieces of steel, so language is far more interesting if you know something of how it was made. It gives a fresh interest to words to know their origins. For instance, how much more vivid such an ordinary word as " engine " becomes when we find that it has developed from a Latin word **ingenium,** which meant first *cleverness* or *ability* and then a *clever idea*. Again, take the word " omnibus." This is not merely derived from Latin, but is an actual Latin word meaning *for all*. Not a bad name for a public conveyance !

Already you know Latin enough to trace quite a number of English words to their Latin beginnings, and hence find out their meaning. See if you can tell from their root meanings what are meant by : a *portable* gramophone, a short *narrative*, a *devastating* wind, an *insuperable* difficulty, a *habitable* country, a *laudable* attempt, a *vulnerable* point.

V

THE FIRST DECLENSION

§ 4. **mēnsa, mēnsae,** *f.,* a table.

CASE	SINGULAR		PLURAL	
Nom.	**mēns-ă**	a table (*subj.*)	**mēns-ae**	tables (*subj.*)
Voc.	**mēns-ă**	table! O table	**mēns-ae**	tables ! O tables !
Acc.	**mēns-am**	a table (*obj.*)	**mēns-ās**	tables (*obj.*)
Gen.	**mēns-ae**	of a table	**mēns-ārum**	of tables
Dat.	**mēns-ae**	to, for a table	**mēns-īs**	to, for tables
Abl.	**mēns-ā**	by, with, from a table	**mēns-īs**	b y, w i t h, from tables

Notes.—(1) The *Nominative* is the case of the subject.

The *Vocative* corresponds to English Nominative of Address.

The *Accusative* is the case of the direct object.

The *Genitive* corresponds to English Possessive Case.

The *Dative* is the case of the indirect object (usually marked in English by the presence of " to " or " for ").

The *Ablative* has a meaning marked in English by the prepositions " by," " with," " from."

The *Accusative* and *Ablative* cases also occur in Latin after certain prepositions.

(2) Latin nouns fall into five classes called *Declensions*. The declension to which a noun belongs is indicated by the ending of the Genitive Singular.

(3) Words which indicate males are *Masculine Gender*; those which indicate females are *Feminine*; the gender of every other noun is indicated not by its meaning but by its form.

EXERCISE 4

1. The normal order of words in a Latin sentence is:

	SUBJECT	OBJECT	VERB
e.g.	**Rēgīna**	**puellam**	**amat.**

2. Interrogative words like **quō ?**, **ubi ?**, **unde ?** stand first in the sentence.

(*Note.*—If it is desired to emphasise a particular word the normal order is often abandoned, the important word being placed first. Thus we frequently find sentences of the type:

Puellam amat rēgīna—The queen loves the *girl*;
or Amat puellam rēgīna—The queen *loves* the girl.

Hence we must use *Inflections*, not the *Order of Words*, to find the subject and object of a Latin sentence and so arrive at its general meaning. Never *assume* that the first noun you meet is the subject !)

A

1. Rēgīnam amāmus.
2. Unde festīnās, puella ?
3. Fābulam nārrant.
4. Rēgīnam vulnerābunt.
5. Quō festīnātis, puellae ?
6. Ad silvam festīnāmus.
7. Ubi puellae habitant ?
8. Puellae in īnsulā habitant.
9. Puellae mēnsās portābant.
10. Valē, rēgīna !

B

1. Good morning, girls ! Hail, O queen !
2. They love the woods.
3. She lives in the wood.
4. Where are you (*s.*) hurrying to ?
5. Where are you (*pl.*) hurrying from ?
6. Where does the queen live ?
7. She lives on the island.
8. We shall lay waste the island.
9. The queen loved the woods.
10. Farewell, girls !
11. They wounded the queen.
12. The girls were hurrying to the wood.

WORD STUDY

You probably know quite well what a peninsula is ; but your Latin will show you how aptly it is so called. Two Latin words **paene,** almost, and **īnsula,** an island, give us peninsula—an almost-island.

A LATIN PROVERB

Surdō fābulam nārrās, You tell your story to a deaf man.

A ROMAN COIN

VI

THE FIRST DECLENSION—*continued*

§ 5. Nouns of the first declension are feminine, except names of males or male occupations, which are masculine, e.g. :

> **poēta, -ae,** *m.,* a poet.
> **agricola, -ae,** *m.,* a farmer.
> **nauta, -ae,** *m.,* a sailor.

§ 6. The nouns **dĕa, dĕae,** *f.,* a goddess ; **fīlia, fīliae,** *f.,* a daughter, have **dĕābus, fīliābus,** respectively in the dative and ablative plural. Their full declension is as follows :

	SINGULAR	PLURAL	SINGULAR	PLURAL
Nom.	dĕa	dĕae	fīlia	fīliae
Voc.	dĕa	dĕae	fīlia	fīliae
Acc.	dĕam	dĕās	fīliam	fīliās
Gen.	dĕae	dĕārum	fīliae	fīliārum
Dat.	dĕae	dĕābus	fīliae	fīliābus
Abl.	dĕā	dĕābus	fīliā	fīliābus

EXERCISE 5

Remember that :

 (*a*) The possessor stands in the genitive case.

 (*b*) The indirect object (generally marked in English by the preposition " to " or " for ") stands in the dative case.

 (*c*) The instrument by means of which an action is done stands in the ablative case.

Note.—The possessive pronouns which appear in the following exercises are not to be expressed in Latin.

A

1. Cūr mēnsam ōrnātis, puellae ?
2. Ad tabernam festīnō.
3. In tabernā habitant.
4. Rēgīnam īnsulae laudāmus.
5. Rēgīna ad īnsulam festīnat.
6. Quō festīnās, fīlia ?
7. Ubi habitant deae ?
8. Cūr fābulam rēgīnae nārrās ?
9. Mēnsam puellīs parābit.
10. Quō rēgīna festīnat ?

B

1. Where are you hastening from, O queen ?
2. Why did you tell the story, girl ?
3. Hail, O queen !
4. Where are you hurrying to, sailor ?
5. I am hurrying to the inn.
6. The daughter used to adorn the table with roses.
7. Why are they carrying the spears ?
8. They are carrying the spears to the island.
9. Why do you (*pl.*) praise the goddess ?
10. Hail, native land !
11. You (*pl.*) love your native land.
12. Where do you (*s.*) live ?
13. I live in the inn.
14. We shall love our native land.
15. The queen's daughters live on the island.

WORD STUDY

Here are two interesting little problems. Try to discover the origin, and hence the meaning, of *patriot* and *patriotic*. The second problem is rather more difficult. We have taken the word **taberna** over into English with a slight change of form. How does it appear in English ?

VII

FIRST CONJUGATION—*continued*

§ 7. Perfect Indicative Active of **amāre**, to love.

PERSON	SINGULAR		PLURAL	
1	**amāv-ī**	I have loved, *or*, I loved	**amāv-imus**	we have loved, *or*, we loved
2	**amāv-istī**	you have loved, *or*, you loved	**amāv-istis**	you have loved, *or*, you loved
3	**amāv-it**	he, she, it has loved, *or*, he, she, it loved	**amāv-ērunt**	they have loved, *or*, they loved

Notes.—(1) The perfect stem of any verb is found by dropping the -ī of 1st person singular of the Perfect Indicative Active. Thus the perfect stem of **amāre** is **amāv-**.

(2) The 3rd Plural Perfect Indicative Active sometimes ends in -**ēre** instead of -**ērunt**.

EXERCISE 6

The negative **nōn** stands immediately before the word to which it belongs, e.g. **Poētam nōn laudat,** He does not praise the poet.

A

1. Poētae deās laudāvērunt.
2. Cūr deās laudāvistī, poēta ?

3. Deae patriam servāvērunt.
4. Quō ambulātis, nautae ?
5. Ad silvam, agricola, festīnāmus.
6. Nautae īnsulam nōn oppugnāvērunt.
7. Quandō ad silvam ambulāvistis, puellae ?
8. Agricola nautam hastā vulnerāvit.
9. Salvēte, agricolae ! Unde festīnātis ?
10. Ē tabernā, poēta, festīnāmus.
11. Nautam, agricola, superāvistī.
12. Festīnant nautae ; poētam servābunt.
13. Cūr hastās et sagittās nautīs parāvistis ?
14. Agricolae hastīs et sagittīs nautās oppugnāvērunt.
15. Ubi habitāvistī, poēta ? In īnsulā habitāvī,
puella.

B

1. You (*s.*) have saved your native land.
2. When did the farmer tell the story to his daughters ?
3. We shall prepare spears and arrows.
4. Why have you (*pl.*) not adorned the table with roses ?
5. They have wounded the poet with a spear.
6. When did the sailors hasten from the wood ?
7. Where did you (*s.*) carry the roses from ?
8. I carried the roses from the wood to the shop.

A FARMER AT THE PLOUGH IN ANCIENT ITALY

(How many points of difference do you notice between this farmer and
those of to-day ?)

9. The sailors of the queen will save their native land.
10. Why did the sailors not overcome the farmers ?
11. The queen's daughter hurried from the island.
12. We shall walk to the shop.
13. The queen and her daughters were walking in the woods.
14. The poet's daughters loved roses.
15. Good morning, girls !   Good-bye, girls !

C

From the list given below select a word to complete each of the following sentences :

(a) Quō ——, nautae ?

(b) Cūr hastīs et sagittīs agricolās —— ?

(c) Mēnsās —— ōrnābunt.

(d) Cūr nautae poētam nōn —— ?

(e) Poēta —— nārrāvit.

(f) Nautae —— vāstābunt.

Rosīs : īnsulam : servābant : festīnātis : vulnerāvistis : fābulās.

WORD STUDY

You will find that Latin crops up in most unexpected places. For example, when the electrician wishes to cover up a live wire out of reach of danger, he *insulates* it. Use your Latin to reach the real meaning of this.

When you go to the railway station, and wish a man to carry your luggage, whom do you hail ? From what Latin verb is his name derived ?

In the Government there is a Minister who looks after farming. What is his title ? With what Latin word that you have learned is that title connected ?

Some people might describe the amount of money required to run the country as *fabulous*. What does this word mean ? From what Latin word is it derived ?

You may be sure that a ship's captain has among his books a *nautical* almanac. What kind of almanac is this, and whence does it derive its name ?

VIII

FIRST CONJUGATION—*continued*

§ 8. Future Perfect Indicative Active of **amāre**, to love.

PERSON	SINGULAR	PLURAL
1	**amāv-erō** I shall have loved	**amāv-erimus** we shall have loved
2	**amāv-eris** you will have loved	**amāv-eritis** you will have loved
3	**amāv-erit** he, she, it will have loved	**amāv-erint** they will have loved

Note.—FORMATION. The Future Perfect Indicative Active of all Latin verbs is formed by adding **-erō, -eris, -erit, -erimus, -eritis, -erint** to the Perfect Stem.

§ 9. Pluperfect Indicative Active of **amāre**, to love.

PERSON	SINGULAR	PLURAL
1	**amāv-eram** I had loved	**amāv-erāmus** we had loved
2	**amāv-erās** you had loved	**amāv-erātis** you had loved
3	**amāv-erat** he, she, it had loved	**amāv-erant** they had loved

Note.—FORMATION. The Pluperfect Indicative Active of all Latin verbs is formed by adding **-eram, -erās, -erat, -erāmus, -erātis, -erant** to the Perfect Stem.

EXERCISE 7

A

1. Vāstābis : festīnāvimus : laudāverās : vulner-
   āvērunt : servāverant.
2. Parātis : ōrnāverātis ; amāmus : portāverit :
   portāverat.
3. Fābulam rēgīnae nārrāverāmus.
4. Nautae patriam servāverant.
5. Rosās, puellae, portāveritis.
6. Nautae victōriam nūntiāvērunt.
7. Hastās agricolārum vītāverātis.
8. Quandō ad villam ambulābimus ?
9. Patriam victōriīs servāvistis.
10. Cūr sagittās nautārum nōn vītāverant ?
11. Salvēte, puellae ! Salvē, poēta !
12. Ē vīllā ad silvam festīnāmus.
13. Cūr victōriam nōn nūntiāverās ?
14. Salvēte, puellae ! Quo ambulātis ?
15. Quō ambulās ? Ubi habitat ? Cūr nōn festīnās ?
    Unde festīnant ? Quandō victōriam nūntiā-
    bunt ?

B

1. Why had they attacked the islands ?
2. He had announced a victory to the queen.
3. When will the poet tell the story ?
4. The poet had avoided the battle.
5. The farmers do not love battles.
6. Hail, queen ! We announce a victory.
7. Why had you (*pl.*) not walked to the wood ?

8. The poets will have told stories to their daughters.
9. She will have adorned the tables with roses.
10. We had saved the islands by our victory.
11. We shall have reported the victory of the sailors.
12. The sailors will have overcome the farmers.
13. They had wounded the farmers with spears and arrows.
14. By your victory you (*pl.*) will have saved your native land.
15. Good morning, farmer ! Where are you hurrying from ?
Why did you avoid the battle ?

AN EXAMPLE OF LATIN BREVITY

One of the most striking characteristics of Latin is its brevity. No language can say so much in so few words. You have already noticed, no doubt, how often it takes two or three English words to translate a single Latin word. Often, also, by dropping out a verb or other word which the reader or hearer can easily supply, a Roman writer gives us a marvellously concise and yet clear phrase. Here is one which you have Latin enough to appreciate :

Unde et quō Catius ? Whence (comes) Catius, and where (goes he) ? *or,* as we might say in English : *Whence and whither away, Catius ?*

A FAMOUS MOTTO

Nēmō mē impūne lacessit, Who dare meddle with me ? (Literally ' No one assails me with impunity.')

IX

THE VERB "TO BE"

§ 10. Present, Future and Imperfect Indicative of **esse,** to be.

Tense	Pers.	Singular		Plural	
Present	1	**sum**	I am	**sumus**	we are
	2	**es**	you are	**estis**	you are
	3	**est**	he, she, it is	**sunt**	they are
Future	1	**érō**	I shall be	**érimus**	we shall be
	2	**éris**	you will be	**éritis**	you will be
	3	**érit**	he, she, it will be	**érunt**	they will be
Imper-fect	1	**éram**	I was	**erāmus**	we were
	2	**érās**	you were	**erātis**	you were
	3	**érat**	he, she, it was	**érant**	they were

Notes.—1. The verb **esse,** to be, frequently requires a noun or adjective to complete the sense, e.g. :

Nauta est, He is a sailor.
Poēta est agricola, The poet is a farmer.

This noun or adjective is called the *complement,* and is always in the same case as the subject.

2. **Est,** there is ; **sunt,** there are—generally stand first in their clause : similarly with **erat,** there was ; **erant,** there were ; **erit, erunt,** there will be.

EXERCISE 8

A

1. Ubi est poēta ?
2. Poēta in Galliā est.
3. Rēgīna et fīlia in Britanniā erunt.
4. Sunt agricolae in īnsulā.

2

5. Nōn sunt poētae in Galliā.
6. Patria nautārum est Britannia.
7. Britannia patria est nautārum.
8. Puella fīlia rēgīnae erat.
9. Rosae in mēnsā sunt.
10. In Galliā, nautae, erātis.
11. Ubi est vīlla poētae ?
12. Vīlla poētae nōn est in īnsulā.
13. Sunt silvae in Britanniā.
14. Quō ambulātis ? Ad tabernam ambulāmus.
15. Quandō erunt rosae in mēnsīs ?

B

1. Where is the poet ?
2. The poet is in his country house.
3. We are sailors, O queen.
4. The queen was in Britain.
5. You will not be a sailor.
6. There are not woods in the island.
7. Where is he walking from ?
8. He is walking from his daughter's country house.
9. They are carrying arrows to the battle.
10. Britain is the girl's native land.
11. There will be a queen in the island.
12. There was a goddess in the island.
13. The girl had hurried to the wood.
14. By our victory we shall save our native land.
15. Britain is an island ; Gaul is not an island.

C

1. Compose and translate an answer in Latin to each of the following questions :

(a) Ubi habitat fīlia rēgīnae ?
(b) Quō ambulās, puella ?
(c) Ubi est vīlla poētae ?
(d) Cūr fābulam nōn nārrās, poēta ?
(e) Ubi sunt rosae, ō puella ?
(f) Cūr īnsulam vāstāvistis, nautae ?

LIFE AT A ROMAN VILLA

REVISION EXERCISES

A

1. We were ; they will have loved ; you (*s.*) were reporting ; we had saved ; we have prepared ; you (*pl.*) will adorn ; she is.
2. Where do the sailors live ?
3. When shall we walk from the shop ?
4. Why have you (*pl.*) not adorned the table ?
5. Where are you (*s.*) carrying the roses to ?
6. The sailor told stories to his daughters.
7. Where did you (*s.*) live in Britain ?
8. We do not praise the farmer's daughter.
9. The farmers were not in the battle.
10. The poet praised his native land.

B

1. By battles ; of stories ; for the farmer ; of the girl ; to the daughters ; by an arrow.
2. The poet will tell a story to his daughters.
3. Good morning, girls ! Where are you hurrying from ?
4. When will you (*s.*) walk to the wood ?
5. Farewell, daughter ! I am hurrying to the shop.
6. The poet's daughters loved roses.
7. A poet saved the sailors by his stories.
8. The queen will not praise the sailor's story.
9. Why did they attack the sailors with arrows ?
10. When will the farmers prepare their arrows ?

C

Complete the unfinished words in, and then translate the following sentences :

1. Naut— in īnsul— habitant.
2. Rēgīna īnsul— nautās nōn am—.
3. Cūr ad tabern— nōn ambulāb—, puellae ?
4. Quandō fīli— fābul— nārrābis, poēta ?
5. Puell— mēnsām ros— ōrnant.
6. In pugn— agricola sagitt— naut— vītāb—.
7. Quō festīn—, puella ? Ad tabern— festīn—, nauta.
8. Unde ros— port—, agricola ? Ē silv— rosās port—.
9. Cūr nōn festīn—, nautae ?
10. Nautae vīll— agricol— oppugnāvērunt.

X

ADJECTIVES OF THE FIRST DECLENSION

§ 11. Adjectives of the first declension are all feminine, and are declined like **mēnsa.**

SINGULAR

Nom.	bŏna	puella	a good girl (*subj.*).
Voc.	bŏna	puella	good girl ! O good girl !
Acc.	bŏnam	puellam	a good girl (*obj.*).
Gen.	bŏnae	puellae	of a good girl.
Dat.	bŏnae	puellae	to, for a good girl.
Abl.	bŏnā	puellā	by, with, from a good girl.

PLURAL

Nom.	bŏnae	puellae	good girls (*subj.*).
Voc.	bŏnae	puellae	good girls ! O good girls !
Acc.	bŏnās	puellās	good girls (*obj.*).
Gen.	bŏnārum	puellārum	of good girls.
Dat.	bŏnīs	puellīs	to, for good girls.
Abl.	bŏnīs	puellīs	by, with, from good girls.

Note.—In Latin, adjectives must agree in number, gender and case with the noun to which they belong.

It follows that adjectives of the first declension can be used only with feminine nouns e.g. :

> **magna mēnsa,** a large table.
> **parva īnsula,** a small island.
> **multae puellae,** many girls.
> **via longa,** a long road.

POSITION OF ADJECTIVES.—As a general rule, when an adjective qualifies a noun in Latin, it may either precede or follow the noun.

EXERCISE 9

By this time you are quite familiar with Latin questions introduced by an interrogative word like **cūr, quandō, quō,** etc. Even where there is no interrogative word, we may convert a statement into a question by attaching **-ně** to the first word of the sentence, e.g. :

Statement : **Sagittās vītāvistī,** You avoided the arrows.
Question : **Sagittāsně vītāvistī ?** Did you avoid the arrows ?

A

1. Vīlla nōn est parva.
2. Estne magna silva in īnsulā ?
3. Sunt in Galliā multae vīllae.
4. Suntne in Britanniā vīllae ?
5. Quandō pugnābitis, nautae ?
6. Sunt in tabernā multae puellae.
7. Crās pugnābimus et patriam servābimus.
8. Cūr nōn festīnātis, agricolae ?
9. Via est longa, puellae. Nōn festīnābimus.
10. Sagittāsne vītāvistis, agricolae ?
11. Sagittās, ō puella, et hastās nautārum vītāvimus.
12. Quandō victōriam nūntiāvistis ?
13. Herī, fīlia, māgnam victōriam nūntiāvimus.
14. Quandō ad silvam ambulābimus ?
15. Crās ad silvam ambulābimus. Hodiē fābulan nārrābimus.

B

1. Why do you tell a long story, poet ?
2. To-day we are not hurrying, girls.
3. There is a large country house on the island.
4. It is the country house of the queen.
5. Is the island large, farmer ?
6. The island is not large ; it is small.
7. Do farmers live on the large island ?
8. To-morrow we shall hasten to the island.
9. By your victory, sailors, you saved your native land.
10. We love our native land, O queen !
11. Where do you live, little girl ?
    I live on a great island.
    Do sailors love the island ?
    The island is the native land of sailors.
    Are there country houses on the island ?
    There are many country houses and big woods on the island.

WORD STUDY

Have you ever heard a proverb which speaks of something as being the " thief of time " ? The " something " is a big word meaning *the habit of putting off till to-morrow*. See whether you can think of it. Here is a clue. Part of it is a Latin word contained in to-day's vocabulary.

In your grammar lesson you have met the word **esse,** and have learned its meaning. Now see whether you can use your knowledge to find the meaning of the words *essence* and *essential*. Compose an English sentence in which *essential* is correctly used.

XI

THE SECOND DECLENSION

§ 12. dominus, dominī, *m.,* a master (of slaves).

CASE	SINGULAR		PLURAL	
Nom.	**domin-us**	a master (*subj.*)	**domin-ī**	masters (*subj.*)
Voc.	**domin-ĕ**	master ! O master !	**domin-ī**	masters ! O masters!
Acc.	**domin-um**	a master (*obj.*)	**domin-ōs**	masters (*obj.*)
Gen.	**domin-ī**	of a master	**domin-ōrum**	of masters
Dat.	**domin-ō**	to, for a master	**domin-īs**	to, for masters
Abl.	**domin-ō**	by, with, from a master	**domin-īs**	by, with, from masters

Note.—The above is the only type of Latin noun in which the vocative singular is not the same as the nominative singular.

§ 13. Adjectives of the second declension ending in **-us.**

These are all masculine, and are declined like **dominus.**

	SINGULAR		PLURAL	
Nom.	**bonus**	**dominus**	**bonī**	**dominī**
Voc.	**bone**	**domine**	**bonī**	**dominī**
Acc.	**bonum**	**dominum**	**bonōs**	**dominōs**
Gen.	**bonī**	**dominī**	**bonōrum**	**dominōrum**
Dat.	**bonō**	**dominō**	**bonīs**	**dominīs**
Abl.	**bonō**	**dominō**	**bonīs**	**dominīs**

EXERCISE 10

Two adjectives qualifying the same noun are regularly joined
by **et**, e.g. :
Multī et bonī agricolae, Many good farmers.

A

1. Sunt in vīllā multī servī.
2. Servōs bonōs dominus līberābit.
3. Servīne dominum amant ?
4. Cūr dominum amātis, servī ?
5. Bonus est dominus et servōs saepe laudat.
6. Quō hodiē festīnābimus, domine ?
7. Ad silvam, servī, hodiē ambulābitis.
8. Crās ad tabernam festīnābimus.
9. Herī dominus festīnāvit ē vīllā.
0. Quandō nautae magnam victōriam nūntiābunt ?
1. Herī, puellae, nautae longōs mūrōs servāvērunt.
2. Cūr nōn sunt multī captīvī ?
3. Nautae multōs captīvōs nōn servāverant.
4. Suntne in Britanniā multī nautae ?
5. Sunt in Britanniā multī et bonī nautae.

B

1. Give the Latin word for *good* to agree with each of the
   following nouns : Captīvōrum ; nautās ; puellae (*dat.*) ;
   domine ; agricola (*voc.*).
2. Why do the good slaves not praise their master ?
3. The master is not good.
4. Is the slave big ?   The slave is small, master.

5. When shall we set free the little slave ?
6. To-morrow, daughter, we shall free many good slaves.
7. There will be many captives.
8. The sailors have announced a great victory.
9. There were long walls in the island.
10. Where were the long walls, farmer ?
11. Where do you live, slaves ?
12. We live in the master's country house.
13. Why did you (*pl.*) not walk to the inn yesterday ?
14. The way was long.
15. Farewell, master ! We shall often praise the good master.

WORD STUDY

To-day try to use your Latin to find out the meaning of th
following expressions :

> a *mural* decoration,
>
> the prisoner was *immured* in a fortress,
>
> a *domineering* character,
>
> a *predominant* feature,
>
> the *dominions*.

Can you find any more words in English which are derive
from the Latin **dominus** ?

It is interesting to note that in some parts of Scotland th
schoolmaster is still called the " *Dominie*."

A Butcher's Shop in Ancient Rome

XII

THE SECOND DECLENSION—*continued*

§ 14. Fīlius, *m.*, a son, is declined thus:

	SINGULAR	PLURAL
Nom.	fīlius	fīliī
Voc.	fīlī	fīliī
Acc.	fīlium	fīliōs
Gen.	fīlī or fīliī	fīliōrum
Dat.	fīliō	fīliīs
Abl.	fīliō	fīliīs

§ 15. Proper names ending in **-ius** are declined like **fīlius**.

§ 16. **Deus,** *m.*, a god, is declined thus:

	SINGULAR	PLURAL
Nom.	děus	dī or děī
Voc.	děus (but see note)	dī or děī
Acc.	děum	děōs
Gen.	děī	děōrum
Dat.	děō	dīs or děīs
Abl.	děō	dīs or děīs

Notes.—(1) The vocative form **děus** is not found in pre-Christian Latin. In pagan Rome when a man prayed to a god he addressed the god by his specific name, Jupiter or Mars or Mercury, or whatever god it happened to be.

EXERCISE 11

A

1. Valerius est amīcus bonī poētae.
2. Poēta Valerium amīcum appellat.
3. Ubi habitat amīcus poētae ?
4. Ōlim in Galliā Valerius et fīlius habitābant.
5. Iam in īnsulā est magna vīlla Valeriī.
6. Īnsulam Britanniam appellāmus.
7. Salvē, Britannia, patria nautārum !
8. Nautae deōs et deās saepe laudant.
9. Dī nautās saepe servāvērunt.
10. In pugnā nautae sagittās vītāverant.
11. Quō festīnātis, servī ? Ubi habitat dominus ?
12. Iam in Britanniā habitāmus. In Galliā ōlim habitābāmus.
13. Valē, amīce ! Ad Galliam festīnō.
14. Dī amīcī agricolārum semper sunt.
15. Amāsne parvās puellās, Valerī ? Puellās nōn amō, amīce.

B

1. Where does Valerius live ?
2. Valerius always lives in Gaul.
3. We used to live in a large country house.
4. Why are you praising the sailors now, poet ?
5. To-day the sailors by their victory have saved the long walls.
6. You once saved many captives by your stories, poet.
7. Why did the master not free the slaves, Valerius ?
8. The slaves have now laid waste the islands.
9. The slave had once saved his master in the battle.

10. The poet told a long story to the queen's sons.
11. To-day Gallus is a slave ; yesterday he was a captive.
12. Are the friends of Valerius in the inn ?
13. The poet is the friend of the gods.

C

1. Complete the following sentences :
    (a) Ōlim mult— servī bonōs agricol— oppugnā-
    vērunt.
    (b) Bon— serv— mēnsam Valeriō parat.
    (c) Ad silv— parvae puell— festīnant.
    (d) Sunt in silv— mult— puell—.

2. Compose and translate :
    (a) A Latin sentence containing the verb **vītābimus.**
    (b) A Latin sentence containing the verb **servāverant.**
    (c) A Latin sentence containing the verb **appellātis.**
    (d) An answer in Latin to the question: **Quandō
    festīnābitis ad vīllam ?**
    (e) An answer in Latin to the question: **Ubi est
    dominus servī ?**
    (f) An answer in Latin to the question: **Unde servus
    herī festīnāvit ?**

WORD STUDY

The English language is derived from several sources. The
chief of these are Anglo-Saxon and Latin. We frequently find
that by means of a single Latin word we can express an idea
which it would take several words of Anglo-Saxon origin to
express. For example, we speak of settling a dispute *in a
friendly way.* Can you think of one word of Latin origin which
could replace these four words ? Again, can you suggest an
adjective of Latin origin to describe the affection which a son
or daughter should show to father or mother ?

XIII

THE SECOND DECLENSION—*continued*

§ 17. Masculine nouns ending in **-er : ager, agrī,** *m.,* a field.

Case	Singular		Plural	
Nom.	**ager**	a field (*subj.*)	**agr-ī**	fields (*subj.*)
Voc.	**ager**	field ! O field !	**agr-ī**	fields ! O fields !
Acc.	**agr-um**	a field (*obj.*)	**agr-ōs**	fields (*obj.*)
Gen.	**agr-ī**	of a field	**agr-ōrum**	of fields
Dat.	**agr-ō**	to, for a field	**agr-īs**	to, for fields
Abl.	**agr-ō**	by, with, from a field	**agr-īs**	by, with, from fields

Notes.—(1) Most nouns of the second declension ending in **-er** are declined as above.

(2) Several masculine adjectives ending in **-er** are declined like **ager,** e.g. **pulcher,** beautiful.

§ 18. Some masculine nouns of the second declension ending in **-er** keep **e** throughout, e.g. **puer, puerī,** *m.,* a boy.

Case	Singular		Plural	
Nom.	**puer**	a boy (*subj.*)	**puer-ī**	boys (*subj.*)
Voc.	**puer**	boy ! O boy !	**puer-ī**	boys ! O boys !
Acc.	**puer-um**	a boy (*obj.*)	**puer-ōs**	boys (*obj.*)
Gen.	**puer-ī**	of a boy	**puer-ōrum**	of boys
Dat.	**puer-ō**	to, for a boy	**puer-īs**	to, for boys
Abl.	**puer-ō**	by, with, from a boy	**puer-īs**	by, with, from boys

Notes.—(1) **vir, virī,** *m.,* a man, is declined like **puer.**

(2) Many masculine adjectives in **-er** follow the declension of **puer,** e.g. **miser,** wretched.

EXERCISE 12

A

1. Cūr miserī estis, puerī ?
2. Captīvī sumus, nautae. In Ītaliā servī erimus.
3. Pulchrī estis, captīvī.
4. Vir bonus pulchrōs servōs līberābit.
5. Quandō ad Ītaliam nāvigābimus, Valerī ?
6. Crās, virī, ē Britanniā festīnābimus.
7. Miserī enim in Britanniā semper sumus.
8. Magnum mūrum semper servāmus.
9. Cūr Ītaliam, poēta, semper laudās ?
10. Dī et deae Ītaliam semper amābant.
11. Estisne miserī, agricolae ?
12. In Ītaliā agricolae miserī nōn sunt.
13. Vir bonus parvum puerum līberābit.
14. Cūr inter captīvōs es, pulcher puer ?
15. Fīlius agricolae sum, nauta. Ōlim in Britanniā habitābam. Iam ad Ītaliam nāvigāvī. Nautae enim patriam oppugnāvērunt et agrōs vāstāvērunt. Sed puerōs et puellās servāvērunt. Iam servī erimus. Valēte, pulchrī agrī Britanniae !

B

1. To-morrow, men, we shall sail to Italy.
2. Hail, Italy ! Italy is the native land of many poets.
3. Now we shall not be unhappy, girls.
4. For there are many beautiful roses in the wood.
5. Does the master praise the good slave ?

6. Little boys will not always be unhappy.
7. To-morrow the good master will set free the boys.
8. Are there large fields in the island, sailor ?
9. The fields of the island are large and beautiful.
10. The wretched slaves laid waste their masters' fields.
11. Among the captives were many little boys.
12. To-morrow we shall sail from Italy to Britain.
13. Valerius was a great and good man.
14. Good men are not unhappy. The gods love good men.

WORD STUDY

From the Latin words in to-day's lesson come many English words. From **ager,** for instance, come *agriculture,* which means the tilling of fields and lands, *agricultural* and *agrarian.* Look up the meaning of these two. **Miser** gives us *miserable* and *misery.* Then notice how many modern names in geography come from Latin originals. That is not surprising when you remember that the Romans once held an empire comprising a great part of Europe. Already you can tell us the Latin names from which are derived *Britain* and *Italy.* As you go on with Latin you will find out that *Greece* comes from the Latin **Graecia,** that *Spain* is from the Latin **Hispania,** that *Germany* is from **Germania,** and that *Africa* is a pure Latin word.

To end with a little problem : If you read that the Romans were a *virile* race, or hear somebody say that so-and-so's speech was a *puerile* composition, what do these words mean and what is their derivation ?

A LATIN PROVERB

Ligna ferre in silvam, To carry logs to the wood, i.e. To carry coals to Newcastle.

XIV

THE SECOND DECLENSION—*continued*

§ 19. Neuter nouns ending in **-um : bellum, bellī,** *n.*, a war.

Case	Singular		Plural	
Nom.	**bell-um**	a war (*subj.*)	**bell-ă**	wars (*subj.*)
Voc.	**bell-um**	war ! O war !	**bell-ă**	wars! O wars!
Acc.	**bell-um**	a war (*obj.*)	**bell-ă**	wars (*obj.*)
Gen.	**bell-ī**	of a war	**bell-ōrum**	of wars
Dat.	**bell-ō**	to, for a war	**bell-īs**	to, for wars
Abl.	**bell-ō**	by, with, from a war	**bell-īs**	by, with, from wars

Notes.—(1) In all declensions Neuter Nouns have the same endings for Vocative and Accusative Singular as for Nominative Singular.

    (2) In all declensions Neuter Nouns have the ending **-ă** in Nominative, Vocative and Accusative Plural.

    (3) Many Neuter Adjectives belong to the second declension. These all end in **-um,** and are declined like **bellum,** e.g. **bonum,** good ; **longum,** long, etc.

EXERCISE 13

A

1. Rēgīna est pulchra : fīlius poētae est pulcher : templum est pulchrum.
2. Bonus poēta pulchra templa laudat.
3. Cūr puerī et puellae ad templa deōrum festīnant?
4. In Galliā multīs et magnīs victōriīs, Gallōs superāvimus, ō nautae.
5. Miserae puellae bellum nōn amant.
6. Puerī et puellae templa deōrum rosīs ōrnāverint.
7. Multōs servōs agricola comparāverat.
8. Servī agricolae captīvī ōlim erant.
9. Ubi habitās, puer? In templō deī semper habitō, rēgīna.
10. Quō festīnās, poēta? Hodiē ad vīllam festīnō ; crās in silvīs ambulābō. Silvās semper laudō et amō.
11. Cūr poēta Britanniam laudat?
12. Britannia est patria poētae. Poēta patriam semper laudat.
13. Herī ad Britanniam nāvigāvimus.
14. Unde nāvigāvistis ad Britanniam, puellae?
15. Poēta victōriam amīcīs nūntiāverat.

B

1. To-day we shall hasten to the long walls.
2. Yesterday the slave hurried to the temple.
3. In the war they have laid waste many beautiful islands.
4. Why do you love your native land, good poet?

5. Many good poets have praised Britain.
6. Did the poet praise the queen ?
7. To-morrow the poet will announce the victory to his friends.
8. When did you set the captive free, Valerius ?
9. Between Britain and Gaul there are many small islands.
10. Valerius always tells good stories to the boys.
11. A great goddess lives in the temple.
12. Why are you always praising the slave, Valerius ?
13. He fought in Italy in the great war.
14. There are many tables in the great temple.
15. Where were you yesterday, poet ? Why were you not in the queen's country house ?

C

A Speed Test

(Write down the Latin for as many of the following words and phrases as you can in 10 minutes.)

of temples.
by war.
of farmers.
for daughters.
we have avoided.
yesterday.
whence ?
spears (*acc.*).
in the beautiful temple.
10 why do you (*s.*) fight ?

we had told.
he will have set free.
once upon a time.
in the native land.
of a son.
farewell, girls !
by long walls.
good poets (*nom.*).
of many good farmers.
30 to-morrow.

in the wood.
does he praise ?
of wretched slaves.
we had sailed.
gods and goddesses (*nom.*).
when ?
for the slave.
good day, sailor !
they have laid waste.
20 of a good friend.

they had saved.
by great victories.
you (*pl.*) have sailed.
where do you live, boy ?
he was carrying arrows.
we were walking to the wood.
there were.
with many roses.
the queen is beautiful.
40 stories (*acc.*).

XV

ADJECTIVES OF FIRST AND SECOND DECLENSIONS

Summary

§ **20.** There are three types:

(1) The masculine ends in -**us**, and is declined like **dominus**, e.g.
bŏnus, bŏna, bŏnum, good.

No.	Case	Masculine	Feminine	Neuter
Singular	*Nom.*	**bŏnus**	**bŏna**	**bŏnum**
	Voc.	**bŏne**	**bŏna**	**bŏnum**
	Acc.	**bŏnum**	**bŏnam**	**bŏnum**
	Gen.	**bŏnī**	**bŏnae**	**bŏnī**
	Dat.	**bŏnō**	**bŏnae**	**bŏnō**
	Abl.	**bŏnō**	**bŏnā**	**bŏnō**
Plural	*Nom.*	**bŏnī**	**bŏnae**	**bŏnă**
	Voc.	**bŏnī**	**bŏnae**	**bŏnă**
	Acc.	**bŏnōs**	**bŏnās**	**bŏnă**
	Gen.	**bŏnōrum**	**bŏnārum**	**bŏnōrum**
	Dat.	**bŏnīs**	**bŏnīs**	**bŏnīs**
	Abl.	**bŏnīs**	**bŏnīs**	**bŏnīs**

(2) The masculine ends in -er, and is declined like **ager**, e.g. **pulcher, pulchra, pulchrum,** beautiful.

No.	CASE	MASCULINE	FEMININE	NEUTER
SINGULAR	*Nom.*	pulcher	pulchra	pulchrum
	Voc.	pulcher	pulchra	pulchrum
	Acc.	pulchrum	pulchram	pulchrum
	Gen.	pulchrī	pulchrae	pulchrī
	Dat.	pulchrō	pulchrae	pulchrō
	Abl.	pulchrō	pulchrā	pulchrō
PLURAL	*Nom.*	pulchrī	pulchrae	pulchră
	Voc.	pulchrī	pulchrae	pulchră
	Acc.	pulchrōs	pulchrās	pulchră
	Gen.	pulchrōrum	pulchrārum	pulchrōrum
	Dat.	pulchrīs	pulchrīs	pulchrīs
	Abl.	pulchrīs	pulchrīs	pulchrīs

(3) The masculine ends in -er, and is declined like **puer**, e.g. **tener, tenera, tenerum,** tender:

SINGULAR.

Nom. **tener, tenera, tenerum,** etc.

PLURAL.

Nom. **tenerī, tenerae, teneră,** etc.

Note.—A Latin adjective may serve as a noun, e.g.

> **bonī,** the good, i.e. good men;
> **multī,** many, i.e. many men ;
> **multa,** many things.

EXERCISE 14

A

The New Slave

[VALERIUS *tells his son,* QUINTUS, *that he has procured a new slave to take the place of Syrus who, after long and faithful service, is to receive his liberty.*]

VALERIUS: Novum servum, Quīnte, comparāvimus.

QUĪNTUS: Cūr? Sunt multī et bonī servī in vīllā nostrā. Cūr novum servum comparāvistī?

VALERIUS: Crās Syrum, Quīnte, līberābō. Syrum amō, et saepe laudāvī. In agrīs nostrīs et in vīllā nostrā diū labōrāvit. Crās, igitur, līber erit. Nōn servus sed amīcus Valeriī erit. Lībertum Valeriī Syrum appellābimus.

QUĪNTUS: Et Syrum, novum lībertum nostrum, amābimus. Sed cūr nōn nārrās dē novō servō? Unde comparāvistī? Ubi est? Estne puer? Estne pulcher?

VALERIUS: Longa fābula est, Quīnte, sed nārrābō. Hodiē enim nōn festīnō ē vīllā nostrā.

Herī ad oppidum ambulāvī. Erant in forō multī captīvī. Multī puerī erant, multī virī, multae fēminae. In Galliā ōlim habitābant, sed Rōmānī māgnō bellō Galliam oppugnāvērunt. Multīs pugnīs nostrī Gallōs superāvērunt. Multa oppida Gallōrum vāstāvērunt. Multī igitur Gallōrum captīvī sunt, et in Ītaliā servī Rōmānōrum erunt. Servus noster puer est, pulcher puer, fīlius magnī virī. Servum nostrum Gallum appellābimus.

THE SLAVE MARKET

QUĪNTUS : Estne Gallus miser ?

VALERIUS : Est miser, Quīnte. Amābat enim patriam. Sed nōn diū miser erit. Habitābit enim in pulchrā vīllā nostrā, et Gallum amābimus. Bonī et iūstī dominī erimus. Gallum ōlim līberābimus et lībertus noster et amīcus erit.

B

1. Decline together, with meanings :
    miserum bellum ; bonus agricola ; pulcher servus.

2. Give Latin for :
    With long spears ; of a great war ; O good poet ; in small country houses ; wretched slaves (obj.).

3. Give the correct Latin word for good, to agree with the following nouns :
    Poētam ; Rōmānī (nom.) ; ō puer ; virō (abl.) ; agricolārum.

4. Translate into Latin :
    (a) The slaves always praise their masters.
    (b) The captives will work in the fields of the Romans.
    (c) The freedman of Valerius once lived in Britain.
    (d) Our men have overcome the Gauls.
    (e) Our master is good and just.
    (f) I do not praise the small slaves.
    (g) Great was the victory of our men.
    (h) The poet's freedman is hastening to the temple.
    (i) The fields of Italy are beautiful.
    (j) There are many beautiful fields between our country house and the temple.

A LATIN MOTTO

Labōrāre est ōrāre, To work is to pray.

XVI

THE VERB " TO BE "—*continued*

§ 21. Perfect, Future Perfect and Pluperfect Indicative of **esse,** to be.

Tense	Pers.	Singular		Plural	
Perfect	1	**fú-ī**	I have been, *or*, I was	**fú-imus**	we have been, *or*, we were
	2	**fu-istī**	you have been, *or*, you were	**fu-istis**	you have been, *or*, you were
	3	**fú-it**	he, she, it has been, *or*, was	**fu-ērunt**	they have been, *or*, they were
Future Perfect	1	**fú-erō**	I shall have been	**fu-erimus**	we shall have been
	2	**fú-eris**	you will have been	**fu-eritis**	you will have been
	3	**fú-erit**	he, she, it will have been	**fú-erint**	they will have been
Pluperfect	1	**fú-eram**	I had been	**fu-erāmus**	we had been
	2	**fú-erās**	you had been	**fu-erātis**	you had been
	3	**fú-erat**	he, she, it had been	**fú-erant**	they had been

EXERCISE 15

A

1. Salvēte, puerī! Quō festīnātis?
2. Ad lūdum, Valerī, festīnāmus.
3. In vīcō nostrō est lūdus Orbiliī.
4. Suntne in lūdō discipulī?
5. Semper in lūdō nostrō multī puerī sunt.
6. Cūr discipulī ad lūdum māne festīnant?
7. Magister īgnāvōs puerōs culpat.
8. Iam multī puerī et multae puellae in lūdum intrāvērunt.
9. Dē magistrīs poētae multās fābulās nārrant.
10. Discipulī Orbiliī semper labōrābant.
11. Hodiē in Britanniā puerī multōs librōs ad lūdum portant.
12. Cūr nōn multōs librōs puer Rōmānus portābat?
13. Ōlim nōn erant multī librī.
14. Servus librōs puerō portābat.
15. Iam puerī et puellae ē lūdō festīnant; magistrum salūtant.

B

1. They will have been; we had been; she has been; she was; you (*pl.*) had not been; is he?; had we been?
2. Why did you (*s.*) not hasten to school?
3. To-day boys and girls carry beautiful books.
4. In a Roman school there were not many books.
5. Where is the school of Orbilius?
6. The school is in our street.
7. Where are you hurrying from, girls?

8. We are hurrying from the school, friend.
9. The pupils love the master, for he is good and just.
10. When will you tell the pupils a story, master ?

WORD STUDY

We have some very interesting words in this lesson. Now that you know the word **discipulus** you can tell what is really meant by Christ's *disciples*.

Other words, to the meaning of which you now possess the key, are : *discipline, disciplinary, disciplinarian.*

Next, see how many English words you can derive from **lĭber**. But you must be careful here, for there is another Latin word **lība̅ber**, meaning *free*, which has also given us many English words.

It may surprise you to learn that **lūdus**, the Latin word for school, really means " a game " or " play." **Lūdus** was the place where one played at, and so trained for, real life.

Salūtāre is another fascinating word. **Salus** means " safety " or " welfare " : so **salūtāre** is to wish someone safety or welfare. You will find the word *salute* used quite often in this sense in the Epistles of the New Testament. Look up your Bible and find an instance.

Landesmuseum, Trier

SCHOOLMASTER AND PUPILS

REVISION EXERCISES

A

1. Gallus is walking to the temple.
2. Why does Gallus not hasten ?
3. The slaves were working in the master's country house.
4. The master is good and just.
5. The slaves love the just master.
6. Do the pupils always love their master ?
7. To-day we shall tell a story about a Roman schoolmaster.
8. To-morrow we shall walk to the wood.
9. Yesterday we were in the country house.
10. Good-bye, boys and girls ! To-day we shall sail to Britain.

B

1. The sailors have attacked the long walls.
2. They will save the temples of the gods.
3. Why do you not tell a story to the pupils, master ?
4. The farmer has avoided the sailors' arrows.
5. The pupils are entering the school.
6. The master will greet the boys and girls.
7. Good morning, boys and girls ! Good morning, master !
8. The idle pupils are not working.
9. Valerius has procured many slaves.
10. The unhappy prisoners will be slaves. They will work in the fields.

C

Complete the unfinished words in the following sentences :

    (a) Magister īgnāvum discipul— herī culpāb—.
    (b) Sunt in pulchrā īnsul— multae et magn— silv—.
    (c) Valerius bonum serv— comparāver—.
    (d) Cūr nōn ad lūd— festīn—, puerī ?
    (e) In pugn— agricolae sagitt— nautār— vītāb—.

XVII

THE SECOND CONJUGATION

§ 22. Present, Future and Imperfect Indicative Active of **monēre**, to advise, *or* warn.

Tense	Pers.	Singular	Plural
Present	1	**móně-ō** I advise	**monē-mus** we advise
	2	**móně-s** you advise	**monē-tis** you advise
	3	**móne-t** he, she, it advises	**móne-nt** they advise
Future	1	**monē-bō** I shall advise	**monē-bimus** we shall advise
	2	**monē-bis** you will advise	**monē-bitis** you will advise
	3	**monē-bit** he, she, it will advise	**monē-bunt** they will advise
Imperfect	1	**monē-bam** I was advising	**monē-bāmus** we were advising
	2	**monē-bās** you were advising	**monē-bātis** you were advising
	3	**monē-bat** he, she, it was advising	**monē-bant** they were advising

EXERCISE 16

The preposition **ad** followed by the accusative case may indicate place
near or at which, e.g. :
Puer amīcum ad iānuam lūdī exspectat, The boy awaits his friend
at the school door.

A

1. Ubi magister discipulōs exspectat ?
2. Magister ad iānuam discipulōs exspectat.
3. Cūr festīnant discipulī ?
4. Magister discipulōs saepe monet.
5. Magister in lūdō discipulōs multa docet.
6. Puellae rosās ad iānuam lūdī collocāvērunt.
7. Cūr dominus servōs nōn laudat ?
8. Servī īgnāvī sunt ; dominum igitur timent.
9. Servus ad iānuam lūdī fīlium dominī exspectat.
10. Magister multōs discipulōs in lūdō docēbat.
11. Puellae māne lūdum multīs rosīs ōrnābunt.
12. Servī librōs puerōrum portābunt.
13. Cūr puerī magistrum nōn timēbunt ?
14. Puerī nōn sunt īgnāvī sed bonī. Bonōs puerōs
    magister laudat.
15. Cūr magister puerōs herī monēbat ?   Puerī ad
    lūdum māne nōn festīnāverant.

B

1. Orbilius has placed many tables in the school.
2. In the morning he will await the boys at the door.
3. Gallus is our friend's freedman. He was once a slave.

ON THE WAY TO SCHOOL

Here you see Sextus on his way to school. He is accompanied by his
"paedagogus," an intelligent and educated slave who acts as his companion and guardian on his way to and from school and even waits for
him at the school all day. Being the son of a well-to-do father, Sextus
also has another slave to carry his books and writing tablets, and on winter
mornings his lantern; for Sextus begins his school day at a very early hour.

4. We have carried beautiful roses for our friend.
5. Why did the slaves fear their master ?
6. They used to fear the master, for he was not always just.
7. Are there many slaves in the fields ?
8. Once upon a time slaves used to teach their masters' sons.
9. Why will the wretched poet not live in Italy ?
10. A Roman poet was once a slave. A just master freed the poet.
11. Why do you praise the slave, Valerius ?
12. He has worked for a long time in our country house.

C

1. Give the Latin for :

   Often, once upon a time, therefore, an arrow, to overcome, to procure, our men, a friend, a story, to prepare.

2. Give the Latin for :

   He advises, we shall teach, they were fearing, you (*pl.*) fear, I used to teach, he will fear, you (*s.*) were advising, they are teaching, we advise, she feared.

3. Compose a Latin sentence using the following words :
   (*a*) māne, salūtāre, agricola, fīlius, magister.
   (*b*) discipulus, lūdus, festīnāre, nōn, īgnāvus, māne, ad.
   (*c*) iūstus, servus, crās, dominus, līberāre, bonus.
   (*d*) multī, vīlla, captīvus, labōrāre, dominus, in.

3

XVIII

THE SECOND CONJUGATION—*continued*

§ 23. Perfect, Future Perfect and Pluperfect Indicative Active of **monēre,** to advise, *or* warn.

TENSE	PERS.	SINGULAR	PLURAL
PERFECT	1	**monu-ī** I have advised, *or* I advised	**monu-imus** we have advised, *or* we advised
	2	**monu-istī** you have advised, *or* you advised	**monu-istis** you have advised, *or* you advised
	3	**monu-it** he, she, it has advised, *or* he, she, it advised	**monu-ērunt** they have advised, *or* they advised
FUTURE PERFECT	1	**monu-erō** I shall have advised	**monu-erimus** we shall have advised
	2	**monu-eris** you will have advised	**monu-eritis** you will have advised
	3	**monu-erit** he, she, it will have advised	**monu-erint** they will have advised
PLUPERFECT	1	**monu-eram** I had advised	**monu-erāmus** we had advised
	2	**monu-erās** you had advised	**monu-erātis** you had advised
	3	**monu-erat** he, she, it had advised	**monu-erant** they had advised

EXERCISE 17

A

A ROMAN SCHOOL

[*Time: Early morning. Place: The house of* VALERIUS.
TULLIUS, *who is staying with* VALERIUS, *sees his
host's son* SEXTUS *bustling about in a great hurry.
The following conversation ensues.*]

TULLIUS : Salvē, Sexte !

SEXTUS : Salvē, ō Tullī !

TULLIUS : Quō festīnās hodiē māne ?

SEXTUS : Ad lūdum, Tullī, festīnō.

TULLIUS : Ubi est lūdus ? Et cūr festīnās ? Castī-
gābitne puerōs magister sī sērō intrāverint ?

SEXTUS : Ita vērō, Tullī. Orbilium, magistrum
lūdī, timēmus et plāgōsum appellāmus. Ignāvōs
enim semper culpat, semper verberat.

TULLIUS : Semper verberat ignāvōs ? Edepol,
plāgōsus est Orbilius. Sed ubi est lūdus ?

SEXTUS : Est in nostrō vīcō. Ad lūdum māne
semper ambulāmus.

TULLIUS : Portantne puerī multōs librōs ?

SEXTUS : Non portāmus librōs, Tullī ; sed servus
portat ad iānuam lūdī.

TULLIUS : Multane puerōs docet Orbilius ?

SEXTUS : Ita vērō, Tullī. Prīmum in sellīs puerōs
collocat. Puerī librōs, cērās, stilōs parant.
Deinde fābulās poētārum Orbilius puerīs recitat,
et puerī fābulās Orbiliō recitant. Bonōs
discipulōs laudat, sed ignāvōs culpat Orbilius.

IN A ROMAN SCHOOL

From this picture of Sextus and his companions at school you will see that the Roman school was something very different from the modern one. It was a private concern, and might be held in a room open to the street, on a verandah or any odd corner. Note the small number of pupils; twenty or thirty would be quite a big roll.

TULLIUS : Laudatne semper Sextum ?

SEXTUS : Ō ! . . . nōn semper, Tullī. Sed bona hodiē nārrō. Litterās puerōs docet Orbilius ; et saepe in lūdō numerāmus. Ecce, Tullī—

Ūnus et ūnus duo : duo et duo quattuoꞋ !

Sed ad lūdum festīnō. Iam ad iānuam lūdī Orbilius puerōs exspectābit. Valē, Tullī !

TULLIUS : Valē, Sexte, bone discipule Orbiliī !

B

1. The master had often warned the lazy slaves.
2. The master will have warned the lazy pupils.
3. Does Orbilius teach many boys ?
4. Yes, indeed ; many boys are the pupils of Orbilius.
5. The slave does not fear his master's son.
6. The masters will teach the sons of Valerius.
7. Why are you beating the slave, Valerius ?
8. Why does the master not read a story to the pupils ?
9. To-day we shall count ; to-morrow we shall carry pens and tablets to the school.
10. The pupils had not feared the good master.
11. Valerius and the farmer's son were walking in the field.
12. When will the master warn the slave ?
13. Where do you live, Sextus ? I live in Italy, master.
14. Yesterday the master warned the idle pupils.
15. The pupils love the master ; for he is good and just.

WORD STUDY

Your Latin continues to give you interesting connections between words. You could guess that *janitor* had something to do with **iānua** ; but who would imagine that there is any connection between *janitor* and *January* ? The connection arises in this way. *January* (in Latin **Iānuārius**) was the month sacred to and named after the god *Janus* (in Latin **Iānus**) who was the god of beginnings, entrances, *doors* and gates.

And the *doctor* whom you call in when you are ill—what connection has he with the verb **docēre** ? Originally, *doctor* meant a teacher, then a person skilled in some branch of learning, e.g. *Doctor of Divinity* (*D.D.*) ; *Doctor of Literature* (*D.Litt.*) ; *Doctor of Laws* (*LL.D.*) ; *Doctor of Science* (*D.Sc.*). Nowadays the word is especially applied to a *Doctor of Medicine* (*M.D.*), so much so that he is usually simply called the *Doctor*.

If you have no *monitors* in your school, you have probably read about them in school stories. Using your knowledge of Latin, say what their job really is.

XIX

THE THIRD DECLENSION

§ 24. Increasing Nouns, Masculine and Feminine.

An increasing noun is one which has a syllable more in the Genitive Singular than in the Nominative Singular:

rēx, rēgĭs, *m.*, a king.
legiō, legiōnĭs, *f.*, a legion.

Case	Singular		Plural	
Nom.	**rēx**	a king (*subj.*)	**rēg-ēs**	kings (*subj.*)
Voc.	**rēx**	king ! O king !	**rēg-ēs**	kings ! O kings !
Acc.	**rēg-em**	a king (*obj.*)	**rēg-ēs**	kings (*obj.*)
Gen.	**rēg-ĭs**	of a king	**rēg-um**	of kings
Dat.	**rēg-ī**	to, for a king	**rēg-ibus**	to, for kings
Abl.	**rēg-ĕ**	by, with, from a king	**rēg-ibus**	by, with, from kings

Case	Singular		Plural	
Nom.	**legiō**	a legion (*subj.*)	**legiōn-ēs**	legions (*subj.*)
Voc.	**legiō**	legion ! O legion !	**legiōn-ēs**	legions ! O legions !
Acc.	**legiōn-em**	a legion (*obj.*)	**legiōn-ēs**	legions (*obj.*)
Gen.	**legiōn-ĭs**	of a legion	**legiōn-um**	of legions
Dat.	**legiōn-ī**	to, for a legion	**legiōn-ibus**	to, for legions
Abl.	**legiōn-ĕ**	by, with, from a legion	**legiōn-ibus**	by, with, from legions

EXERCISE 18

Note carefully the following interrogative pronouns :

Quis ?, Who ?
Quem ?, Whom ?
Quid ?, What ?

A

1. Cūr nōn labōrant mīlitēs Rōmānī ?
2. Imperātor in oppidō est. Mīlitēs igitur īgnāvī sunt.
3. Quis ad castra festīnat, mīlitēs ?
4. Edepol ! Imperātor est ! Īgnāvōs semper castīgat.
5. Quid puerōs terruit ?
6. Hastae et sagittae mīlitum parvōs puerōs terrēbant.
7. Amātisne rēgem, mīlitēs ?
8. Ita vērō ; rēx enim bonus et iūstus est.
9. Cūr Rōmānī rēgēs nōn amābant ?
10. Rōmānī rēgēs ōlim habēbant. Sed nōn bonī erant.
11. Imperātor legiōnem nostram saepe laudat.
12. Quis poētam docuit ? Orbilius poētam docuit.
13. Quem timēs, miser puer ?
14. Lūdī magister puerōs terret, bone mīles.
15. Orbilius mīles ōlim erat. Discipulīs fābulās dē bellō saepe nārrat.

B

1. Why does the general chide the soldiers ?
2. The soldiers are idle.   They do not work in the camp.
3. What will you read to-day, pupils ?
4. To-day we shall read about the Roman kings.
5. To-morrow the story will be about a Roman soldier.
6. What has frightened the farmers ?   Whom did they fear ?
7. The spears of the soldiers have frightened the wretched farmers.
8. Yesterday the second legion entered the town.
9. Did the soldiers frighten the girls ?
10. Yes indeed ; the girls always fear the soldiers' spears.
11. Does the slave carry the boy's books ?
12. Yes, indeed ; Roman boys often had slaves.
13. The slaves are waiting for the boys at the door of the school.
14. Roman boys used to hasten to school in the morning.
15. In our school there are many boys and many girls.

C

This simple cross-word will give you some practice in words and terminations most of which you have already learnt.

Copy out the pattern to avoid putting marks on your book.

CLUES ACROSS

1. A tiller of the soil.
6. 14 reversed.
8. Your first Latin noun.
12. A book.
13. In English or Latin it's *in*.
14. To.
15. 13 reversed.
16. O good (man) !
19. *Just* needs *us* to make it Latin.
21. See 18 down.
23. Neuter nouns of the second declension end in this.
24. And reversed.
26. I adorn.
27. With pens.
30. See 18 down.
32. Good morning !
34. A rose.
35. Slaves (*dative*).
37. See 14.
39. Shops.
41. Two-thirds of but.
42. Legion (*ablative*).

CLUES DOWN

1. A friend.
2. All first and second declension dative and ablative plurals end in this.
3. Once upon a time.
4. By a book.
5. Preposition governing ablative.
6. Another preposition governing ablative.
7. To love ends in this.
9. For.
10. For sailors.
11. Preposition governing accusative.
17. 26 reversed.

18. Reversed or not, remains the negative.
20. A chair.
22. New (*vocative singular*).
25. To be.
28. Your (*ablative singular*).
29. Proper names ending in this have vocative in -i.
30. I relate.
31. To-morrow.
33. Ways.
36. But.
38. See 6.
40. Genitive singular of the first declension ends in this.

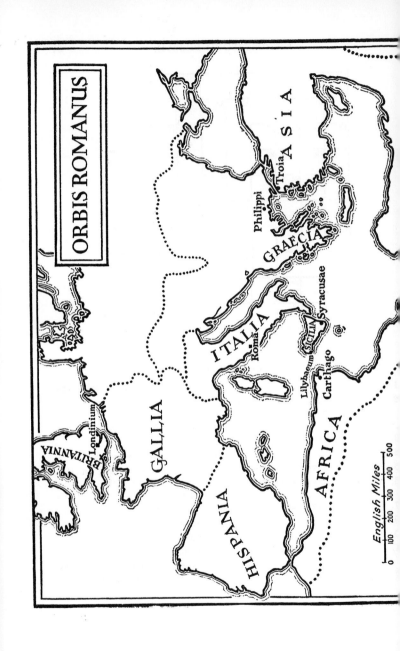

ORBIS ROMANUS

BRITANNIA
Londinium
GALLIA
HISPANIA
ITALIA
Roma
SICILIA
Lilybaeum
Syracusae
Carthago
AFRICA
GRAECIA
Philippi
Troia
ASIA

English Miles
0 100 200 300 400 500

XX

THE THIRD DECLENSION—*continued*

§ **25.** Increasing Nouns, Neuter:

nōmen, nōminĭs, *n.*, a name.
ŏnus, ŏnerĭs, *n.*, a burden.

CASE	SINGULAR		PLURAL	
Nom.	**nōmen**	a name (*subj.*)	**nōmin-ă**	names (*subj.*)
Voc.	**nōmen**	name! O name!	**nōmin-ă**	names ! O names !
Acc.	**nōmen**	a name (*obj.*)	**nōmin-ă**	names (*obj.*)
Gen.	**nōmin-ĭs**	of a name	**nōmin-um**	of names
Dat.	**nōmin-ī**	to, for a name	**nōmín-ibus**	to, for names
Abl.	**nōmin-ĕ**	by, with, from a name	**nōmín-ibus**	by, with, from names

CASE	SINGULAR		PLURAL	
Nom.	**ŏnus**	a burden (*subj.*)	**ŏner-ă**	burdens (*subj.*)
Voc.	**ŏnus**	burden ! O burden !	**ŏner-ă**	burdens ! O burdens !
Acc.	**ŏnus**	a burden (*obj.*)	**ŏner-ă**	burdens (*obj.*)
Gen.	**ŏner-ĭs**	of a burden	**ŏner-um**	of burdens
Dat.	**ĕner-ī**	to, for a burden	**ŏnér-ibus**	to, for burdens
Abl.	**ŏner-ĕ**	by, with, from a burden	**ŏnér-ibus**	by, with, from burdens

EXERCISE 19

A

Oh, for the Life of a Soldier!

Titus : Ō mē miserum ! Semperne labōrābō in fundō ? Semperne onera portābō ex agrīs in vīllam, et ē vīllā in agrōs ? Quam miseram vītam habeō ! Est enim vīta servī, sed nōn virī Rōmānī. Nōn agricola erō, sed ē fundō ad Galliam ad castra imperātōris festīnābō. Mīles erō ; in multīs terrīs contrā barbarōs pugnābō. Magnam glōriam habēbō. Ōlim imperātor erō, et Rōmānī Titum laudābunt. Sed quis in agrum festīnat ? Marcus est. Salvē, Marce !

A Roman Legionary Soldier

Marcus : Salvē, Tite ! Sed cūr miser es ? Quid timēs ?

Titus : Nihil timeō, Marce ; sed vītam agricolārum nōn amō. Semper labōrō in agrīs. Multa et magna onera portō.

Ō mē miserum ! Dūrī hominis fīlius sum. Fīlium semper īgnāvum appellat ; semper castīgat ; numquam laudat. Marce, ē fundō festīnābō ad Galliam et mīles erō. Sed quid nārrās dē vītā mīlitum ? Estne bona vīta ?

MARCUS : Bona vīta est, sī pugnās, perīcula, castra nōn timēs.

TITUS : Nōn timeō, ō Marce, sed dē Secundā legiōne quid ? Estne bona legiō ?

MARCUS : Ita vērō, Tite. Secunda legiō castra in Galliā habet, sed in Britanniam cum imperātōre festīnābit. Britannī enim barbarī sunt : Rōmānōs nōn amant : contrā Rōmānōs in Galliā saepe pugnant.

TITUS : Edepol, Marce, mīles Secundae legiōnis erō. In Britanniam cum mīlitibus Secundae legiōnis nāvigābō. Pugnābimus contrā barbarōs. Erunt multae pugnae, perīcula multa ; sed Secundam legiōnem nōn terrēbunt. Barbarōs virtūte superābimus, et ad silvās ex pugnīs festīnābunt. Magnam glōriam habēbimus. Magna erit virtūs et glōria Titī. Magnam glōriam habēbit Marcus.

MARCUS : Bonus vir es, Tite. Quam bonus mīles eris ! Imperātor et mīlitēs Secundae legiōnis bonōs virōs semper amant, semper laudant. Hodiē ad Galliam festīnābimus. Eris enim mīles, Tite.

B

1. The boys' names are Sextus and Lucius.
2. The life of Roman slaves was not always unhappy.
3. What has terrified the unhappy girls ?
4. Hail, general ! Great is the glory of the Second legion.
5. The slaves' burdens are great.
6. The idle boys did not carry books to school.
7. The Roman soldiers had saved the camp by their valour.
8. We shall salute the great general.

9. Where are Sextus and Lucius? They are among the soldiers.
10. Where has the legion sailed to?
11. Why do the Romans not fear the barbarians?
12. Who will terrify the soldiers of our legion?
13. He used to have a farm in Britain.
14. Good men do not fear danger. They love glory.
15. What had Lucius feared? Lucius feared nothing.

WORD STUDY

Can you give an English word meaning *danger* which is derived from **perīculum**?

What are *onerous* duties? Why are they so called?

What is meant by *culpable homicide*?

A LATIN MOTTO

Via, Vēritās, Vīta, The Way, the Truth, the Life.

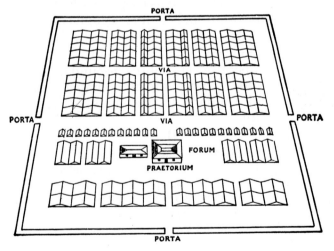

PLAN OF A ROMAN CAMP

XXI

THE THIRD DECLENSION—*continued*

§ 26. Non-increasing Nouns, Masculine and Feminine, Neuter.

A non-increasing noun is one which has the same number of syllables in the Genitive Singular as in the Nominative Singular.

The Genitive Plural of non-increasing nouns regularly ends in -ium.

cīvĭs, cīvĭs, *m.*, a citizen.
cubīle, cubīlĭs, *n.*, a couch, bed.

Case	Singular		Plural	
Nom.	cīvĭs	a citizen (*subj.*)	cīv-ēs	citizens (*subj.*)
Voc.	cīvĭs	citizen! O citizen!	cīv-ēs	citizens! O citizens!
Acc.	cīv-em	a citizen (*obj.*)	cīv-ēs	citizens (*obj.*)
Gen.	cīv-ĭs	of a citizen	cīv-ium	of citizens
Dat.	cīv-ī	to, for a citizen	cīv-ibus	to, for citizens
Abl.	cīv-ĕ	by, with, from a citizen	cīv-ibus	by, with, from citizens

Case	Singular		Plural	
Nom.	cubīlĕ	a couch (*subj.*)	cubīl-ĭă	couches (*subj.*)
Voc.	cubīlĕ	couch! O couch	cubīl-ĭă	couches! O couches!
Acc.	cubīlĕ	a couch (*obj.*)	cubīl-ĭă	couches (*obj.*)
Gen.	cubīl-is	of a couch	cubīl-ium	of couches
Dat.	cubīl-ī	to, for a couch	cubīl-ibus	to, for couches
Abl.	cubīl-ī	by, with, from a couch	cubīl-ibus	by, with, from couches

EXERCISE 20

A

1. Nautae mare timent ; terram dēsīderant.
2. Cūr cīvēs virtūtem imperātōris laudant ?
3. Terrā marīque imperātor hostēs Rōmānōrum superāvit.
4. Miserī nautae in nāvibus cubīlia nōn habent.
5. Imperātor noster cum multīs nāvibus longīs ad Britanniam festīnābit.
6. Corpora barbarōrum magna sunt.
7. Quō festīnātis hodiē, puerī ? Ad mare festīnāmus, ō poēta ; nāvēs enim pulchrās amāmus.
8. Cūr nautae ex īnsulā festīnābant ?
9. Hostēs īnsulam oppugnāverant, et magnā virtūte nautās terruerant.
10. Quis puerōs terruit ? Quem puerī timent ? Quid puerī portant ?

B

1. The citizens are counting the warships.
2. Our warships will protect Britain. The enemy will fear our warships.
3. The ships have carried the soldiers to the island.
4. There was once a camp of Roman soldiers on our farm.
5. By land and sea we have overcome the enemy, O citizens.
6. The sailors love the sea, but the farmers love the land.
7. Where will you walk to to-morrow, citizens ?
8. To-day I walked to the sea, but to-morrow I shall walk to the wood.

(*Top*) Hadrian's Wall at the present time and (*below*) as it would have appeared
in Roman times

9. Are there many boys in our street?
10. Yes, indeed; for it is a long street.
11. For a long time a poet lived on our island. He loved sailors and the sea.
12. When will you tell the boys a story about the sea, master?

WORD STUDY

What is the origin and hence the meaning of *annihilate*? The word **nāvis** has given us many English words. You have *navy* and *naval*; and what about the *nave* of a cathedral? Find out what this is, and you will soon see why it received its name. Everyone has seen a *navvy* working with pick and shovel. His name is also connected with the Latin **nāvis**. For *navvy* is just a very much shortened form of the word *navigator*, which was once applied to a labourer employed in making a harbour or canal, and later came in its shortened form to mean a labourer engaged in any work where there is a lot of digging to be done.

A ROMAN WARSHIP

XXII

THE THIRD DECLENSION—*continued*

§ 27. Monosyllabic Nouns ending in two consonants.

The Genitive Plural of these nouns ends in **-ium.**
urbs, urbĭs, *f.,* a city.

Case	Singular		Plural	
Nom.	**urbs**	a city (*subj.*)	**urb-ēs**	cities (*subj.*)
Voc.	**urbs**	city! O city!	**urb-ēs**	cities! O cities!
Acc.	**urb-em**	a city (*obj.*)	**urb-ēs**	cities (*obj.*)
Gen.	**urb-ĭs**	of a city	**urb-ium**	of cities
Dat.	**urb-ī**	to, for a city	**urb-ibus**	to, for cities
Abl.	**urb-ĕ**	by, with, from a city	**urb-ibus**	by, with, from cities

Note.—The following nouns also belong to the above class:

nŏx, nŏctĭs, *f.* night.
ŏs, ossis, *n.* a bone.

EXERCISE 21

A

Some Articles of Roman Dress

In Ītaliā hominēs in sōle saepe ambulant et labōrant. Rōmānī igitur onus multōrum vestīment-ōrum nōn amābant. Vestīmenta pulchra erant. Prīmum, enim, cīvis Rōmānus tunicam semper habēbat. In vīllā et in agrīs tunica satis erat ; sed in urbe et in forō et in cūriā super tunicam togam longam et albam semper habēbat. Toga pulchrum vestīmentum fuit. Togam albam et longam Rōmānī laudābant; sed togam parvam et sordidam culpābant. Poētae Rōmānī togam saepe laudant, et cīvēs Rōmānōs gentem togātam appellant. Servī enim togās nōn habuērunt. Cīvium Rōmānōrum fīliōrumque toga vestīmentum fuit; sed servus tunicam modo habēbat. In pedibus calceōs habēbat cīvis Rōmānus. Capite nūdō saepe ambulābat et labōrābat; sed in sōle et in longō itinere petasum habēbat.

B

1. I am a Roman citizen.
2. Where is my toga, Syrus? It is on the chair, master.
3. What beautiful clothes Valerius has! How long his toga is!
4. Upon my word! The boy has a new tunic and new shoes!
5. How dirty the farmer is! How dirty the farmer's shoes are!
6. Why have you not a hat on your head, boy?
7. I always walk bareheaded to school.
8. To-morrow the slave will have a new tunic.
9. Sextus loves cities; Titus loves fields and woods.
10. Who has my hat? Where is my hat? Hang it all, I haven't a hat!
11. The Roman legions will attack the walls.
12. There are large shops in our city.
13. The women love the shops; for there are many beautiful garments in the shops.
14. The poet will procure a new tunic for his son.
15. Valerius longs for his country house. He does not love the city.

C

A Morning Scene

(*Note.*—**māter**, mother)

SEXTUS : Māter ! māter ! māter !

MĀTER : Quid est, Sexte ?

SEXTUS : Ubi est tunica mea ?   Herī in sellā collocāvī.
Hodiē māne in sellā nōn est.   Ubi est ?   Quis habet ?

MĀTER : Ecce, Sexte, in cubīlī sunt vestīmenta.

SEXTUS : Edepol, tunica est in cubīlī ; sed ubi est toga ?
Togam nōn videō (*I see*).

MĀTER : Ecce, īgnāve puer ; toga est in sellā.

SEXTUS : Ō māter !   Quam alba est !   Nova toga est !

MĀTER : Sed sērō in lūdum intrābis, sī nōn festīnābis.   Et
magister īgnāvōs puerōs semper castīgat, et saepe
verberat.

SEXTUS : Ō mē miserum !   Tunicam habeō et togam, sed
ubi sunt calceī meī ?   Pedibus nūdis ad lūdum nōn
festīnābō hodiē.   Ō māter, calceōs nōn videō.   Ubi
calceōs collocāvistī ?

MĀTER : Ubi Sextus collocāvit ?   Ecce, īgnāve puer, sunt
inter sellam et cubīle.   Sed cūr nōn festīnās, Sexte ?
Iam puerī in lūdum intrant.

SEXTUS : Ita vērō, māter.   Festīnō ; sed ubi sunt librī ?

MĀTER : Servus librōs habet, et ad lūdum portābit.   Sed
cūr nōn festīnās ?

SEXTUS : Festīnō.   Sed ubi est——.

MĀTER : Iam satis est.   Abī ! (*Be off !*)

SEXTUS : Valē. māter !   Abeō (*I'm off*).

WORD STUDY

1. The Latin word **caput** gives us the English word *capital*. This English word has come to have a great many different shades of meaning as the following examples will show; but notice that behind every particular meaning there is the general idea of the head or top or chief part of a thing, of greatness or of importance:

    (*a*) London is the *capital* of England.
    (*b*) Every sentence should begin with a *capital* letter.
    (*c*) *Capital* punishment has been abolished in many countries.
    (*d*) The fleet has many *capital* ships.
    (*e*) We admired the *capital* of the pillar.
    (*f*) The firm was obliged to draw on its *capital*.

2. What is meant by the *suburbs* of a city? (In Latin the preposition **sub** means " under," " up to," " close to.")

A ROMAN TAILOR AND HIS CUSTOMERS

XXIII

THE THIRD DECLENSION—*continued*

NOTES

§ 28. (1) **păter, pătrĭs,** *m.,* father
māter, mātris, *f.,* mother
frāter, frātrĭs, *m.,* brother
cănĭs, cănĭs, *m.,* dog
iuvenĭs, iuvenĭs, *m.,* young man

} have **-um** in Genitive Plural.

(2) **senex, senĭs,** old man, is declined thus:

		SINGULAR.	PLURAL.
Nom.	*Voc.*	senex	sen-ēs
	Acc.	sen-em	sen-ēs
	Gen.	sen-ĭs	sen-um
	Dat.	sen-ī	sen-ibus
	Abl.	sen-ĕ	sen-ibus

Note.—Remember that the father, mother, brother, the young man, the old man and the dog all have **-um** in the Genitive Plural. We might call it a family peculiarity.

(3) **Iūppiter, Iŏvis,** *m.,* Jupiter, is declined thus:

Nom.	*Voc.*	Iūppiter
	Acc.	Iŏv-em
	Gen.	Iŏv-ĭs
	Dat.	Iŏv-ī
	Abl.	Iŏv-ĕ

(4) **bōs, bovis,** *m.,* an ox, or *f.,* a cow, is declined thus:

		SINGULAR.	PLURAL.
Nom.	*Voc.*	bŏs	bŏv-ēs
	Acc.	bŏv-em	bŏv-ēs
	Gen.	bŏv-ĭs	bŏum
	Dat.	bŏv-ī	bōbus or būbus
	Abl.	bŏv-ĕ	bōbus or būbus

(5) **vīs,** *f.*, force (in plural, strength), is declined thus :

	SINGULAR.	PLURAL.
Nom.	vīs	vīr-ēs
Acc.	vĭm	vīr-ēs
Gen.	—	vīr-ium
Dat.	—	vīr-ibus
Abl.	vī	vīr-ibus

(6) **moenia, moenium,** *n.*, city walls, is used only in the plural. (Decline like the plural of **cubīle.**)

EXERCISE 22

After words of number or quantity, such as **multī,** many, **pars,** part, a genitive case may be used as in English, e.g. :

> **Multī mīlitum,** Many of the soldiers.
> **Pars urbis,** Part of the city.

This is called the Partitive Genitive.

A

1. Poēta patrem laudat ; erat enim pater poētae vir bonus.
2. Salvē, agricola ! Edepol, multōs bovēs comparāvistī !
3. Magnum fundum, ō poēta, habeō. Sunt semper multī bovēs in agrīs meīs.
4. Cūr iuvenēs arma parant et ad moenia festīnant?
5. Barbarī in Ītaliam intrāvērunt ; multa oppida vāstāvērunt ; ad urbem festīnant.
6. Magnā vī iuvenēs castra hostium oppugnābunt.
7. Capite nūdō et nūdīs pedibus miser servus in agrīs labōrat.
8. Pater fīlium castīgat ; iuvenis enim est īgnāvus.

9. Iuvenēs ad bellum festīnant ; senēs moenia servant.

10. Mīlitēs Rōmānī magna onera portābant.

11. Salvē, Syre ! Unde festīnās ? Edepol, magnum onus habēs. Quid portās ?

12. Ex oppidō, Galle, festīnō. Novam tunicam et calceōs novōs dominō nostrō portō.

13. Puerum videō in nostrō vīcō. Quis est ? Edepol, Sextus est, frāter meus.

14. Salvē, Sexte, cūr nōn festīnās ē lūdō ?

15. Timeō patrem et mātrem. In lūdō hodiē duo puerī mē oppugnāvērunt ; puerōs superāvī ; magna victōria mea erat ; magna est glōria mea inter puerōs nostrī lūdī. Sed post pugnam sordida est nova tunica mea ; nusquam est toga, nusquam sunt librī meī. Pater igitur et māter mē castīgābunt. Ō mē miserum !

B

1. The barbarians have laid waste a large part of the city.
2. The old man praises the valour of the young men.
3. A long life teaches many things.
4. The farmer's brother has many dogs.
5. Young men often love dogs.
6. My brother has a large part of the farm.
7. My father has many books in his country house.
8. The enemy feared the valour of our men.
9. The poet used to live in Italy with his brother.
10. By his great valour Horatius saved the city.
11. On our farm there are many beautiful oxen.
12. The name of the poet's friend is Gallus.

13. The little boy longs for a dog.
14. The citizens are preparing many warships, for the danger is great.
15. Whom do I see ? Is it Sextus ? It is. Goodness gracious ! he has a hat on his head. Where is he hurrying to ? **He** is hurrying to the temple of Jupiter.

WORD STUDY

Use your Latin to find out what is meant by : *paternal* authority, *maternal* affection, *fraternal* love.

You have learned the Latin names for certain animals. These names will enable you to understand what is meant by *canine* teeth, and by a *bovine* expression. Here are some more English words derived from Latin names of animals. Try to find out their meaning, and, if possible, what they come from : *feline, asinine, equine.*

The names of gods give us many interesting words. A *jovial* fellow was one supposed to have been born under the influence of the planet *Jupiter*. A *martial* shout is a warlike shout, from *Mars*, the Roman god of war. Ask your teacher to go over and explain the following list : *Bacchic, cereal, mercuric* and *mercurial, volcano* and *volcanic, saturnine.*

A LATIN IDIOM

Vī et armīs, By force of arms.

REVISION EXERCISES

A

1. We shall fear : they have taught : you (*s.*) have had : you (*pl.*) warn : he was fearing : we were seeing : they will have taught.
2. Of fathers : for an old man : of heads : feet (*obj.*) : by burdens : by land and sea : by valour : strength (*subj.*).
3. Whom will the master blame ?
4. The master always blamed the lazy pupils.

5. The farmer has many oxen on the farm.
6. Why does the master not greet the father and mother of the pupil ?
7. My father is a hard man : he has beaten the wretched slave.
8. The big dog has frightened the old man.
9. Why do you walk to the city with bare feet ?
10. The farmer's oxen had big bodies and small heads.

B

1. Docēbitis : exspectātis : monuerāmus : timent : terrueris : monēbimus : terrēbās : monuērunt : collocāmus : recitābis.
2. Dūrī hominis : magnā virtūte : multōrum mīlitum : magnīs oneribus : vīrium : bōbus : in castrīs imperātōris : marī.
3. Cum patre et mātre ad urbem ambulābō.
4. Cūr nōn contrā barbarōs terrā marīque pugnāmus ?
5. Quam dūra est vīta agricolārum !
6. Cūr togam et tunicam in cubīlī collocās ?
7. Dūrum est cubīle : misera est vīta mea.
8. Quid hodiē in lūdō nārrābātis ?
9. Hodiē dē rēgibus Rōmānīs magister fābulās recitāvit.
10. Herī magister īgnāvōs discipulōs verberābat. Edepol, magnae sunt magistrī vīrēs !

C

1. Who is waiting for me at the door of the school ?
2. Where have you placed my books ? They are on the seat.
3. Why have you entered the school late to-day ?
4. Yesterday we saw the great walls of the city.
5. You have never read aloud the names of the idle pupils.
6. The danger of the citizens is great.
7. Why have the generals not warned the unhappy citizens ?
8. We shall hasten in the morning ; for the journey is long.
9. The Romans overcame many great nations.
10. We saw four young men in the street.

TYPES OF ROMAN DRESS

Here we see Sextus in his home. Being under sixteen, he wears the toga praetexta. His father, being a senator, also wears the toga praetexta. His mother is dressed in the stola, and his elder brother wears the plain white toga virilis.

ROMAN DRESS

Well, you have read a good deal lately about the toga and its importance. As an article of dress it had its disadvantages. Being made of wool it was heavy, and it was difficult to put on properly. A Roman gentleman who was keen on appearances might require the assistance of three slaves to get his toga into position, with every fold gracefully arranged.

The Roman boy wore a toga with a broad purple edge, called the **toga praetexta.** When he came of age—i.e. when he was about sixteen or seventeen—he laid aside the toga of boyhood. The occasion was quite a ceremony. Friends of the family gathered in the home, the father offered sacrifice, and then arrayed his son in a plain white toga—the **toga virīlis.** Then by his friends and relations the young Roman was escorted to the forum and registered in the official list of citizens. He was no longer a **puer** but a **iuvenis,** now liable for military service. It is interesting to note that Roman magistrates as a sign of office wore the **toga praetexta.** All other citizens, however, wore the plain white toga.

Roman ladies at home wore the **stola.** This was a long gown tied in with a girdle at or a little above the waist. Outside her home the Roman lady wore the **palla.** This was not unlike the toga, and was worn draped about the person in pretty much the same way.

When his toga became dirty, the Roman sent it to the cleaner (**fullō, -ōnis,** *m.*). The Romans—except the poorest of the poor—did no washing of clothes at home. At Pompeii, the city which was buried in the eruption of Vesuvius in A.D. 79, a **fullōnia** or laundry has been excavated, and as its walls had paintings showing the whole process of cleaning we know fairly accurately how it was done.

The dirty toga was put first in a tub or vat of water. The Romans hadn't anything like our soap ; so with the water was mixed a kind of potash called lye, or **nitrum,** which was just washing-soda in its natural state. Then, bare-footed and barelegged, the **fullō** or his assistant got into the vat and treaded the toga with his feet. It reminds you, does it not, of the way Scottish peasant women used to wash their blankets? After it was thoroughly washed in this way, the toga was dried in the open air, and then brushed and carded to bring up the pile of the wool. Lastly it was hung over an arrangement like a big cage and some sulphur was burned underneath. The fumes whitened the cloth. Then, washed, dried, brushed and bleached, the toga returned to its owner.

A candidate for a magistracy, while doing his canvassing, was not content with an ordinary dull white toga. He wanted his to be **candida**—shiny white. This effect was obtained by treating the toga with **crēta,** which was pretty much our pipe-clay. The word **candidātus** means clad in a pipe-clayed toga, and has given us our word *candidate*. Think of that next time you read about an election.

A ROMAN FULLER AT WORK

XXIV

PRINCIPAL PARTS OF VERBS

§ 29. A Latin verb has usually four *Principal Parts*, so called because from them every other part of the verb can be found.

The principal parts are :

(*a*) The 1st person singular present indicative active.
(*b*) The present infinitive active.
(*c*) The 1st person singular perfect indicative active.
(*d*) The supine. (The meaning and use of this part will be learned later.)

Thus the principal parts of **amāre** and **monēre** are:

amō	**amāre**	**amāvī**	**amātum**
moneō	**monēre**	**monuī**	**monitum**

To conjugate a verb is to give in order its principal parts. All regular verbs of the first conjugation are conjugated like **amāre,** e.g. :

oppugnō	**oppugnāre**	**oppugnāvī**	**oppugnātum**
nāvigō	**nāvigāre**	**nāvigāvī**	**nāvigātum**

All regular verbs of the second conjugation are conjugated like **monēre,** e.g. :

terreō	**terrēre**	**terruī**	**territum**

§ 30. However, some verbs of the first and second conjugations are irregular in the perfect and supine, e.g. :

dō	**dăre**	**dĕdī**	**dătum,** to give.
stō	**stāre**	**stĕtī**	**stātum,** to stand.
maneō	**manēre**	**mānsī**	**mānsum,** to remain.
videō	**vidēre**	**vīdī**	**vīsum,** to see.

Given the principal parts, the endings in each tense are regular. Thus, once it is known that the first person singular perfect indicative active of **dare** is **dedī,** the remainder of the tense is known, for it is formed with the same endings as **amāvī**. Hence we have : **dedī, dedistī, dedit, dedimus, dedistis, dedērunt.**

Similarly, knowing that the 1st person singular perfect indicative active of **manēre** is **mānsī**, we say : **mānsī, mānsistī, mānsit, mānsimus, mānsistis, mānsērunt,** using the endings of **monuī, monuistī, monuit,** etc.

Also, knowing the 1st person singular perfect indicative active of any Latin verb, we can form the future perfect indicative active by adding to the perfect stem the endings **-erō, -eris, -erit,** etc., and we can form the pluperfect indicative active by adding to the perfect stem the endings **-eram, -erās, -erat,** etc.

Note.—From this point onward, always learn and state the principal parts of verbs.

EXERCISE 23

A

THE SIGHTS OF ROME. I

[MARCUS *and his young friend* SEXTUS, *to whom he is showing the sights of the city, have just arrived at the top of the Capitoline Hill.*]

MARCUS : Ecce, Sexte, in Monte Capitōlīnō stāmus. Iam magnam urbis Rōmae partem vidēs.

SEXTUS : Edepol, Marce, magna urbs est et pulchra.

MARCUS : Ita vērō, Sexte. Vidēsne flūmen Tiberim ? In rīpīs Tiberis Rōmānī Rōmam aedificāvērunt.

SEXTUS : Tiberim, ō Marce, videō, et in flūmine pontēs multōs. Quid dē pontibus nārrās ?

MARCUS : Prīmus fuit Pōns Sublicius.

SEXTUS : Ō ! iam meminī (*I remember*). Dē
Ponte Subliciō magister pulchram fābulam
saepe nārrābat. Vir Rōmānus ōlim Pontem
Sublicium contrā hostēs Rōmānōrum servāvit.
Sed quid nōmen virī fuit ? Meminī. Horātius
erat.

MARCUS : Ita vērō, Sexte. Pōns Sublicius ligneus
est. Sed multī pontēs sunt. Est enim Pōns
Aemilius et Pōns Fabricius et Pōns Cestius.

SEXTUS : Pōns Fabricius ? Pontem Fabricium nōn
videō. Ubi est ?

MARCUS : Vidēsne in Tiberī īnsulam parvam ?

SEXTUS : Videō, Marce.

MARCUS : Est inter īnsulam et urbem Pōns Fabricius ; sed inter īnsulam et agrōs est Pōns
Cestius.

SEXTUS : Videō pontēs, Marce. Sed dē portīs urbis
quid ? Habetne Rōma multās portās ?

MARCUS : Ita vērō ; multās habet et pulchrās.
Multīs enim viīs ex urbe in multās Ītaliae partēs
Rōmānī festīnant. Viam Appiam et Viam
Flāminiam semper laudāmus.

SEXTUS : Ō ! dē Viā Appiā magister multa nārrat.
Viam Appiam rēgīnam viārum appellat.

MARCUS : Sed iam satis. Sērō est, Sexte. Ad
cēnam festīnābimus. Crās montēs et magna
aedificia urbis vidēbis.

4

B

1. The boys stand on the Mons Capitolinus.
2. What do the boys see ?
3. They see the river Tiber.
4. When shall we see the forum ?
5. To-morrow, Sextus, we shall walk to the forum.
6. Why do we not hasten to the forum to-day ?
7. It is late, Sextus. Our fathers are standing at the gate.
8. Once upon a time Rome was a small city.
9. We shall build a city, O citizens, on the banks of the river.
10. Many poets have praised the Tiber.
11. The poet calls the Romans the toga-clad race.
12. Look ! The boy has white garments.
13. How beautiful his toga is !
14. The first Roman bridge was of wood.
15. How beautiful were the buildings of ancient Rome !

WORD STUDY

What is an *antiquary* ? What sort of things interest him ?
Now follow up this clue and see how many English words you
can find derived from **antīquus.**

Prīmus is worth following up in the same way. What do
you call the first minister in the government ? Go ahead and
see how many more descendants of **prīmus** you can find.

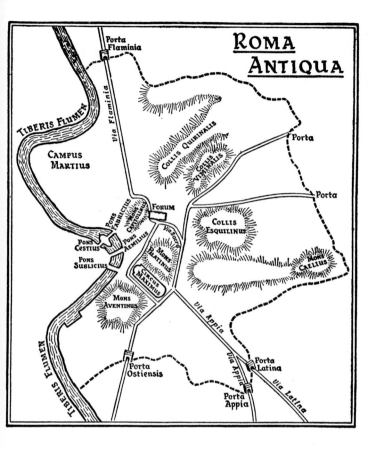

EXERCISE 24

A

THE SIGHTS OF ROME. II

SEXTUS : Salvē, Marce ! Herī pontēs et portās
urbis vidēbāmus. Quid hodiē vidēbimus ?

MARCUS : Ad Montem Capitōlīnum festīnābimus.
Ecce, vidēsne moenia antīqua urbis Rōmae ?

SEXTUS : Videō, Marce. Edepol, intrā moenia multī collēs sunt. Ūnum videō, duo—quattuor —sed quot sunt, Marce ?

MARCUS : Septem sunt, Sexte. Sunt enim Mōns Capitōlīnus, Mōns Palātīnus, Mōns Aventīnus, Mōns Caelius, Collis Esquilīnus, Collis Vīminālis, Collis Quirīnālis.

SEXTUS : Quid ? Videōne extrā mūrum lātum campum ?

MARCUS : Ita vērō, Sexte. Est enim extrā mūrum Campus Mārtius. In Campō Mārtiō imperātōrēs Rōmānī mīlitēs ōlim exercēbant. Hodiē cīvēs Rōmānī post negōtia ad Campum festīnant, et cum amīcīs ambulant et sedent. Saepe etiam pĭlā multīsque lūdīs corpora exercent.

SEXTUS : Sed intrā moenia multa aedificia videō. Ubi est Forum Rōmānum ?

MARCUS : Est inter Capitōlīnum et Palātīnum. Vidēsne Viam Sacram et templum Vestae et Rōstra et Cūriam ?

SEXTUS : Videō. Quam pulchrīs aedificiīs Rōmānī Forum ōrnāvērunt ! Sed Circum Maximum magister meus saepe laudat. Ubi est Circus Maximus ?

MARCUS : Est inter Aventīnum et Palātīnum, Sexte. Sed hodiē Circum Maximum nōn vidēbimus. Festīnābimus enim ad vīllam nostram. Māter enim bonam cēnam parāvit.

B

1. How many young men do you see ?
2. I see seven young men and four old men.
3. Where is the dog ?   Nowhere do I see the dog.
4. See ! How white Marcus's toga is !
5 . Why has Sextus a hat on his head ?   He is working in the sun.
6. Once upon a time Roman generals trained soldiers outside the walls.
7. Now the Romans often walk in the Campus Martius.
8. After dinner we shall sit outside the gate.
9. Why does Marcus walk to school with bare feet ?
10. Poor (*miser*) Marcus has not shoes. Where are Marcus's shoes?
11. The slave is counting the master's oxen.
12. The boy has a little dog. The dog's name is Hylax. (**Hylax, -acis :** the name really means " Barker.")
13. The Temple of Jupiter used to stand on Mons Capitolinus.
14. After business we shall walk with our friends in the Campus.
15. Where is the ball, Sextus ?   Hang it all ! the master has the ball.

WORD STUDY

Do you play golf yet ? If so, you may have spoken, or heard someone speak of his golf-ball as a " pill." That is slang English, but good Latin ! In the chemist's shop you may find the word **pilula** on the pots where he keeps his pills. Now **pilula is a** Latin word meaning " a little ball."

What is meant by *extraordinary* ?

What shade of blue is *ultramarine* ?

You often hear of people or of nations *negotiating* about something. What exactly does that mean ?

Some people are engaged in *sedentary* occupations. Can you give examples of such occupations ?

We saw in an earlier lesson that **longus** gave us the English word *longitude*; and that **magnus** gives us *magnitude,* and **multus** gives *multitude.* What do we get from **lātus ?**

XXV

THE THIRD CONJUGATION

§ 31. Present, Future and Imperfect Indicative Active of **regō**
regĕre, rēxī, rēctum, to rule.

Tense	Pers.	Singular		Plural	
Present	1	**rég-ō**	I rule	**rég-imus**	we rule
	2	**rég-is**	you rule	**rég-itis**	you rule
	3	**rég-it**	he, she, it rules	**rég-unt**	they rule
Future	1	**rég-am**	I shall rule	**reg-ēmus**	we shall rule
	2	**rég-ēs**	you will rule	**reg-ētis**	you will rule
	3	**rég-et**	he, she, it will rule	**rég-ent**	they will rule
Imperfect	1	**reg-ēbam**	I was ruling	**reg-ēbāmus**	we were ruling
	2	**reg-ēbās**	you were ruling	**reg-ēbātis**	you were ruling
	3	**reg-ēbat**	he, she, it was ruling	**reg-ēbant**	they were ruling

EXERCISE 25

A

1. Cūr rēgēs Rōmānōs nōn regēbant ?
2. Rōmānī nōmen rēgis nōn amābant.
3. Quid Valerius fīliō dedit ? Valerius parvum canem fīliō dedit.
4. Cūr imperātor mīlitēs ad Campum Mārtium dūcet ?
5. In Campō imperātor mīlitēs exercet.
6. Cūr senēs ad arcem nōn festīnant ?
7. Senēs contrā barbarōs nōn pugnābunt. Iuvenēs igitur ad arcem mittunt.
8. Iuvenēs enim fortiter pugnābunt et arcem servābunt.
9. Barbarī senēs in urbe necāvērunt.
10. Ad rēgiam hodiē ambulābimus ; rēgem et rēgīnam vidēbimus.
11. Rēx enim et rēgīna ē rēgiā ad urbem festīnābunt.
12. Quam pulchrum aedificium est rēgia ! Patrem et mātrem ad rēgiam crās dūcēmus.

B

1. When shall we send our son to school ?
2. To-morrow we shall take (lead) the boy to the school of Orbilius.
3. Shall I have new shoes, mother ?
4. I shall not send my son to school with dirty shoes.
5. We have not seen the citadel. Where is it ?
6. The master will take (lead) the boys to the citadel.

Ander

THE FORUM IN ROME
(*above*) as it was, and (*below*) as it is to-day

7. The master used to lead the boys out of the city.
8. The plain is outside the walls of the city.
9. Has the soldier killed the slave ?
0. The king and queen live in the palace.
1. After business the citizens often walk in the plain.
2. Horatius bravely defended the bridge.
3. How bravely our men fight ! They will overcome the enemy.
4. We shall stand on the hill. We shall see the wooden bridge.
5. They are sending soldiers to the king's palace.

WORD STUDY

To-day, instead of tracing derivations, let us have a look for Latin in our everyday lives. In the first place, most of us are probably carrying some Latin in our pockets. Take out a penny and have a look at that side of it which bears the queen's head.

The words inscribed there are all Latin words. Some of them are not given in full ; but still you know enough Latin by this time to recognise most of them. Try to read and translate the inscription. Your teacher will help you if you are stuck.

Again, we use a great many sets of initials which are really the initial letters of Latin words. For example, on a Royal Mail van, or indeed on any piece of Government property, you may see the letters *E.R.* What do these stand for ? Here are some other sets of initials which you might try to find out about :

N.B. ; *P.S.* ; *A.M.* ; *P.M.*, etc.

Lastly, here are a few Latin words and phrases, many of which you have used in conversation, and all of which you will no doubt use sooner or later. Search and ask till you discover the exact meaning of each :

Curriculum, sub rosa, infra dig., status quo, quid pro quo, exit, requiem, sub judice, interim.

XXVI

THE THIRD CONJUGATION—*continued*

§ 32. Perfect, Future Perfect and Pluperfect Indicative Active of **regĕre,** to rule.

Tense	Pers.	Singular	Plural
Perfect	1	**rēx-ī** I have ruled, *or* I ruled	**rēx-imus** we have ruled, *or* we ruled
	2	**rēx-istī** you have ruled, *or* you ruled	**rēx-istis** you have ruled, *or* you ruled
	3	**rēx-it** he, she, it has ruled, *or* ruled	**rēx-ērunt** they have ruled, *or* they ruled
Future Perfect	1	**rēx-erō** I shall have ruled	**rēx-erimus** we shall have ruled
	2	**rēx-eris** you will have ruled	**rēx-eritis** you will have ruled
	3	**rēx-erit** he, she, it will have ruled	**rēx-erint** they will have ruled
Pluperfect	1	**rēx-eram** I had ruled	**rēx-erāmus** we had ruled
	2	**rēx-erās** you had ruled	**rēx-erātis** you had ruled
	3	**rēx-erat** he, she, it had ruled	**rēx-erant** they had ruled

EXERCISE 26

A

THE TROJAN WAR. I

[DIDO, *queen of Carthage on the North coast of Africa, is entertaining the Trojan* AENEAS *and his followers who have reached Carthage in their wanderings. As the banquet ends,* DIDO *prevails upon* AENEAS *to tell the tale of Troy. The story begins with the love of* PARIS *and* HELEN, *Helen's flight to Troy, and the Greek expedition to win her back.*]

DĪDŌ : Dē bellō Trōiānō, ō Aenēā, multī multa iam nārrāvērunt. Ēheu! quam longum bellum fuit! Quam fortiter urbem contrā dūrōs hostēs dēfendistis! Sed cūr Graecī Trōiānōs oppugnāvērunt? Quid initium bellī fuit?

AENĒĀS : Ēheu!

Īnfandum, rēgīna, iubēs renovāre dolōrem.[1]

Multa enim et misera in bellō vīdī. Quam pulchram, quam antīquam urbem Graecī vāstāvērunt! Multōs virōs necāvērunt. Multae fēminae, multī puerī iam miserī in Graeciā captīvī sunt. Ēheu! miserī sumus Trōiānī. Patriam enim vidēbimus numquam. Patria nusquam est. Ab initiō, tamen, dē bellō nārrābō.

Trōia urbs antīqua fuit. Magna moenia, arcem magnam, lātōs agrōs habēbat. Priamus, rēx Trōiae, multās gentēs regēbat. Paris, fīlius Priamī, ad Graeciam ōlim nāvigāvit. Ecce initium dolōrum nostrōrum! In itinere enim in urbem Menelāī, rēgis Spartae, intrāvit. Mene-

---

[1] With this line the great Roman poet Virgil begins the tale of Troy his epic poem, "The Aeneid." The meaning is: "O queen, thou iddest me renew unspeakable grief."

THE SIEGE OF TROY

lāus Paridem salūtāvit ; ad rēgiam iuvenem
dūxit ; multa et pulchra dedit. Sed in rēgiā
Paris Helenam, uxōrem Menelāī, vīdit et amāvit.
Helena enim pulchra erat. Deam inter mortālēs
cīvēs Helenam appellābant. Ad patriam,
igitur, Paris cum Helenā festīnāvit. Menelāus
ex multīs Graeciae partibus mīlitēs comparāvit.
Multās nāvēs longās aedificāvit. Graecī ex
patriā ad Asiam nāvigāvērunt. Magna castra
collocāvērunt ; agrōs Priamī vāstābant. Multa
erant in campō proelia. Multōs hominēs Graecī
necāvērunt ; captīvōs multōs in Graeciam
mīsērunt. Urbem magnā vī oppugnābant ; sed
Hector, frāter Paridis, magnā virtūte Trōiam
dēfendēbat.

B

1. Hector had defended the city.
2. The Greeks built a wooden horse.
3. The Trojans have led the wooden horse within the walls.
4. Why are the citizens unhappy ?
5. Alas ! the Greeks have killèd Hector.
6. The Greeks will send the wretched women to Greece.
7. There are many soldiers in Priam's palace.
8. The citizens will bravely defend the walls and temples.
9. The Greeks will have laid waste the ancient city.
10. The Romans used to rule many races.
11. Where are the old men ?   They are in the citadel.
12. Alas ! the gods have given many griefs to mortals.
13. Who defended the bridge ?   Horatius defended the bridge against the enemy.
14. Why have you entered the school late, boy ?   Four boys attacked me in the street, master.
15. We shall lead the young man to the palace, citizens.   He is the son of a great king.

WORD STUDY

Mittere gives us the words *mission* and *missionary*.   A *mission* is really a " sending "—some duty to which one is sent or a body of people sent on some duty.   A *missionary* is a person sent to carry out a duty ; and usually the word is applied to the person sent to carry out the duty of spreading religion.   Notice that when the Latin word **mittere** has a prefix it often seems to lose its meaning " to send " and to acquire the meaning " to let."   Thus **āmittere** means " to let away," and **omittere** means " to let go."   This explains the meaning of many English words like *admit, admittance, omit, omission, demit.*

XXVII

THE THIRD CONJUGATION—*continued*

§ 33. Verbs ending in **-iō**. Active voice, Indicative mood of **capiō, capere, cēpī, captum**, to take, to capture.

The Perfect, Future Perfect and Pluperfect Tenses are perfectly regular. The Present, Future and Imperfect Tenses are as follows :

PRESENT.

capiō, I take.	**capĭmus,** we take.
capĭs, you take.	**capĭtis,** you take.
capĭt, he, she, it takes.	**capiunt,** they take.

FUTURE.

capiam, I shall take.	**capiēmus,** we shall take.
capiēs, you will take.	**capiētis,** you will take.
capiet, he, she, it will take.	**capient,** they will take.

IMPERFECT.

capiēbam, I was taking.	**capiēbāmus,** we were taking.
capiēbās, you were taking.	**capiēbātis,** you were taking.
capiēbat, he, she, it was taking.	**capiēbant,** they were taking.

EXERCISE 27

A

THE TROJAN WAR. II

[AENEAS *continues his story :* HECTOR *was slain by* ACHILLES, *but still the Greeks could not take Troy. The stratagem of the wooden horse.* SINON *appears on the scene.*]

DĪDŌ : Quid ? Graecīne Hectorem superāvērunt ?

AENĒĀS : Ita vērō, rēgīna. Achillēs enim in pugnā Hectorem superāvit et necāvit.

DĪDŌ : Quid ? Tum Graecī urbem cēpērunt ?

AENĒĀS : Cēpērunt, sed nōn statim. Diū enim urbem fortiter dēfendēbāmus. Saepe Graecōs in campō oppugnāvimus et superāvimus. Sed tandem novum cōnsilium cēpērunt. Auxiliō deae equum ligneum aedificāvērunt. Multōs virōs in equō collocāvērunt. Tum ē castrīs ad nāvēs festīnāvērunt et statim ad īnsulam parvam—Tenedos nōmen erat—nāvigāvērunt. Nihil iam timēbāmus : magnum erat gaudium nostrum. Exclāmābāmus enim " Nusquam in campō sunt Graecī. Bellō dēfessī ad Graeciam iam nāvigant. Dī patriam nostram perīculīs bellī tandem līberāvērunt. Victōriam Graecīs nōn dedērunt, sed urbem Trōiam servāvērunt."

Festīnāmus igitur ad castra Graecōrum ; in castrīs ambulāmus ; equum ligneum vidēmus. Paucī equum timent ; multī laudant. Exclāmāmus " Cūr Graecī equum aedificāvērunt ? Quid est ? Cūr in campō stat ? Quid faciēmus ? Equumne ad urbem trahēmus et in arce collocābimus ? "

Sed tum pāstōrēs ad Priamum rēgem iuvenem trāxērunt. Graecus erat ; Sinōn nōmen erat. Cum amīcīs ad īnsulam nōn nāvigāverat, sed in agrīs pāstōrēs exspectāverat.

B

1. The general will adopt a new plan.
2. Why did Valerius send his brother to the city ?
3. Where is the poet's wife ? She has journeyed to the city with her daughters.
4. The shepherds had dragged the young man to the king.

5. When did Sextus warn the citizens about the danger ?
6. I do not see my shoes, boy. Where are they ?
7. The shoes are on the chair, master.
8. What did you do in school to-day, Quintus ?
9. I read a story about the Trojan war.
10. Who is sitting in our seat ? Upon my word, it is Gallus, the poet's freedman.
11. Alas ! the Greeks have killed Hector. Great is the grief of the Trojans.
12. The shepherd works on the hills. He has many dogs.
13. The queen was sitting in the palace with her daughters.
14. To-morrow, citizens, we shall drag the wooden horse to the citadel.
15. Valerius has given new tunics to the slaves. Upon my word, he is a good master.

C

THE INQUISITIVE SON

FĪLIUS : Ō pater, quid erat Trōia ?

PATER : Trōia urbs antīqua Asiae fuit.

FĪLIUS : Et Achillēs ? Quis Achillēs fuit ?

PATER : Vir Graecus erat. Hectorem imperātōrem Trōiān-ōrum in pugnā ōlim necāvit, et——.

FĪLIUS : Iam satis, pater, dē Achille nārrāvistī. Sed quid est caput ?

PATER : Caput ? Caput est . . . Caput est . . . Edepol nesciō (*I don't know*).

FĪLIUS : Ō pater, quam stultus (*foolish, stupid*) es ! Caput est locus (*place*) ubi (*where*) petasum habēs. Ha ! ha ! ha !

PATER : Ō ! Ecce, petasum in mēnsā collocō. Estne mēnsa caput ? Ha ! ha ! ha !

FĪLIUS : Quōmŏdŏ (*how*), elephantus (*guess this word*) rosā differt (*is different from*) ?

PATER : Nesciō.

FĪLIUS : Ō ! Quam stultus homō es, pater ! Edepol numquam ā tē (*from you*) rosās petam (**petere,** *to seek,
to ask*). Sī enim rosās petam, fortasse (*perhaps*)
elephantōs dabis !

WORD STUDY

Many English nouns which indicate the doer of an action
end in **-or.** For example, a conductor is one who conducts, a
liberator is one who sets free. Such words, you will find, mostly
come from Latin without any change of form at all. In to-day's
lesson we have the word **pāstor,** shepherd, really one who *feeds*
sheep or cattle. This word has passed into English, but what
has its meaning become ? How has this modern meaning come
about from the original one ? Perhaps a look at your New
Testament, St. John's Gospel, xxi. 15–17, will help to suggest
the answer.

REVISION EXERCISES

A

1. Give principal parts of the Latin verbs meaning : to stand :
    to lead : to teach : to do : to take : to give : to send :
    to kill : to have : to frighten.
2. The soldier has bravely defended the gate.
3. The master has adopted a new plan.
4. He always sends lazy pupils to their fathers.
5. The old men praised the ancient buildings of the city.
6. At length, by the help of the gods, they took the city.
7. We have never seen the hills of Rome.
8. What are you doing, shepherds ?
9. We are defending the oxen against the dogs.
10. Why are you standing on the bridge ? I am waiting for
    my brother.

B

1. The river is broad : the bridge is beautiful : the burdens are great : of the ancient city walls : our wide plains.
2. We shall send : they had dragged : we were giving : you (s.) will lead : they are standing : they will take.
3. Whom are the shepherds dragging to the king ?
4. To-morrow we shall lead the horses to the farm.
5. The farmer had built a country house on the bank of the broad river.
6. There are many hills within the city walls.
7. The old man will bravely defend the gates.
8. Kings did not rule the Romans for a long time.
9. Few citizens have adopted the general's plan.
10. In the battle the horse saved his master.

C

1. On the hills : about the Roman kings : at the door : in the field : on the bank : after business : against the enemy : above the tunic : into the sea : out of the city.
2. To-day we shall have games in the Campus.
3. Great is the joy of the boys. For they love games.
4. The soldier bravely defended the ancient bridge.
5. The master is not a hard man.
6. For he has given shoes and garments to the old men.
7. What are the shepherds doing ?
8. They are leading the oxen to the city.
9. Who has taken my hat ?
10. I placed my hat on the table.

XXVIII

ADJECTIVES OF THE THIRD DECLENSION

§ 34. (a) audāx, audācis, bold.

NUMBER	CASE	MASCULINE	FEMININE	NEUTER
SINGULAR	Nom.	audāx	audāx	audāx
	Voc.	audāx	audāx	audāx
	Acc.	audācem	audācem	audāx
	Gen.	audācis	audācis	audācis
	Dat.	audācī	audācī	audācī
	Abl.	audācī	audācī	audācī
PLURAL	Nom.	audācēs	audācēs	audāciă
	Voc.	audācēs	audācēs	audāciă
	Acc.	audācēs	audācēs	audāciă
	Gen.	audācium	audācium	audācium
	Dat.	audācibus	audācibus	audācibus
	Abl.	audācibus	audācibus	audācibus

(b) ingēns, ingentis, huge.

NUMBER	CASE	MASCULINE	FEMININE	NEUTER
SINGULAR	Nom.	ingēns	ingēns	ingēns
	Voc.	ingēns	ingēns	ingēns
	Acc.	ingentem	ingentem	ingēns
	Gen.	ingentis	ingentis	ingentis
	Dat.	ingentī	ingentī	ingentī
	Abl.	ingentī	ingentī	ingentī
PLURAL	Nom.	ingentēs	ingentēs	ingentiă
	Voc.	ingentēs	ingentēs	ingentiă
	Acc.	ingentēs	ingentēs	ingentiă
	Gen.	ingentium	ingentium	ingentium
	Dat.	ingentibus	ingentibus	ingentibus
	Abl.	ingentibus	ingentibus	ingentibus

EXERCISE 28

A

The Trojan War. III

[Aeneas *tells* Dido *how, deceived by* Sinon, *the Trojans dragged the wooden horse into Troy.*]

Dīdō : Ēheu ! quid Sinōn fēcit ?

Aenēās : " Ab initiō bellī," inquit, " pater ad castra Graecōrum mē mīsit. Magnum gaudium meum erat. Inter Graecōs enim erat Palamēdes, amīcus noster. Auxiliō Palamēdis et virtūte meā glōriam comparāvī et partem praedae semper habēbam. Diū fēlīx eram. Ecce, tamen, initium dolōris meī ! Dēfessī enim bellō Graecī Palamēdem culpābant ; hostem appellābant ; tandem necāvērunt. Ēheu ! quam miseram vītam tum trahēbam ! Amīcum Palamēdem semper dēsīderō ; mox terret mē perīculum ingēns. Exclāmant enim ducēs Graecōrum, ' Numquam, ō cīvēs, urbem Priamī capiēmus. Ad Graeciam igitur festīnābimus. Sed prīmum ingentem equum ligneum aedificābimus : deinde hominem Graecum necābimus. Dī enim, sī equum ligneum et sanguinem iuvenis Graecī dederimus, nostrōs terrā marīque servābunt et in patriam dūcent.' Terret mē, ō Trōiānī, cōnsilium ducum ; ex castrīs festīnō ; diū in agrīs maneō ; tandem in agrīs pāstōrēs mē capiunt. Graecī ad patriam iam nāvigant, sed perīculum nōn vītāvī. Ēheu ! miser captīvus sum : numquam patriam vidēbō ; nusquam amīcum habeō.''

)ĪDŌ : Quid tum fēcistis ?

ᴀᴇɴᴇ̄ᴀꜱ : Vītam miserō Sinōnī dedimus. Priamus
enim, " In urbem," inquit, " Sinōnem dūcēmus.
Sinōn noster erit. Graecōs patriamque nōn
dēsīderābit. Sed dē equō ligneō, Sinōn, quid
monēs ? " Tum Sinōn, " Sī equum," inquit,
" dēlēveritis, Graecī urbem ōlim capient : sī
equum in urbem traxeritis et in arce collo-
cāveritis, urbem contrā hostēs semper dēfendet."
Tum puerī et puellae equum rosīs ōrnant : virī
magnam partem moenium dēlent et magnō
gaudiō equum in urbem trahunt.

B

1. Good morning, boys ! Have you seen my dog ?
2. See, master ! The dog is sitting at the door.
3. When will the bold young men journey to the city ?
4. To-morrow we shall hurry to the city. Great will be the joy
of our friends.
5. What beautiful garments Sextus has ! Where is he hurrying
to ?
6. What a huge horse Marcus has !
7. Where is the palace ? When shall we see the king and
queen ?
8. The leaders of the Greeks have adopted a new plan.
9. The wretched citizens have not destroyed the huge horse.
10. The shepherds are dragging a prisoner to the king.
11. By the help of the gods the Greeks have taken the city.
12. The enemy have dragged the king's wife to the ships.
13. See ! I have a new ball. How lucky I am !
14. Where is the temple of Jupiter ? See ! it stands on the
Mons Capitolinus.
15. The Romans used to exercise their bodies with many games.
16. How bold the citizens are ! They are walking to the camp.

C

THE LATE-COMERS

MAGISTER : Cūr nōn videō Marcum, Sextum, Septimum ?
Ubi sunt ? Quid faciunt ? (*To a pupil.*) Ubi habitant ?

DISCIPULUS : In nostrō vīcō habitant, magister, sed hodiē
puerōs nōn vīdī. Fortasse aegrotant. (*Perhaps they are
ill.*)

MAGISTER : Quid ? Aegrotantne hodiē trēs (*three*) discipu-
lōrum meōrum ? . . . Fortasse !

DISCIPULUS : Ecce, magister ! Trēs puerī iam ad lūdum
festīnant. Marcum videō, et Sextum et Septimum.

MAGISTER : Ita vērō. Sed cūr sērō ad lūdum festīnant ?
Mox vidēbimus. (*The late-comers enter.*)

TRĒS PUERĪ (*cheerfully*) : Salvē, magister ! (*Affecting vast
surprise.*) Quid ? Sērōne intrāmus ?

MAGISTER : Ita vērō. Iam diū in lūdō labōrāmus. Marce,
quid hodiē faciēbās ?

MARCUS : Ō mē miserum ! Hodiē diū in cubīlī manēbam.
Dēfessus enim eram. Herī cum patre meō iter longum
fēcī.

MAGISTER : Videō : et quid Sextus fēcit ?

SEXTUS : Ad lūdum festīnābam. Ecce, in vīcō canem
nostrum vīdī. Canem domum (*home*) traxī. Sērō
igitur lūdum intrō.

MAGISTER : Quid Septimus nārrat ?

SEPTIMUS : Ēheu, magister ! aeg-aeg-aegrotō. Sed lūdum
amō. Domī (*at home*) igitur nōn mānsī sed ad lūdum
iter fēcī.

MAGISTER : Marcus in cubīlī mānsit : Sextus canem domum
trāxit : Septimus aegrotat. Edepol, pulchrās fābulās
nārrāvistis. Cūr, tamen, in lūdum intrātis **simul** (*at
the same time*) ? Quid Marcus portat ? Pilamne videō ?
Ita vērō. Ō puerī īgnāvī, edepol crās ad lūdum māne
festīnābitis. (*And he administers justice in the old-
fashioned way.*)

WORD STUDY

To-day's words give us many English derivatives. When you read about a *predatory* expedition, you will recognise a connection with **praeda**. Again, distinguish the English *sanguine* and *sanguinary*, and consider how each is derived from **sanguis**. **Fēlīx** gives us *felicity* and *felicitous*. From **audāx** we have *audacity* and *audacious*. Very often in filling up a form you will come across the instruction " *Delete* what is not applicable." What does all that mean ? In English also we frequently speak of an *indelible* impression. What is the meaning and derivation of that word ?

To go back upon our vocabulary a little, have you been noticing how **initium** helps you not only to arrive at the meaning of a phrase like *initial* letter but to see what is meant by expressions like " His *initial* error lay in his doing so-and-so." Have you paused to study **trahō** ? It gives us *traction*, *tractor*, *contract*, *contraction*, and helps us to see what is meant by *detracting* from a reputation.

A BRONZE STAND

XXIX

ADJECTIVES OF THIRD DECLENSION—
continued

§ 35. (a) **fortis, fortis, fortĕ,** brave.

NUMBER	CASE	MASCULINE	FEMININE	NEUTER
SINGULAR	*Nom.*	fortis	fortis	fortĕ
	Voc.	fortis	fortis	fortĕ
	Acc.	fortem	fortem	fortĕ
	Gen.	fortis	fortis	fortis
	Dat.	fortī	fortī	fortī
	Abl.	fortī	fortī	fortī
PLURAL	*Nom.*	fortēs	fortēs	fortiă
	Voc.	fortēs	fortēs	fortiă
	Acc.	fortēs	fortēs	fortiă
	Gen.	fortium	fortium	fortium
	Dat.	fortibus	fortibus	fortibus
	Abl.	fortibus	fortibus	fortibus

(b) **ācer, ācris, ācrĕ,** keen, eager, spirited, fierce.

NUMBER	CASE	MASCULINE	FEMININE	NEUTER
SINGULAR	*Nom.*	ācer	ācris	ācrĕ
	Voc.	ācer	ācris	ācrĕ
	Acc.	ācrem	ācrem	ācrĕ
	Gen.	ācris	ācris	ācris
	Dat.	ācrī	ācrī	ācrī
	Abl.	ācrī	ācrī	ācrī
PLURAL	*Nom.*	ācrēs	ācrēs	ācriă
	Voc.	ācrēs	ācrēs	ācriă
	Acc.	ācrēs	ācrēs	ācriă
	Gen.	ācrium	ācrium	ācrium
	Dat.	ācribus	ācribus	ācribus
	Abl.	ācribus	ācribus	ācribus

Note.—**celer, celĕris, celĕrĕ,** swift, is declined like **ācer,** but keeps the **e** throughout.

EXERCISE 29

A

The Trojan War. IV

*[*Aeneas *tells of the entry of the Greeks into the city and the horrors of the last night of Troy.]*

Aenēās : Nox erat : in cubīlibus cīvēs omnēs erant. Tum ex īnsulā Graecī festīnāvērunt et signum Sinōnī dedērunt. Sinōn signum vīdit, et ex equō sociōs audācēs statim līberāvit. Festīnāvērunt ad portās : fortēs custōdēs oppugnāvērunt et omnēs necāvērunt. Iam ex nāvibus ad moenia mīlitēs Graecī festīnāverant. Tum per portās in urbem et in arcem intrāvērunt.

Dīdō : Ēheu! quam misera, Aenēā, nārrās!

Aenēās : Ita vērō, rēgīna. Festīnant enim Graecī per omnēs partēs urbis. Multa aedificia dēlent ; cīvēs multōs necant ; fēminās capiunt et ad nāvēs trahunt. Praedam comparant magnam et ad castra portant. Oppugnant rēgiam antīquam Priamī : post ācrem pugnam fortēs custōdēs necant et in aedificium intrant. Priamum, miserum senem, fīliōsque necant. Hecubam, uxōrem Priamī, cum multīs captīvīs ad nāvēs trahunt. Ēheu! quam misera nox est! Est in omnibus urbis partibus sanguis fortium virōrum : sunt clāmōrēs hostium cīviumque. Omnia vāstant Graecī ; omnia dēlent. Nōn deōrum auxilium, nōn hominum virtūs urbem iam servat.

B

1. The ships of the Greeks are swift.
2. Throughout the night the shouts frightened the citizens.
3. What are you doing, soldiers? We give a signal to the guards.
4. Have the Greeks taken many prisoners?
5. Yes, indeed. They are dragging many captives to the ships.
6. Alas! the valour of the brave citizens will not save the town.
7. How spirited are the horses of the allies!
8. By the help of a goddess the Greeks made the wooden horse.
9. The enemy will destroy the sacred buildings of Troy.
10. After business the citizens walk in the Campus Martius.
11. What are the soldiers doing on the bank of the river?
12. They are building a wooden bridge.
13. Complete the unfinished words in the following sentences:
    (a) Cūr miser—— puellās ad nāv—— magnam trahit——, mīlitēs?
    (b) Cūr nūd—— capite labōr——, puer? In sōl—— nōn labōrō.
    (c) Puer—— in Camp—— Martiō corpor—— exercent.
    (d) Cūr can—— ad iānuam lūd—— sedet? Parvum fīli—— agricolae exspectat.

C

Solve the following cross-word puzzle:

CLUES ACROSS

1. A Roman god.
8. And.
10. Of oxen.
11. Many infinitives end thus.
12. This noun-ending indicates the doer of an action.
13. Force.
14. I attack.
15. This prep. can govern acc. or abl.
17. A number.
20. The Latin negative.
22. He overcomes.
24. This Latin word is often seen on railway posters.
26. First syllable of a " great " word.
27. Some neuter nouns of 3rd declension end in this.

28. Alas reversed.

30. How many ?

31. For lives.

33. Prep. governing abl.

34. You will find 4th declension neuter plurals ending in this.

35. It is human to do this.

37. All men are this.

CLUES DOWN

1. The genitive of 1 across.

2. Where ?

3. Prep. governing acc.

4. A general.

5. 8 across reversed.

6. They will be.

7. I rule.

8. I advise ends in this.

9. A famous city of old.

6. Never.

18. See 7.

19. A Roman greeting.

21. A mere nothing.

23. Not many.

24. Dative sing. of old.

25. What you wear a petasus on.

28. For a long time (rev.).

29. You are.

32. Prep. governing acc.

36. The singular of 29.

XXX

ADJECTIVES OF THIRD DECLENSION—
continued

§ 36. The following Adjectives require special attention :
    (*a*) **vetus, vetĕris,** old.

NUMBER	CASE	MASCULINE	FEMININE	NEUTER
SINGULAR	*Nom.*	**vetus**	**vetus**	**vetus**
	Voc.	**vetus**	**vetus**	**vetus**
	Acc.	**veterem**	**veterem**	**vetus**
	Gen.	**veteris**	**veteris**	**veteris**
	Dat.	**veterī**	**veterī**	**veterī**
	Abl.	**vetere**	**vetere**	**vetere**
PLURAL	*Nom.*	**veterēs**	**veterēs**	**veteră**
	Voc.	**veterēs**	**veterēs**	**veteră**
	Acc.	**veterēs**	**veterēs**	**veteră**
	Gen.	**veterum**	**veterum**	**veterum**
	Dat.	**veteribus**	**veteribus**	**veteribus**
	Abl.	**veteribus**	**veteribus**	**veteribus**

    (*b*) **dīvĕs, dīvĭtis,** rich.

CASE	SINGULAR Masculine and Feminine	PLURAL Masculine and Feminine
Nom.	**dīvĕs**	**dīvĭtēs**
Voc.	**dīvĕs**	**dīvĭtēs**
Acc.	**dīvĭtem**	**dīvĭtēs**
Gen.	**dīvĭtis**	**dīvĭtum**
Dat.	**dīvĭtī**	**dīvĭtibus**
Abl.	**dīvĭte**	**dīvĭtibus**

(c) **pauper, paupĕris,** poor.

CASE	SINGULAR	PLURAL
	Masculine and Feminine	Masculine and Feminine
Nom.	pauper	paupĕrēs
Voc.	pauper	paupĕrēs
Acc.	paupĕrem	paupĕrēs
Gen.	paupĕris	paupĕrum
Dat.	paupĕrī	paupĕribus
Abl.	paupĕre	paupĕribus

Note.—Of the above, **dīvĕs** and **pauper** have no neuter; the
ablative singular (all genders) ends in **-ĕ**; the genitive
plural (all genders) ends in **-um.**

EXERCISE 30

A

THE TROJAN WAR. V

[AENEAS *tells how with a few companions he attempted re-
sistance, and then despairing of success escaped from
the doomed city. They built a fleet and set out to
found a new Troy somewhere in the West.*]

AENĒĀS : Arma capiō et in viam festīnō. Auxiliō
paucōrum sociōrum hostēs oppugnō; multōs
superō; multōs necō. Diū et fortiter pugnāmus,
sed post multa et ingentia proelia sociīs dēfessīs
exclāmō, " Virtūte nostrā, sociī, Trōiam numquam servābimus. Partem urbis hostēs iam
cēpērunt ; partem incendērunt. Mox omnia
Graecī dēlēbunt : omnēs, fortēs ignāvōsque,
dīvitēs pauperēsque necābunt."

Ad montēs, igitur, ex urbe iter fēcimus.
Patrem, iam senem, servāvī et in montēs

portāvī. Deōs deāsque omnēs patriae servāvi-
mus. Deinde nāvēs aedificāvimus et ad mare
trāximus. Ex Asiā cum sociīs nāvigāvī. Per
multa maria, ō rēgīna, errāvimus : perīcula
saepe mē sociōsque terruērunt ingentia. Ad
sōlem occidentem, tamen, iter semper facimus.
Dī mē sociōsque in Ītaliam ōlim dūcent et in
Ītaliā novam Trōiam aedificābimus. Patriam
novam comparābimus : erit ā sanguine Trōiānōrum gēns nova et dīves, fortis et ācris bellō.
Multōs hominēs superābit : multās deinde
terrās, multās gentēs reget. Glōriam habēbit
aeternam.

B

1. Yesterday I saw a poor old man in the street.
2. He was wandering through the town with his wife.
3. I gave my father's old shoes to the poor man.
4. The slave's master is rich. How many horses has he ?
5. He has seven horses, many oxen and a huge farm.
6. The gods will give eternal glory to the Roman race.
7. The shouts of the barbarians did not frighten our men.
8. The Greeks have taken Troy. They have burned the temples.
9. After the battle the general gave the booty to the soldiers.
10. With a few companions Columbus (**Columbus, -ī**) sailed toward the West.
11. After the victory the general sent a swift messenger to the city.
12. How keen our men are ! They will fight bravely against the enemy.
13. Yes, indeed ; they are all awaiting the signal.
14. The guards are dragging a prisoner to the palace.
15. Where is the ball, my son (**mī fīlī**) ? I gave my ball to a poor boy.

C

Post Negōtia

QUINTUS : *Assistant to a rich old uncle who keeps a shop.*
LUCIA : *wife of Quintus.* QUINTUS *has just returned home after a particularly trying day.*

QUĪNTUS : Ō mē miserum! Dēfessus sum. Quam dūra vīta est! Et avunculus (*uncle*) noster! Dī immortālēs! bēlua (*brute*) est, nōn homō. In tabernā enim, sī stō semper, sī labōrō, sī festīnō, sī omnia parō, quid avunculus facit? Laudatne mē? *Nōn.* Collocatne mē in sellā? *Nōn.* Exclāmatne " Mī Quīnte, dēfessus es. Videō. Sed satis hodiē labōrāvistī." *Nōn*; sed semper, " Quīnte," inquit, " sī nihil faciēs, numquam dīves et fēlīx eris." Et statim cum oneribus multīs et ingentibus in omnēs partēs urbis mē mittit. Novam togam Marcō portō, petasōs Septimō, calceōs Valeriō, rosās fīliābus poētae, librōs fīliīs imperātōris, canem Sextō.

Sed līber sum, mea Lūcia, nōn servus. Vir fortis erō, et audāx cōnsilium capiam. Per noctem tabernam incendam ; avunculum, dūrum senem, ad Tiberim traham et——

LŪCIA : Satis est, mī Quīnte. Ecce, quam bonam cēnam parāvī! Post cēnam in Campum ambulābis ; amīcōs vidēbis ; pilā corpus exercēbis.

QUĪNTUS : Ō! quam bonam uxōrem habeō! Edepol, sī fēlīx homō in urbe est, Quīntus est.

GAMES

Just as nowadays so in ancient Rome, the earliest games that children played were with their toys. The Roman infant had its rattle, its little drum, its ball, bells, toy carts and models of horses, birds and other animals. There were also dolls, of course, and, just as to-day, these appealed to girls rather than boys. Dolls varied very much in size, material and expense. They were very commonly made of terra-cotta, but we also hear of wooden ones, wax ones and ivory ones. We don't hear of sleeping or squeaking dolls ; but dolls with movable legs and arms were quite common. The older boy had his hoop, which was made of bronze and sometimes hung with bells. He propelled it by means of a wooden handle with a hook at the end. And, of course, there were tops, both whipping-tops and humming tops spun by means of a string.

Apart from toys the children had definite games. We hear a good deal about a game called " **Rēx.**" It was played in a ring. One player was chosen " king " ; another was " out." The one who was " out " had to do exactly and correctly whatever the " king " commanded. And while the game was going on, the rest of the players kept singing a sort of rhyme, part of which was :

Rēx eris sī rēctē faciēs, sī nōn faciēs nōn eris.

But it is time to speak about the games played by Romans of all ages. A favourite was the game called **Pār impar,** or odds and evens. You took a handful of knucklebones or dice or pebbles or anything, and your opponent had to guess whether the number was odd or even. Another game which is played in Italy to the present day was called **mora.** In this game you and your opponent at precisely the same instant hold up your right hands with a certain number of fingers extended, and like a flash you call out the number of fingers you think he has extended and he calls out the number he guesses to be extended on your hand. The player to make the first correct guess opens a finger of the left hand. The winner is the first to open all his left hand ; that is, he who first guesses right five times.

The Romans were keen on physical fitness, and had many games designed to secure this. Apart from walking, running, jumping, skipping and exercise with things like dumb-bells, the great game was ball. This took several forms. Two or more players might have a simple game of " catch." In the favourite ball game, which was called **trigōn,** there were three players who stood so as to form a triangle. The balls were thrown from player to player. Expert players threw and caught with the left hand only. Points were scored according to the catches made. **Trigōn** was an exceedingly fast and heating game, and after playing it the Roman liked to visit one or other of the magnificent and splendidly equipped public baths which were a feature of the city.

Century	Vital Dates	Periods and Notes
	B.C. 753	Descendants of Aeneas rule Alba Longa
700 B.C.		Romulus–founds city 753 B.C.
		Numa – founds state religion
		Tullus Hostilius – warrior king
600 B.C.		Aneus Martius–extends Roman power
		Tarquinius Priscus – great builder
		Servius Tullius – reorganises people
500 B.C.	B.C. 510	Tarquinius Superbus–tyrant; expelled 510 B.C.
400 B.C.		Long series of wars ending with defeat of Pyrrhus 275 B.C. leaves Rome mistress of Italy
300 B.C.		
	B.C. 275	
	B.C. 234	
	B.C. 241	First Carthaginian War 264-241 B.C.
200 B.C.	B.C. 218	Second Carthaginian War 218-202 B.C.
	B.C. 202	
	B.C. 133	Rome becomes mistress of the Mediterranean world 202-133 B.C.
100 B.C.		A century of revolution and civil wars. Sulla and Marius: Caesar and Pompey: Octavius and Antony. Octavius master of Roman world, 31 B.C. Founds empire, and receives name Augustus.
	B.C. 31	
		THE EMPIRE

(Vertical labels: THE PERIOD OF THE KINGS; THE PERIOD OF THE REPUBLIC)

ROMAN HISTORY, 753–31 B.C.

Your reading lessons in the later part of this book will gain much in interest from study of, and frequent reference to, the above chart.

5

XXXI

FOURTH CONJUGATION

§ 37. Indicative Active of **audīre,** to hear.

(a) Present, Future and Imperfect Tenses.

Tense	Pers.	Singular	Plural
Present	1	**aúdi-ō** I hear	**audī-mus** we hear
	2	**aúdī-s** you hear	**audī-tis** you hear
	3	**aúdi-t** he, she, it hears	**aúdi-unt** they hear
Future	1	**aúdi-am** I shall hear	**audi-ēmus** we shall hear
	2	**aúdi-ēs** you will hear	**audi-ētis** you will hear
	3	**aúdi-et** he, she, it will hear	**aúdi-ent** they will hear
Imperfect	1	**audi-ēbam** I was hearing	**audi-ēbāmus** we were hearing
	2	**audi-ēbās** you were hearing	**audi-ēbātis** you were hearing
	3	**audi-ēbat** he, she, it was hearing	**audi-ēbant** they were hearing

(b) Perfect, Future Perfect and Pluperfect Tenses.

TENSE	PERS.	SINGULAR	PLURAL
PERFECT	1	audīv-ī I have heard, *or*, I heard	audīv-imus we have heard
	2	audīv-istī you have heard, *or* you heard	audīv-istis you have heard, *or* you heard
	3	audīv-it he, she, it has heard, *or* heard	audīv-ērunt they have heard, *or* they heard
FUTURE PERFECT	1	audīv-erō I shall have heard	audīv-erimus we shall have heard
	2	audīv-eris you will have heard	audīv-eritis you will have heard
	3	audīv-erit he, she, it will have heard	audīv-erint they will have heard
PLUPERFECT	1	audīv-eram I had heard	audīv-erāmus we had heard
	2	audīv-erās you had heard	audīv-erātis you had heard
	3	audīv-erat he, she, it had heard	audīv-erant they had heard

Note.—Verbs of the Fourth Conjugation may form the Perfect, Future Perfect and Pluperfect Tenses without the letter **v**, e.g.:

Perfect   .   .   .   **audiī, audiistī, audiit,** etc.
Future Perfect   .   **audierō, audieris, audierit,** etc.
Pluperfect   .   .   **audieram, audierās, audierat,** etc.

EXERCISE 31

A

THE BEGINNINGS OF ROME. I

[RHEA SILVIA, *a princess descended from* AENEAS, *bears to* MARS, *god of war, twin sons,* ROMULUS *and* REMUS. *Their wicked uncle,* AMULIUS, *who had usurped the throne, orders the boys to be flung into the Tiber.*]

Vēnit tandem ad Ītaliam cum sociīs Aenēās. Post multa perīcula et proelia ingentia hostēs superāvit omnēs, et urbem Laurentum occupāvit. Rēgēs gentis Trōiānae cīvēs diū regēbant. Tandem Albam Longam, urbem pulchram, occupāvērunt. Multī rēgēs Albae Longae erant ; tandem Numitor, vir bonus et iūstus, cīvēs regēbat. Contrā Numitōrem frāter Amūlius arma cēpit. Vī et armīs Numitōrem superāvit. Numitor ē patriā festīnāvit. Rhea Silvia, tamen, fīlia Numitōris, in rēgiā manēbat. Amūlius enim, " Rhea Silvia," inquit, " mē nōn terret. Puella est. Nōn fortis, nōn audāx est. Numquam mē oppugnābit : nihil contrā mē faciet.' Filiōs tamen Rhea Silvia habēbat, Rōmulum e Remum. Pater puerōrum Mārs erat, deus bellī Amūlius puerōs timēbat. " Puerī," inquit, " iuvenēs fortēs et audācēs ōlim erunt. Sī dē Numitōre audīverint, arma capient, et auxiliō cīvium mē superābunt. Quid ? Vītamne puerīs dabō ? Perīculumne semper exspectābō ? Nōn faciam ! Mīlitēs ad Tiberim puerōs portābunt et in flūmen conicient. Tum perīculō līber erō : per omnem vītam fēlīx erō."

B

1. I shall come : she had heard : you (*pl.*) will have come : we had heard : it will hear : you (*s.*) throw : they were throwing : they threw : they are coming : we shall hear : we shall throw.

2. When will you come to the river, Titus ?

3. I shall come in the morning.

4. The citizens had remained a long time in the forum.

5. He has thrown the ball into the river.

6. We shall soon hear the shouts of the guards.

7. How many bridges do you see, boys ? We see seven.

8. The wives of the citizens heard the poet's story.

9. The soldiers and sailors have burned the palace.

10. The enemy have seized the citadel by force of arms.

11. The shepherd's dog is wandering on the mountain.

12. He has given the shoes to the poor man.

13. I heard the shouts of the slaves. They were working on the ship.

14. The rich man is in his country house. When will he come to the city ?

15. Complete each of the following sentences by selecting the one most suitable verb from the list which accompanies it :

   (a) Uxōrēs et fīliī Trōiānōrum in moenibus—— (*sedeō, stat, festīnābimus, stant, vēnerant*).

   (b) Mīlitēs rēgis puerōs in flūmen—— (*portābam, vidēbō, coniēceram, capiunt, conicient*).

   (c) Quandō, puerī, ad cēnam——? (*festīnāveris, capiētis, veniētis, occupāverāmus, monēbitis*).

   (d) Mīlitēs fortiter pugnant, sed urbem nōn—— (*laudant, manēbunt, nāvigant, docēbimus, servābunt*).

XXXII

THE FOURTH DECLENSION

§ 38. (*a*) **Exercitus, exercitūs,** *m.*, an army.

Case	Singular		Plural	
Nom.	**exercit-us**	an army (*subj.*)	**exercit-ūs**	armies (*subj.*)
Voc.	**exercit-us**	army ! O army !	**exercit-ūs**	armies ! O armies !
Acc.	**exercit-um**	an army (*obj.*)	**exercit-ūs**	armies (*obj*).
Gen.	**exercit-ūs**	of an army	**exercít-uum**	of armies
Dat.	**exercit-uī**	to, for an army	**exercít-ibus**	to, for armies
Abl.	**exercit-ū**	by, with, from an army	**exercít-ibus**	by, with, from armies

(*b*) **cornū, cornūs,** *n.*, a horn.

Case	Singular		Plural	
Nom.	**corn-ū**	a horn (*subj.*)	**corn-uă**	horns (*subj.*)
Voc.	**corn-ū**	horn ! O horn !	**corn-uă**	horns ! O horns !
Acc.	**corn-ū**	a horn (*obj.*)	**corn-uă**	horns (*obj.*)
Gen.	**corn-ūs**	of a horn	**corn-uum**	of horns
Dat.	**corn-ū**	to, for a horn	**corn-ibus**	to, for horns
Abl.	**corn-ū**	by, with, from a horn	**corn-ibus**	by, with, from horns

Note.—**cornū** commonly means also *the wing* (*of an army*).

EXERCISE 32

A

THE BEGINNINGS OF ROME. II

[ROMULUS *and* REMUS *are thrown into the Tiber, but drift
to the bank where they are first befriended by a she-
wolf, and later rescued by a shepherd named* FAUS-
TULUS.]

Mīlitēs igitur Rōmulum et Remum ē rēgiā ad
Tiberim portant. Ēheu! quam trīste iter fuit!
Puerī nihil timēbant ; saepe enim rīdēbant et cum
rīsū parvās manūs ad mīlitēs tendēbant. Mīlitēs
tamen, saepe stābant ; saepe exclāmābant, " Quid ?
Puerōsne tam pulchrōs in flūmen coniciēmus ? Nōn
faciēmus. Sed Amūlium timēmus. Sī puerōs
servāverimus, nōs statim capiet et necābit." Tandem ad flūmen vēnērunt ; puerōs in Tiberim coniēcērunt et trīstēs ad rēgem festīnāvērunt. Mārs
tamen, ab ingentī perīculō parvōs fīliōs servāvit.
Cōnsiliō enim deī, flūmen puerōs nōn dēlēvit sed ad
rīpam portāvit. Et in rīpā deus puerōs dēfendit.
Prīmum enim lupa vēnit ; puerōs vīdit ; sed puerōs
nōn terruit, nōn vulnerāvit, nōn necāvit. Lupa
puerōs amābat et diū dēfendit. Deinde pāstor,
pauper homō—Faustulus nōmen erat—Rōmulum et
Remum ab omnibus perīculīs servāvit. Ambulābat
per rīpam flūminis. Ecce! puerōs audit, et mox
videt. Festīnat ad puerōs, et statim, " Quam
pulchrī," inquit, " puerī sunt ! Mē nōn timent ;

rīdent enim ; et rīsū mē salūtant." Tum magnō gaudiō puerōs ad uxōrem portāvit. Deinde Faustulus et uxor Rōmulum et Remum servābant.

B

1. Ō mē miserum ! Pilam in mare coniēcī.
2. Ignāvus puer magistrum rīdēbat ; magister puerum castīgāvit.
3. Cūr trīstis es, agricola ? Lupae bovēs meōs necāvērunt.
4. Clāmōrēs captīvōrum audīverāmus. Captīvī in castrīs sedēbant.
5. Valerius is standing in the temple of Jupiter.
6. He stretches out his hands to the god.
7. The old man's oxen have long horns.
8. The army is outside the city walls.
9. The ox had wounded the farmer with its horns.
10. The enemy will never overcome our army.
11. Yesterday my old friend greeted me with a smile.
12. A shepherd heard the boys.
13. The wives of the Trojans burned the ships.
14. Why are the captives sad ? They will never see their native land.
15. In the senate house a messenger announced the victory of the army.

WORD STUDY

Next time you have your Bible in your hands cast a glance at the introduction, which consists of an address to King James. There you will find the expression, " that bright *Occidental* Star, Queen Elizabeth." *Occidental* is by no means a common word, but now, thanks to your knowledge of Latin, you can easily reason out its meaning. At the same time take a moment to think about *oriental*, which *is* a common English word.

What is an *error* ? Just a " wandering " from the proper path. Therefore, in all your doings be careful to follow the *sign*-posts ! You have probably met the word *pauper* in English. Like *dux*, it is one of the words we have taken straight from Latin. *Veteran* you can now explain with ease ; but what is an *incendiary* ?

No part of the language of daily life seems to have escaped the influence of Latin. The *audience* at the theatre, the *signal* at the *station*, the *sign* above the shop door, the *incense* on the *altar*, the knight-*errant* in the story, the *occupant* of the house, would all have had to find other names had not Latin supplied us with these ones.

THE WOLF

As well as **lupa** meaning a she-wolf, there is a Latin word **lupus** which means a he-wolf. We find **lupus** figuring in many Roman sayings and proverbs. Thus, if two Romans were talking of a third party, and he suddenly appeared on the scene, the saying was **Lupus in fābulā**—" Here's the wolf in the story ! " Our corresponding saying is, of course: " Talk of the devil and he appears."

Again, the Romans had an interesting expression to apply to that very awkward predicament when one finds oneself in a tight corner, quite unable to do anything and yet unable to cut and run for it. Their saying was **Lupum auribus teneō**—I'm holding a wolf by the ears !

The wolf comes into the proverbial expression which the Roman applied to a particularly difficult or dangerous task—**Agnum lupō ēripiō.** This means literally: " I'm snatching a lamb from a wolf."

But quite the oddest thing that the Romans believed about the wolf was this : they thought that if a wolf saw a man before the man saw it, then the poor man became dumb !

XXXIII

THE FOURTH DECLENSION—*continued*

§ 39. Declension of **dŏmus, dŏmūs,** *f,.* a house

This noun belongs partly to the Second and partly to the Fourth Declension.

CASE	SINGULAR		PLURAL	
Nom.	**dŏm-us**	a house (*subj.*)	**dŏm-ūs**	houses (*subj.*)
Voc.	**dŏm-us**	house ! O house !	**dŏm-ūs**	houses ! O houses !
Acc.	**dŏm-um**	a house (*obj.*)	**dŏm-ūs,** *or* **dŏm-ōs**	houses (*obj.*)
Gen.	**dŏm-ūs**	of a house	**dŏm-uum,** *or* **dŏm-ōrum**	of houses
Dat.	**dŏm-uī**	to, for a house	**dŏm-ibus**	to, for houses
Abl.	**dŏm-ō**	by, with, from a house	**dŏm-ibus**	by, with, from houses

Note.—(1) With verbs expressing motion, e.g. **festīnāre,** to hasten,

dŏmum=home, homewards.
dŏmō=from home.

(2) **dŏmī**=at home.

This is known as the Locative Case.

EXERCISE 33

A

THE BEGINNINGS OF ROME. III

*[When they grow up, ROMULUS and REMUS attack and defeat
AMULIUS and restore the kingdom to NUMITOR. They
found the city of Rome on the banks of the Tiber.
REMUS mocks at the lowly walls of the new city, and
is killed by his brother. ROMULUS becomes first king
of Rome, which grows into a strong and populous city.]*

Rōmulus et Remus iuvenēs iam erant, fortēs et
ācrēs. Quam audācēs in perīculīs semper erant!
quam strenuī in labōribus! Tandem omnia dē
Numitōre et Amūliō audīvērunt. Tum īrātus Rōmulus frātrī, " Amūliusne," inquit, " homō scelestus,
fēlīx et dīves erit ? Numitorne, vir bonus et iūstus,
ē terrā in terram trīstis et miser semper errābit ?
Age, frāter, exercitum comparābimus. Cīvēs, enim,
veterem rēgem dēsīderant; cum gaudiō contrā
Amūlium, hominem scelestum, arma capient. Nōn
diū patriam nostram Amūlius reget."

Laudābat Remus cōnsilium frātris ; laudābant
et multī cīvēs. Virum enim fortem et strenuum
fortēs virī semper amant. Magnum igitur exercitum
ad urbem Albam Longam frātrēs dūxērunt. Magnā
vī Amūlium oppugnāvērunt et virtūte superāvērunt.
Numitōrī tandem rēgnum antīquum reddidērunt.
Tum frātrēs novum cōnsilium cēpērunt. In rīpā
Tiberis urbem aedificāvērunt et Rōmam appellāvērunt.

Parva initia urbs habēbat. Remus, igitur, magnō rīsū parva moenia urbis vīdit, et statim, " Quid est ? " inquit, " Rōmule ? Cūr moenia urbis nūsquam videō ? " Sed Rōmulus labōribus dēfessus et rīsū frātris īrātus, " Vae tibi," inquit, " sceleste frāter ! Rīdēbisne moenia mea ? " Et frātrem gladiō statim necāvit. Rōmulus igitur prīmus rēx Rōmānōrum erat. Cīvēs diū regēbat. Magnā virtūte et bonīs cōnsiliīs multās gentēs bellō superāvit. Multōs cīvēs glōriamque aeternam urbī comparāvit.

B

1. Valerius is not at home to-day. He will come home to-morrow.
2. The slaves are working in the field. How active they are !
3. Come, boy ! We shall hasten home to-day.
4. The young men will restore the kingdom to the old king.
5. How wicked the boys are ! They have destroyed their books.
6. The barbarians had seized the citadel by force of arms.
7. Come, Marcus, who was the first king of the Romans ?
8. The brave and energetic youths have overcome the wicked king.
9. All the boys and girls have heard about Romulus and Remus.
10. " Woe to thee ! " said he, " you will not laugh at my city."
11. Why did you hasten from home in the morning ?
12. Valerius and his son will journey from home to the country house.
13. The poet is not at home to-day, but he will come home soon.
14. The general praised the guards, for they were brave and energetic men.

WORD STUDY

Do you know :

- (a) Why the *Prime Minister* is so called ?
- (b) What is meant by the expression " He was the *prime* mover in the matter " ?
- (c) What is meant by *prime* condition ?
- (d) What is meant by " in his *prime* " ?
- (e) What a *primer* is ?

REVISION EXERCISES

A

1. We shall come : he had heard : they are burning : you (*s.*) were laughing : I shall hear : we have restored : you (*pl.*) had destroyed : you (*pl.*) will hear : he has come : we are coming.
2. By work we shall do all things.
3. They have not restored the kingdom to the kings.
4. The ox has destroyed the gate with its great horns.
5. The little boys stretched out their hands to the shepherd.
6. We have seen the signal ; we did not hear the shout.
7. The enemy have killed the guards ; they will destroy the city.
8. The bold leader is not always lucky.
9. The brave guards defended the walls throughout the night.
10. Come ! we shall hurry home ; for the master is angry.

B

1. Of rich farmers : for poor citizens : throughout all the night : in the ancient city : for an old friend : of swift horses : of bold leaders : for old allies : swift horses (*acc.*) : by a huge army.
2. Veterem amīcum semper amāmus, semper laudāmus.
3. Strenuī iuvenēs ingentia onera portant.

4. Dabuntne dīvitēs pauperibus praedam ?
5. Quis domum incendit ?   Cūr nōn cūstōs domum dēfendit ?
6. Bovēs ingentia cornua habent.
7. Cūr audācēs puerī in agrum intrāvērunt ?
8. Omnēs omnia nōn laudant.
9. Auxiliō sociōrum fēlīcēs et dīvitēs mox erimus.
10. Puerōrum capita sunt parva, manūs magnae.

C

1. What has the bold young man thrown into the river ?
2. Why is the poor man sad ?
3. He is tired by the journey.
4. What have you in your hand, Marcus ?
5. I have two pens and four books in my hands.
6. The enemy will never restore arms to our allies.
7. By the help of our leaders we shall soon come to the city.
8. " The rich," said he, " are not always happy."
9. The wings of the army are standing on the hills.
10. Throughout the night we had heard the shouts of the young
    men.

D

1. The poor men were wandering in the streets of the great
   city.
2. Why have you (*pl.*) burned the poor men's houses ?
3. When will the messenger come ?
4. We are waiting for the messenger now.
5. The rich will restore everything to the poor citizens.
6. All the pupils are not active ; many are lazy.
7. Why are the old men sad ?
8. Why do they not greet the young men with a smile ?
9. We shall defend our homes bravely.
10. For already we hear the shouts of the allies.

XXXIV

THE FIRST CONJUGATION—*continued*

§ 40. Present, Future and Imperfect Indicative Passive of
amāre, to love.

Tense	Pers.	Singular	Plural
Present	1	**ám-or** I am loved	**amā-mur** we are loved
	2	**amā-ris** you are loved	**amā-minī** you are loved
	3	**amā-tur** he, she, it is loved	**amā-ntur** they are loved
Future	1	**amā-bor** I shall be loved	**amā-bimur** we shall be loved
	2	**amā-běris** you will be loved	**amā-biminī** you will be loved
	3	**amā-bitur** he, she, it will be loved	**amā-buntur** they will be loved
Imperfect	1	**amā-bar** I was being loved	**amā-bāmur** we were being loved
	2	**amā-bāris** you were being loved	**amā-bāminī** you were being loved
	3	**amā-bātur** he, she, it was being loved	**amā-bantur** they were being loved

Note.—All 2nd Persons Singular Passive ending in **-ris** have an alter-
native ending, viz. **-re.** Thus instead of **amāris** we find occasionally
amāre.

EXERCISE 34

With the passive voice of the verb the living person—sometimes called the *agent*—by whom the action is done is in the ablative case with the preposition **ā, ab**; the thing—sometimes called the *instrument*—by which the action is done is in the ablative case without any preposition, e.g.:

> **Captīvus ā mīlite vulnerābātur.** The prisoner
> was being wounded by the soldier.

but **Captīvus sagittīs vulnerābātur.** The prisoner
> was being wounded by the arrows.

A

A TALK ON KINGS

[VALERIUS *has taken his young son* MARCUS *to his country
house for the holidays. But constant rain is spoiling
everything;* MARCUS *is almost reduced to tears. As a
last resort his father leads him to discuss the seven
kings who ruled Rome from its foundation in* 753 B.C.
to the expulsion of the kings in 510 B.C.]

VALERIUS : Quid est, Marce ? Cūr trīstis es ?

MARCUS (*almost in tears*) : Vae tibi, pater ! Dūrus
et scelestus homō es ! Ab urbe, ā lūdīs, ab
amīcīs, ā campō ad vīllam mē traxistī. Quam
miseram vītam habeō ! Cūr ? Semper pluit
Herī pluēbat ; hodiē pluit ; crās, sī domō
ambulāverō, pluet. Vidēbis. Ēheu ! Iovem
Pluvium īrātum habēmus.

VALERIUS : Minimē vērō, Marce. Si hodiē pluit
nōn semper pluet. Mox sōlem vidēbis. Age
Marce, quot rēgēs Rōmānōrum erant ?

MARCUS (*forgetting his sorrows in surprise at the
question*) : Edepol, numquam audīvī. Prīmus
tamen Rōmulus erat. Pater gentis Rōmānae
saepe appellātur. Ab initiō enim urbem Rōman

aedificāvit. Ā cīvibus Rōmānis igitur semper
amātur, semper laudātur. Sed quis secundus
rēx erat ?

VALERIUS : Numa Pompilius, bonus vir et iūstus
Bella Numa nōn amābat sed longam pācem
cīvibus dedit et urbem magnam dīvitemque
fēcit. Cīvēs multa dē dīs docuit et templa
deōrum multa et pulchra aedificāvit.

MARCUS : Rōmulus et Numa . . . deinde quis rēx
erat ?

VALERIUS : Tullus Hostīlius. Ō ! quam fortis vir
erat ! quam audāx ! Saepe contrā hostēs arma
cēpit et multās gentēs vī et armis superāvit.
Deinde rēgnum habuit quārtus rēx, Ancus
Mārtius, vir bellō ācer. Hostēs enim multōs
superāvit et Ītaliam ad ostium (*mouth of a river*)
Tiberis occupāvit.

MARCUS : Rōmulus, Numa, Tullus Hostīlius, Ancus
Mārtius. Multa mē docēs, pater. Quis quīntus
rēx erat ?

VALERIUS : Post Ancum Tarquinius Prīscus cīvēs
regēbat. Aedificiīs multīs et ingentibus urbem
ōrnāvit. Moenia Tarquiniī Prīscī saepe vīdistī.

MARCUS : Vīdī.

VALERIUS : Et templum Iovis in Monte Capitōlīnō
Tarquinius Prīscus aedificāvit. Post Tarquinium Prīscum quis Rōmānos regēbat ?
Quis ? Iam meminī (*I remember*). Servius
Tullius erat. Deinde Tarquinius Superbus
rēgnum occupāvit, homō scelestus et dūrus.
Multōs cīvēs necāvit ; patriam trīstem et
miseram faciēbat. Nōn amābātur, nōn laudā-
bātur. Vī et armīs rēgnum diū habēbat, sed
tandem cōnsiliō Brūtī, bonī cīvēs arma cēpērunt
10

omnēs et magnā virtūte patriam līberāvērunt.
Ecce, Marce, nōmina rēgum Rōmānōrum audi-
vistī.

MARCUS : Ita vērō, pater. Primus fuit Rōmulus,
deinde Numa, deinde Tullus Hostīlius rēx, fuit.
Tum cīvēs regēbat Ancus Mārtius ; deinde—
pater ! pater ! vidēsne ? Nōn pluit ! Sōlem
iam videō. Ubi sunt calceī ? ubi petasus ?
Age, pater, in agrōs festīnābimus ; bovēs,
equōs vidēbimus. Ō, quam amō vīllam nostram !

B

1. Alas ! it is always raining in our island.
2. Peace is loved by all good citizens.
3. Kings were not loved by the Romans.
4. The citadel was being attacked by the barbarians.
5. The pupils will be praised by the master.
6. How dirty your tunics are, boys ! You will be blamed by
   the master.
7. I have often heard the names of the Roman kings.
8. The good slaves will soon be freed by the master.
9. The boy's books were carried home by the slave.
10. The lazy boys will not be praised by the old man.
11. The citizens will be saved by Romulus.
12. Good day, soldiers ! How energetic you are ! You will be
    praised by the general.
13. How dirty your hands are, Marcus ! Were you fighting in
    the street ?
14. The shepherd's dog is carrying a big bone.

C

1. Veniētis : audīverit : reddis : dēlēverās : dēfendam :
   audiētis : audiunt : incendēmus.
2. Fortium cūstōdum : ācrī equō : trīstēs agricolae : ingentem
   praedam : veterī amīcō : audācium iuvenum.

3. Barbarī cornua exercitūs nostrī iam oppugnant.
4. Puerī magnō gaudiō manūs ad pāstōrem tendunt.
5. Audāx iuvenis signum cūstōdibus dedit.
6. Strenuī servī agricolae onera trahunt.
7. Mox ad urbem antīquam veniētis.
8. Quandō equum pauperī reddēs, agricola ?
9. Numquam petasum in flūmen coniēcī.
10. Quid faciēmus ? In proeliō ingentem praedam comparāvimus.

WORD STUDY

The Latin translation of a very beautiful New Testament phrase is **Pāx vōbīscum.** Can you identify it ? Speaking of **pāx,** that is the word which gives us *pacify, pacifist,* and, of course, *peace* itself.

It is now time to give attention to another feature of your word study. Not only are you steadily increasing the number of words you really know in English by your study of Latin, and finding out their derivations, but you are being helped to realise what is a very important truth—a great deal of our language is made up of metaphorical or, one might almost say, pictorial expressions. For example, we have often used the word *derive.* That word comes from the Latin **dērīvāre,** which meant to draw off water from a river or lake in a little stream. What an interesting picture that suggests, and what an appropriate one ! Think of a Latin word as a lake high up in the mountains, as its English and other derivatives as streams tumbling down from it into the world of to-day.

Take another example. You know how a bad illness sometimes makes a person *delirious.* That word comes from the Latin **dēlīrāre,** which expressed what a Latin ploughman did when he swerved from the straight line of his **līra** or furrow. Again, what an apt picture to apply to a departure from the straight line of normal speech or conduct !

XXXV

THE FIRST CONJUGATION—*continued*

§ 41. Perfect, Future Perfect and Pluperfect Indicative Passive of **amāre,** to love.

TENSE	PERS.	SINGULAR	PLURAL
PERFECT	1	**amātus sum** I have been loved, *or* I was loved	**amātī sumus** we have been loved, *or* we were loved
	2	**amātus es** you have been loved, *or* you were loved	**amātī estis** you have been loved, *or* you were loved
	3	**amātus est** he has been loved, *or* he was loved	**amātī sunt** they have been loved, *or* they were loved
FUTURE PERFECT	1	**amātus erō** I shall have been loved	**amātī erimus** we shall have been loved
	2	**amātus eris** you will have been loved	**amātī eritis** you will have been loved
	3	**amātus erit** he will have been loved	**amātī erunt** they will have been loved
PLUPERFECT	1	**amātus eram** I had been loved	**amātī erāmus** we had been loved
	2	**amātus erās** you had been loved	**amātī erātis** you had been loved
	3	**amātus erat** he had been loved	**amātī erant** they had been loved

Note.—In the above tenses **amātus** is inflected (like **bonus -a -um**) to show the number and gender of the subject, e.g. :

　　amāta est, she has been loved.
　　amātum erat, it had been loved.
　　puellae amātae erunt, the girls will have been loved.
　　parva oppida amāta sunt ā barbarīs, small towns were loved
　　　　by the barbarians.

EXERCISE 35

A

How Horatius kept the Bridge

Tarquinius Superbus, septimus rēx Rōmānōrum, dūrus et scelestus homō erat. Tandem cīvēs īrātī Tarquinium ē patriā expulērunt. Statim ad veterem amīcum, Lartem Porsinnam, Clūsīnum rēgem, festīnāvit. Porsinna auxilium dedit, et in agrōs Rōmānōrum cum magnō exercitū iter fēcit. " Rōmānōs," inquit, " mox superābimus ; urbem capiēmus ; rēgnum Tarquiniō reddēmus." Prīmum igitur agrōs Rōmānōrum vāstāvit ; deinde ad Tiberim iter fēcit et in rīpā castra collocāvit. Ēheu ! ingentī iam in perīculō Rōmānī erant. In urbem ex agrīs cīvēs festīnant ; iuvenēs arma capiunt et moenia dēfendunt ; senēs, puerī, fēminae ad arcem fugiunt. Hostēs iam impetum parant ; ex castrīs ad Pontem Sublicium festīnant.

Pōns Sublicius hostibus iter paene dedit ; sed ūnus vir, Horātius Cocles, urbem servāvit. Nōn enim Tarquinium, nōn Porsinnam, nōn impetum hostium, non clāmōrēs timēbat ; sed sociīs, " Cūr et quō fugitis ? " inquit. " Hostēs, sī Pontem Sublicium occupāverint, mox in urbe erunt. Pontem igitur omnī vī dēlēte (*destroy*) ; ego impetum hostium sustinēbō."

Ad aditum pontis cum amīcīs, Spuriō Larciō et Titō Herminiō, Horātius festīnāvit. Virī impetum hostium diū sustinēbant. Deinde Horātius (pars enim parva pontis iam manēbat) amīcōs ad urbem mīsit. Tum Horātius hostēs sustinēbat omnēs. Ō vir fortis et audāx! Attonitī sunt cīvēs virtūte virī; attonitī et hostēs sunt. Multī hostium ab Horātiō necātī, multī vulnerātī sunt. Tandem magnō clāmōre omnēs in Horātium tēla coniēcērunt. Vulnerātus est; stābat tamen semper in aditū pontis et impetum hostium sustinēbat. Ecce, tamen, fragōrem omnēs audiunt: Rōmānī pontem iam dēlēvērunt. Stant hostēs, fragōre pontis attonitī. Tum Horātius, "Tiberīne pater," inquit, "haec (*these*) arma et hunc (*this*) mīlitem servā (*save*)." Tum in flūmen dēsiluit. Tiberīnī patris auxiliō servātus est.

B

1. Kings are never loved by the Romans.
2. The citizens drove out the seventh king.
3. Why are you sad, citizens? To-day the city will be attacked by the enemy.
4. Will the soldiers flee? No, indeed. They will defend the camp.
5. A great danger has been avoided. The city has been saved.
6. The second legion had withstood all the attacks of the barbarians.
7. Astounded by the shouts of our men the enemy fled.
8. The bridge had been saved by the valour of Horatius.
9. When he heard the crash, Horatius leaped down into the river.
10. The soldier had almost avoided the weapons of the enemy.
11. Where are you leading the horse to? I am leading the horse home.

12. Why had he driven out the wretched poet ?
13. Turn the following sentences into passive form :

    (*a*) Mīlitēs perīculum vītāverint.
    (*b*) Graecī audāx cōnsilium laudāverant.
    (*c*) Horātius pontem servābat.
    (*d*) Pulchrae puellae mēnsam ōrnāvērunt.
    (*e*) Parvus servus magnum onus portat.
    (*f*) Hostēs arcem nōn occupābunt.

WORD STUDY

Latin even invades the football field ! You know, of course, that " Soccer " stands for " Association." This word in turn is derived from **socius.** Talking about football, the goalkeeper is sometimes called a " custodian." Why ? And don't forget to ask your teacher to explain the derivation of " referee."

You have met the word **tandem,** and you know that it is an adverb meaning " at length." But what is a " tandem " in English ? Why should it be called by a name which really means " at length " ? See whether your English dictionary tells you : if it fails you, call in your teacher to help.

HEADS OR SHIPS

What did the Roman cry when he tossed a coin ? Let us think a minute. If we could examine a case of Roman bronze coins in, say, the British Museum, we should find that on one side some bore a head—the head of some god or goddess— while on the other side is depicted the prow of a ship. Hence, naturally enough, when the Roman tossed a coin he cried " heads " or " ships." Now, with the teacher's help, translate the following sentence from an old Roman writer :

Puerī denariōs in sublime iactantēs capita aut nāvia exclāmant.

XXXVI

THE FIFTH DECLENSION

§ 42. (a) dĭēs, dĭēī, *m.*, a day.

CASE	SINGULAR		PLURAL	
Nom.	dĭ-ēs	a day (*subj.*)	dĭ-ēs	days (*subj.*)
Voc.	dĭ-ēs	day! O day!	dĭ-ēs	days! O days!
Acc.	dĭ-em	a day (*obj.*)	dĭ-ēs	days (*obj.*)
Gen.	dĭ-ēī	of a day	dĭ-ērum	of days
Dat.	dĭ-ēī	to, for a day	dĭ-ēbus	to, for days
Abl.	dĭ-ē	by, with, from a day	dĭ-ēbus	by, with, from days

(b) rēs, rĕī, *f.*, a thing.

CASE	SINGULAR		PLURAL	
Nom.	r-ēs	a thing (*subj.*)	r-ēs	things (*subj.*)
Voc.	r-ēs	thing! O thing!	r-ēs	things! O things!
Acc.	r-em	a thing (*obj.*)	r-ēs	things (*obj.*)
Gen.	r-ĕī	of a thing	r-ērum	of things
Dat.	r-ĕī	to, for a thing	r-ēbus	to, for things
Abl.	r-ē	by, with, from a thing	r-ēbus	by, with, from things

Notes.—(1) **rēs** is declined like **dĭēs** except that Genitive and Dative Singular end in -ĕī NOT -ēī.

(2) In this declension **dĭēs** and **rēs** only have a complete Plural. **Aciēs, aciēī,** *f.*, line of battle has Nominative and Accusative Plural only.

EXERCISE 36

Note.—You have already learned that **multa** means "many things."
This is only true of the Nominative and Accusative cases. In the other
cases the noun **res** must be used. Thus :

Nom. **multa,** many things,
Acc. **multa,** many things (*obj.*).
Gen. **multārum rērum,** of many things.
Dat. **multīs rēbus,** to, for many things.
Abl. **multīs rēbus,** by, with, from many things.

So also with other Adjectives.

A

THE STORY OF C. MUCIUS SCAEVOLA. I

[LARS PORSENA *now lays siege to Rome. C. MUCIUS, a noble
Roman youth, makes his way to the enemy's camp to
kill* PORSENA *and so free Rome from siege. By mistake
he kills a clerk instead of the king. Being taken
prisoner he hints of perpetual danger to* PORSENA.]

Lars Porsinna, Clūsīnus rēx, Rōmānōs iam obsidēbat ; prīmō enim impetū urbem nōn cēperat.
Rērum omnium in urbe iam magna inopia erat.
Tum C. Mūcius, iuvenis nōbilis, audāx cōnsilium
cēpit. Ad cūriam enim festīnāvit, et senātōribus,
"Trāns Tiberim," inquit, "patrēs, sī cōnsilium meum
laudāveritis, festīnābō et in castra hostium intrābō.
Deinde, sī dī auxilium dabunt, Porsinnam necābō.
Hostēs enim, si rēx necātus erit, domum statim iter
facient." Laudant patrēs cōnsilium. Iuvenis
intrā vestīmenta gladium collocat et ad castra
hostium festīnat.

Vēnit tandem ad castra : stat inter multōs mīlitēs ad sellam rēgis. Stīpendium mīlitibus dabātur ; et scrība cum rēge sedēbat. Mūcius Porsinnam īgnōrābat ; numquam enim hominem vīderat. In scrībam, igitur, nōn rēgem, impetum fēcit ; scrībam, nōn rēgem, gladiō necāvit. Est in castrīs clāmor ingēns : impetum in iuvenem omnēs faciunt. Mūcium capiunt : ad rēgem trahunt. Tum rēx, " Vae tibi," inquit, " sceleste homō ! Quis es ? Unde in castra vēnistī ? Cūr scrībam meum necāvistī ? " Sed Mūcius, " Rōmānus sum," inquit, " cīvis. Cīvēs C. Mūcium appellant. Ego tē hodiē nōn necāvī : alius tamen post mē tē ōlim necābit. Es enim et semper eris in perīculō ingentī. In castrīs, in rēgiā, hostem semper habēbis."

B

1. There will be a lack of many things in our city.
2. The king will not terrify the brave young man.
3. He does not know the courage of the Roman youth.
4. When will pay be given to the sailors ?
5. There was never a scarcity of brave men in our city.
6. Throughout many days the enemy besieged the citadel.
7. The noble youth will be saved by the help of Father Tiber.
8. We shall hasten to the bridge by another approach.
9. Yesterday pay was given to the soldiers in the camp.
10. For a long time our men withstood the attack.
11. Where are you hurrying to, friend ? I am hastening to the senate house.
12. What white togas the senators have ! How beautiful their shoes are !
13. After the battle the booty will be given to the soldiers.

14. Read each of the following sentences carefully, change it
into passive form, and *then* translate into Latin :
  (*a*) The brave young man has saved the bridge.
  (*b*) The master praises the poet's story.
  (*c*) The boys did not love the wicked master.
  (*d*) The enemy were attacking our camp.
  (*e*) The rich man will not save the poor man.
  (*f*) Marcus has read the story aloud.

WORD STUDY

The words given in your last two vocabularies are rich in
interesting derivatives. From **expellere** come *expel* and
expulsion—the ultimate penalty for the bad schoolboy ! **Fugere**
gives us a word of three syllables meaning one who runs away or
escapes, and it gives us a word of two syllables meaning a place
to which one goes for safety. Can you find those two words ?

The explanation of the minister's *stipend*, the derivations
of *noble, ennoble, nobility*, the meaning of *scribe* and *scribble*,
what exactly an *ignoramus* is, what it means to *ignore* a person,
what an *alias* is, what an *alibi* is—all these are problems which
you are now in a position to solve.

Again, what are the *equinoxes* ? What would you expect
to be the chief characteristic of a *nocturnal* raid ? What is a
nocturne ? What is the *accelerator* in a car ? What does *om-
niscient* mean ? And, to end this battery of questions, to what
kind of dispute would you apply the term *acrimonious* ?

By courtesy of the British Museum

A Roman Rag Doll

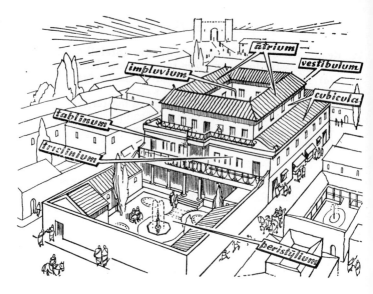

THE HOUSE OF PANSA AT POMPEII

The picture above shows a rich man's house in ancient Pompeii. This is an exceptionally large and handsome house, but illustrates many of the features of more ordinary dwellings. The front rooms on either side of the doorway were usually walled off from the rest of the house and let as shops, as can be seen on the side wall of the House of Pansa above. A short passage led from the street to the door—**iānua,** which in turn opened into the **vestibulum** or entrance hall. The **vestibulum** gave access to the **ātrium,** the central hall of the house, roofed over, except for a square in the middle. This was the **compluvium,** and directly underneath was a tank of equal area—the **impluvium.** To right and left of the **ātrium** were bedrooms—**cubicula**; and behind it the **tablīnum,** a sort of study or library, alongside which was the **triclīnium** or dining-room. Beyond the **tablīnum** was an unroofed courtyard, off which opened numerous rooms—bedrooms, storerooms, kitchen, slaves' quarters. This courtyard, known as the **peristȳlium,** was frequently a spot of great beauty, ornamented with statues and marble pillars and laid out with flower-beds containing a fountain and pool. Sometimes it was planted with one or more trees to give a welcome shelter from the fierce Italian sun.

XXXVII

§ 43. (*a*) Cardinal and Ordinal Numbers, 1–10.

		CARDINAL	ORDINAL	
1	I	ūnus, -a, -um	prīmus, -a, -um	*first*
2	II	duŏ, -ae, -ŏ	secundus, -a, -um	*second*
3	III	trēs, trēs, trĭă	tertius, -a, -um	*third*
4	IV	quattuor	quārtŭs, -a, -um	*fourth*
5	V	quīnque	quīntus, -a, -um	*fifth*
6	VI	sex	sextus, -a, -um	*sixth*
7	VII	septem	septimus, -a, -um	*seventh*
8	VIII	octō	octāvus -a, -um	*eighth*
9	IX	nŏvem	nōnus, -a, -um	*ninth*
10	X	dĕcem	decimus, -a, -um	*tenth*

(*b*) The Cardinal Numbers **ūnus, duŏ, trēs** are declined as follows:

N.	ūnus	ūna	ūnum
Ac.	ūnum	ūnam	ūnum
G.		ūnīus	
D.		ūnī	
Ab.	ūnō	ūnā	ūnō

N.	duŏ	duae	duŏ
Ac.	duŏs / duo	duās	duŏ
G.	duōrum	duārum	duōrum
D.	duōbus	duābus	duōbus
Ab.	duōbus	duābus	duōbus

N.	trēs	trēs	trĭă
Ac.	trēs	trēs	trĭă
G.		trĭum	
D.		trĭbus	
Ab.		trĭbus	

Notes.—(1) The other cardinal numbers are not declined.

(2) The ordinal numbers are declined like **bonus, -a, -um.**

EXERCISE 37

Rules of Time !

1. The time at which or within which an event happens is expressed by the ablative, e.g.:

    (*a*) **Quārtō diē vēnit,** He came on the fourth day.

    (*b*) **Quattuor diēbus vēnit,** He came in four days.

2. The time throughout which something goes on is expressed by the accusative, e.g. :

    Quattuor diēs mānsit, He remained four days.

A

The Story of C. Mucius Scaevola   II

[Porsena *threatens torture to make* Mucius *reveal the details of the danger of which he had spoken. In contempt of the king's threats* Mucius *thrusts his own right hand into a fire already kindled for sacrifice.* Porsena *lets* Mucius *go free. He returns to Rome where the citizens henceforth call him* Scaevola, *the left-handed.*]

Tum Porsinna, " Ēheu ! " inquit, " Quid nārrās ? Semperne in perīculō vītam miseram et sollicitam traham ? Quid, tamen, dē perīculō nārrās ? Quis hostis est ? Ubi est ? Quandō mē oppugnābit ? Age, sī dīxeris, vītam tibi dabō." Mūcius, tamen, " Nōn dīcam," inquit, " Mortem enim nōn timeō ; vītam nōn rogō." Tum rēx īrātus et perīculō sollicitus, " Vae tibi ! " inquit, " Ignēs incendam et circum tē collocābō. Ubi flammae tē superābunt, tum propter dolōrem omnia dīcēs." Sed Mūcius nōn sollicitus, " Ecce ! "

inquit, " Quam vīle corpus est virō Rōmānō, sī
magnam glōriam videt ! " et statim in ignem ad
sacrificium parātum dextram iniēcit. Ō mīrāculum
virtūtis ! Dēlent flammae dextram ; ingēns est
dolor ; stat tamen iuvenis et hostēs, rēgem, flammās,
dolōrēs rīdet. Rēx paene attonitus mīrāculō virtūtis
ē sellā dēsiluit et Mūciō, " Propter virtūtem," inquit,
" tē līberō et ad cīvēs mittō." Tum Mūcius Porsinnae omnia dē perīculō dīxit. " Trecentī iuvenēs
nōbilēs," inquit, " contrā tē coniūrāvērunt. Ego
prīmus tē oppugnāvī : ego tē nōn necāvī, sed paucīs
diēbus veniet secundus. Tum sī perīculum vītā-
veris, post secundum tertius iuvenis tē oppugnābit,
post tertium quārtus, post quārtum quīntus. Nōn
diū perīculum vītābis. Paucīs diēbus, sī in agrīs
Rōmānīs manēbis, necāberis."

Deinde festīnāvit Mūcius ad urbem : cīvēs
propter virtūtem omnēs Mūcium laudāvērunt et
Scaevolam appellāvērunt. Paucīs diēbus Porsinna
ex agrīs Rōmānōrum exercitum dūxit.

B

1. Marcus will come home in three days.
2. Why do the young men stretch out their hands to the gods ?
3. They are conspiring against the king.
4. The king is the enemy of the Roman citizens.
5. I am hastening to the temple of Jupiter. The fire is already
   prepared for (*here use* **ad** *with acc.*) sacrifice.
6. The boys are stretching out their hands to the shepherd.
7. Valerius will remain at home for four days. On the fifth day
   he will come to the forum.

8. In nine days the city will be saved by the allies.
9. The young man thrust his right hand into the flames.
10. The king's soldiers were astounded at the marvel of valour.
11. When I heard the crash, I hastened from the house.
12. To the wicked general the lives of the soldiers were cheap.
13. In a few days pay will be given to the soldiers.
14. The mothers are anxious. Our soldiers have been attacked by the enemy.
15. How many oxen have you, farmer ? I have three hundred, O poet.
16. In the following, translate italicised words only :

    (*a*) We shall stay here *for ten days.*
    (*b*) We shall come home *on the fourth day.*
    (*c*) We shall send a letter *in five days.*

C

Solve the following cross-word puzzle :

CLUES ACROSS

1. A Roman river.
8. " You " (*acc. sing.*).
10. Part of " I thank."
11. I stretch out.
13. Messenger (*ablative case*).
15. " Me."
16. Same as 12 down.
17. " By death."
18. This added to a word makes it interrogative.
19. You will be.
21. " They say."
24. " By a mountain."

26. " With a smile."
28. If you subtract 38 across from 25 down this is the result.
30. The Imperial City (*accus.*).
32. " An attack."
34. An old friend among Latin verbs.
35. Same as 19.
37. A preposition which governs ablative.
38. This is obtained by subtracting 28 across from 25 down.
40. " My " (*feminine*).
41. " An approach."

CLUES DOWN.

1. In Latin an adverb, in English a wheeled vehicle.
2. The 1st plural pres. indic. active of this verb is an English noun meaning "dunce."
3. "Of oxen."
4. A conjunction.
5. The ablative sing. of a 5th declension noun.
6. "A beginning."
7. "A Horn."
8. "However."
9. "Alas!"
12. Same as 16 across.
14. Either "we" or "us."

20. "Scarcity."
21. "To the god."
22. "To-morrow."
23. This word means "in safety."
25. The result of adding 28 across to 38 across.
27. "We are."
28. A day (*accusative case*).
29. A second declension neuter ending.
31. "By hand."
33. "Where?"
36. Same as 5 down.
37. Preposition governing accusative.
39. "If."

6

REVISION EXERCISES

A

1. We have been loved : they will be blamed : we shall praise ı
   you (*pl.*) were being attacked : it will be carried : he
   prepared : I shall have been loved : you (*s.*) are praised :
   it had been prepared : she has been loved.
2. Why have the citizens all conspired against the king ?
3. The king's plans were blamed by the citizens.
4. On account of the scarcity of all things we shall not withstand the attack.
5. Why do you not leap down, soldiers ?
6. You will be praised by all the leaders.
7. Pay will be given to the soldiers to-morrow.
8. The citizens long for peace ; they will conspire against the
   senators.
9. The plan of the noble young man was praised by all.
10. Many weapons had been prepared by the old men.

B

1. What are you (*pl.*) saying ?　You will be rebuked by the
   master.
2. The young man is throwing the weapon with his right
   hand.
3. When has pay been given to the farmers ?
4. The beautiful houses have been destroyed by fire.
5. Have you heard the crash ?
6. Yes, the bridge has been destroyed.
7. The citizens have already driven out the seventh king.
8. It is raining to-day.　We shall sit round the fire.
9. When will you (*s.*) lead me to the city ?　I do not know the
   way.
10 You (*pl.*) will not be praised by good citizens.

C

A Vocabulary Test

1. Give Latin for :
   (1) of senators
   (2) in the fire
   (3) by pain
   (4) attacks (*obj.*)
   (5) things (*subj.*)
   (6) a day (*obj.*)
   (7) of a crash
   (8) the seventh legion (*obj.*)
   (9) by many things
   (10) into the flames

2. Give Latin for :
   (1) he has been loved
   (2) they have conspired
   (3) it had been praised
   (4) you (*pl.*) will leap down
   (5) I shall thrust
   (6) it was avoided
   (7) she has been carried
   (8) you (*pl.*) will be prepared
   (9) they have said
   (10) we shall withstand

3. Give Latin for :
   (1) of noble young men
   (2) by huge weapons
   (3) astounded (*nom. sing.*)
        by the crash
   (4) on the seventh day
   (5) throughout the long war
   (6) of a few senators
   (7) huge flames (*obj.*)
   (8) by great scarcity
   (9) of great pain
   (10) by a noble old man

D

1. We have driven out the kings.
2. We were astounded by the great crash.
3. They have fled into the wood.
4. You (*pl.*) will not withstand the fierce attacks.
5. I shall leap down into the river.
6. They were besieging the ancient city.
7. He thrust his right hand into the fire.
8. He has not said many things.
9. We had conspired against the leaders.
10. They had almost adopted my plan.

XXXVIII

THE SECOND CONJUGATION—*continued*

44. Present, Future and Imperfect Indicative Passive of **monēre**, to advise.

Tense	Pers.	Singular	Plural
Present	1	**mónĕ-or** I am advised	**monē-mur** we are advised
	2	**monē-ris** you are advised	**monē-minī** you are advised
	3	**monē-tur** he, she, it is advised	**mone-ntur** they are advised
Future	1	**monē-bor** I shall be advised	**monē-bimur** we shall be advised
	2	**monē-bĕris** you will be advised	**monē-biminī** you will be advised
	3	**monē-bitur** he, she, it will be advised	**monē-buntur** they will be advised
Imperfect	1	**monē-bar** I was being advised	**monē-bāmur** we were being advised
	2	**monē-bāris** you were being advised	**monē-bāminī** you were being advised
	3	**monē-bātur** he, she, it was being advised	**monē-bantur** they were being advised

§ 45. Perfect, Future Perfect and Pluperfect Indicative Passive of **monēre,** to advise.

Tense	Pers.	Singular	Plural
Perfect	1	**monitus sum** I have been advised, *or* I was advised	**monitī sumus** we have been advised, etc.
	2	**monitus es** you have been advised, etc.	**monitī estis** you have been advised, etc.
	3	**monitus est** he has been advised, etc.	**monitī sunt** they have been advised, etc.
Future Perfect	1	**monitus erō** I shall have been advised	**monitī erimus** we shall have been advised
	2	**monitus eris** you will have been advised	**monitī eritis** you will have been advised
	3	**monitus erit** he will have been advised	**monitī erunt** they will have been advised
Pluperfect	1	**monitus eram** I had been advised	**monitī erāmus** we had been advised
	2	**monitus erās** you had been advised	**monitī erātis** you had been advised
	3	**monitus erat** he had been advised	**monitī erant** they had been advised

Note.—See § 41, note.

EXERCISE 38

A

A Mother's Tears

[*In* 489 *B.C. the Roman hero* Coriolanus *quarrelled with his fellow-citizens and joined the Volsci, who were now attacking Rome. He won victory after victory over his countrymen, and seemed to have Rome at his mercy when he yielded to his mother's prayers and withdrew from before the city.*]

Urbem Coriolōs Rōmānī diū obsidēbant. Tandem urbem virtūte et cōnsiliīs Cn. Marciī, virī fortis et audācis, cēpērunt. Post victōriam Marcius ā cīvibus propter virtūtem laudātus est et Coriolānus appellābātur.

Proximō annō tamen Rōmānī Coriolānum ex urbe expulērunt. Cōnsilium enim dē cīvibus pauperibus dūrum et scelestum cēperat. Īrātus igitur ad Volscōs, hostēs populī Rōmānī, festīnāvit. Cum magnō exercitū Volscōrum in agrōs Rōmānōrum iter fēcit. Saepe Rōmānōs superāvit; multōs cīvēs necāvit. Tandem urbem Rōmam obsidēbat. Tum sollicitī sunt cōnsulēs; sollicitī sunt et omnēs bonī cīvēs. Lēgātōs ad Coriolānum mittunt pācem rogant. Lēgātōs nōn audit. Iterum lēgātōs mittunt; Coriolānus in castra nōn accipit. Sacer dōtēs tandem ad virum festīnant. Ēheu! dūrum e scelestum cōnsilium Coriolānus nōn mūtat.

Tandem Veturia, māter Coriolānī, et Volumnia uxor cum duōbus parvīs fīliīs ad castra Volscōrum

CORIOLANUS AND HIS MOTHER

estīnant. Tum mīles Coriolānō, " Stant in castrīs,"
nquit, " multae et nōbilēs fēminae Rōmānae.
Pācem rogant." Sed Coriolānus, " Fēminās,"
nquit, " nōn audiam. Nōn propter virōs, nōn
propter fēminās cōnsilium mūtābō." Tandem ūnus
ex amīcīs Coriolānī, " Quid est ? " inquit, " Mehercule, māter tua et uxor cum fīliīs in castrīs sunt."
Tum sollicitus ē sellā Coriolānus dēsiluit. Mātrem
salūtat. Veturia tamen īrāta, " Cūr mē," inquit,
" salūtās ? Hostisne es an (or) fīlius meus ? Cap-
īvane sum in castrīs tuīs an māter ? Ēheu ! ad quam
miseram rem longa vīta mē traxit ! Hostem tē
videō. Quid ? patriam tuam vāstābis ? Urbem

Rōmam, sceleste, dēlēbis ? Sed intrā moenia Rōmae
sunt māter tua, uxor, fīliī. Ō mē miseram ! Cūr
fīlium habeō ? Cūr vītam tuam dī servāvērunt ?
Vae tibi ! Propter tē nōn sum lībera in līberā
patriā." Tum lacrimīs mātris Coriolānus superātus
est, exercitumque ē patriā dūxit.

B

1. Alas ! Coriolanus will not be advised by the ambassadors.
2. We shall flee to the city ; we have been warned by many
   things.
3. What do the ambassadors say ? Alas ! the general will not
   change his plan.
4. The soldiers saw a great marvel. The general was overcome
   by his mother's tears.
5. We came home on the next day. We had changed our
   plan.
6. The brave guards will not be terrified by small things.
7. The priests have kindled a fire for (ad) sacrifice.
8. In ten days the city will be besieged.
9. The master will tell a story about Coriolanus.
10. The wicked general will not receive the ambassadors
    again.
11. For many days we were terrified by the shouts of the
    barbarians.
12. Why does the general leap down from his chair ? He is
    terrified by the danger.
13. What are the women doing in the enemy's camp ? They are
    asking peace.
14. Troy was besieged for ten years by the Greeks.

C

THE STORY OF CLOELIA

[*Tired of hearing her father's stories about brave Roman men,*
LUCIA, the little daughter of VALERIUS, herself tells
the story of CLOELIA the brave Roman girl who escaped
from the Etruscans when they were besieging Rome.]

LŪCIA : Pater ! erantne nūllae fēminae in antīquā urbe
Rōmā ?

PATER : Ha ! ha ! ha ! Multae fēminae et puellae multae
erant. Cūr tam stulta es ?

LŪCIA :ʼ Ego nōn stulta sum, mī pater, sed tū et omnēs virī
Rōmānī stultī estis.   Dē virīs enim fābulās semper
nārrātis, dē fēminīs numquam.   Horātium enim et
Scaevolam saepe laudātis ; Cloeliam numquam laudātis. Ego tamen dē Cloeliā audīvī. Fortior erat quam
Horātius ; fortior erat quam Scaevola. Ita enim dīxit
rēx Etruscōrum.

PATER : Cūr igitur fābulam dē Cloeliā nōn nārrās ?

LŪCIA : Sed nārrābō, mī pater.   Obsidēs ōlim Etruscīs ā
Rōmānīs datī sunt. Inter obsidēs Cloelia erat et multae
nōbilēs puellae.   Castra Etruscōrum in rīpā Tiberis
erant.   Ibi Etruscī obsidēs custōdiēbant.   Puellae
tamen parentēs dēsīderābant, et Cloelia tandem cōnsilium audāx excōgitāvit. Puellīs enim, " Ego," inquit,
" dūx erò ; custōdēs vītābimus ; Tiberim trānābimus ;
domum ad parentēs et amīcās festīnābimus." Ita puellae
fēcērunt.   Inter tēla Etruscōrum flūmen trānāvērunt
et prīmum ad rīpam, deinde ad urbem vēnērunt.
Custōdēs tamen ad rēgem festīnant ; rem nārrant.
Prīmō rēx īrātus erat ; deinde, " Mehercule," inquit,
" fortis puella est, fortior quam Horātius, fortior quam
Scaevola."   Nūntiōs igitur ad urbem Rōmam mīsit.
" Obsidēs," inquit, " sī nōn reddētis, bellum geram ;
sī ad mē puellās mīseritis, incolumēs ad parentēs omnēs
mittam."   Rōmānī igitur puellās ad rēgem mīsērunt.

Cloeliam rēx laudat ; multa et pulchra dōna dat ;
tandem incolumem cum amīcis ad parentēs mittit.
Propter mīrāculum virtūtis Rōmānī statuam Cloeliae
in Viā Sacrā collocāvērunt.

PATER : Et iūre, mea Lūcia, Rōmānī virtūtem Cloeliae et
nōbilium puellārum laudāvērunt.

Note :

nūllus, -a, -um (*adj.*), no.
stultus, -a, -um, foolish.
tū, you (*nom. sing.*).
fortior, braver.
quam, than.
ita, so, thus.
obses, -sidis, (*c.*), hostage.
custōdiō, -īre, -īvī, ītum, to
guard.
ibi (*adv.*), there.
parēns, -entis (*c.*), parent.

excōgitō, -āre, -āvī, -ātum, to
think out.
trānō, -āre, -āvī, -ātum, to swim
across.
mehercule, upon my word.
gerō, -ere, gessī, gestum, to
wage, carry on.
incolumis, -is, -e, unharmed.
dōnum, -ī (*n.*), gift.
statua, -ae (*f.*), statue.
iūre (*adv.*), rightly.

WORD STUDY

Here are a few problems for you to-day. Using your recent
vocabularies trace the derivation and hence establish the
meaning of the following words and phrases :

lacrimose, in the *proximity* of the *station, ambidextrous, sacer-
dotal vestments, ignite, ignition, inflammable, vile, injection,
mortal, immortal, mortuary, miraculous, conjurer, iteration*
and *reiterate.*

XXXIX

THE COMPARISON OF ADJECTIVES

§ 46. The General Rule:

To form the Comparative of a Latin Adjective, change **-ī**, or
-is, of the genitive singular into **-ior.**

To form the Superlative, change **-ī**, or **-is**, of the genitive
singular into **-issimus**, e.g. :

Positive.	Comparative.	Superlative.
altus (high)	altior (higher)	altissimus (highest)
lātus (wide)	lātior (wider)	lātissimus (widest)
fortis (brave)	fortior (braver)	fortissimus (bravest)
audāx (bold)	audācior (bolder)	audācissimus (boldest)

§ 47. Adjectives ending in -er.

These form their comparative according to the rule, but to form the Superlative, add **-rimus** to the nom. sing. masculine of the positive, e.g. :

miser (wretched)	miserior (more wretched)	miserrimus (most wretched)
niger (black)	nigrior (blacker)	nigerrimus (blackest)

48. Declension of a Comparative Adjective: **fortior, fortior, fortius,** braver.

Number	Case	Masculine	Feminine	Neuter
Singular	Nom.	fortior	fortior	fortius
	Voc.	fortior	fortior	fortius
	Acc.	fortiōrem	fortiōrem	fortius
	Gen.	fortiōris	fortiōris	fortiōris
	Dat.	fortiōrī ·	fortiōrī	fortiōrī
	Abl.	fortiōre	fortiōre	fortiōre
Plural	Nom.	fortiōrēs	fortiōrēs	fortiōră
	Voc.	fortiōrēs	fortiōrēs	fortiōră
	Acc.	fortiōrēs	fortiōrēs	fortiōră
	Gen.	fortiōrum	fortiōrum	fortiōrum
	Dat.	fortiōribus	fortiōribus	fortiōribus
	Abl.	fortiōribus	fortiōribus	fortiōribus

Note.—The superlative degree of all adjectives is declined like **bonus, -a, -um.**

EXERCISE 39

Notes.—1. The word *than* after a comparative adjective is expressed in Latin by **quam.** Words joined by **quam** are in the same case, e.g. : **Agricola fortior quam poēta est,** The farmer is braver than the poet.

2. The superlative degree can have the meaning *very* . . . e.g. : **miles fortissimus,** a very brave soldier.

A

The Schoolmaster of Falerii

[*In* 394 *B.C. the Romans under* Camillus *were besieging Falerii, the city of the Falisci. A schoolmaster of that city tried to betray his pupils to the Romans.* Camillus *had the rascal whipped back to the town by the boys. This sportsmanship on the part of* Camillus *ended the siege ; the citizens were so impressed by his fair dealing that they voluntarily surrendered.*]

Urbs Falēriī ā M. Fūriō Camillō, imperātōre Rōmānō, obsidēbātur. Magister fīliōrum nōbilium cīvium cōnsilium audāx et scelestum cēpit. Discipulōs extrā moenia saepe dūcēbat. Ita enim corpora puerōrum exercēbat et magna et fortia faciēbat.

Cum discipulīs igitur ex portīs ōlim ambulābat. Prīmum breviōribus, deinde longiōribus spatiīs puerōs ab urbe traxit. Multīs lūdīs, multīs sermōnibus discipulōs in itinere dēlectābat. Omnēs tandem in statiōnēs et ex statiōnibus in castra Rōmānōrum ad Camillum dūxit.

Tum scelestō factō scelestiōrem sermōnem addidit. Camillō enim, " Ecce, imperātor," inquit, " urbem Falēriōs Rōmānīs trādō. Dūxī enim ad vōs fīliōs cīvium nōbilium. Mehercule, prō vītā puerōrum Faliscī urbem Rōmānīs trādent ! "

Camillus tamen, ubi sermōnem magistrī audīvit, irātus, " Vae tibi, sceleste ! " inquit, " Nōn ad populum, nōn ad imperātōrem scelestum vēnistī. Sīcut pācis, sunt bellī iūra. Nōn fortiter modo sed iūstē etiam populus Rōmānus bellum gerit. Contrā virōs, nōn contrā puerōs arma cēpimus. Falēriōs, sīcut multās urbēs, mōre Rōmānō, virtūte, labōribus, vī et armīs capiēmus."

Tum miserum magistrum puerīs nūdum trādidit. Virgās omnibus dedit. Deinde magistrō, " Discipulī," inquit, " ad urbem tē trahent et in itinere virgīs tē verberābunt." Rīdent mīlitēs Rōmānī ; rīdent et Faliscī, ubi clāmōrēs īgnāvī hominis audīvērunt et ad moenia festīnāvērunt. Iūstitiā Camillī paene attonitī, cōnsilia mūtant : lēgātōs, prīmum in castra ad Camillum, deinde ad urbem Rōmam mittunt. Falēriōs Rōmānīs trādunt pācemque rogant. Pāx data est, et Faliscī bonī et fortēs sociī populī Rōmānī semper fuērunt.

B

1. Is there a braver general than Camillus ?
2. Horatius was the bravest of all the citizens.
3. Poets praise the customs of the ancient Romans.
4. The master's toga is very short. Upon my word, it is shorter than mine.
5. Camillus is a very just man. He will always be praised by the citizens.
6. The farmer's dog is more beautiful than mine.
7. Why had the general not adopted a bolder plan ?

8. The barbarians had very swift horses.
9. Why are you laughing, boys ? To-day we have beaten the master with rods.
10. There are many beautiful islands between Gaul and Britain.
11. In Gaul there are very wide plains.
12. Where has the old man come from ? Where is he hurrying to ?
13. He has come from Britain and is sailing to Italy.
14. When he saw the priest, the soldier leapt down from his horse.
15. Good day, Valerius ! Why are you angry ?
16. I gave my son a new ball yesterday. To-day it's nowhere !
17. I have never led braver soldiers into battle.
18. We shall never hand over the citadel to the enemy.

WORD STUDY

To-day you are able to tell what is really meant by the minister's *sermon* ; and you can fully appreciate the point of the saying that *brevity* is the soul of wit. When you read in the *Pilgrim's Progress* of the *delectable* mountains, your Latin will help you to understand why Bunyan gave them that name.

Addō gives us *add* and *addition*. And speaking of *addition* here is an interesting piece of information. You know that the answer to a problem in addition is often called the *sum*. Why is this ? The answer is that when the Romans did an addition they had a habit of writing the answer at the top instead of beneath the items to be added. Now the Latin for the top line is **summa līnea**. Hence the line containing the answer was the **summa līnea**. For short it came to be called simply the **summa,** and people forgot that this word is really an adjective agreeing with **līnea,** and thought of it as a noun meaning " total."

XL

COMPARISON OF ADJECTIVES—*continued*

§ 49. Six Adjectives with Nominative Singular in **-ilis** form Comparative and Superlative Degrees as follows :

facilis	easy	**facilior**	**facillimus**
difficilis	difficult	**difficilior**	**difficillimus**
similis	like	**similior**	**simillimus**
dissimilis	unlike	**dissimilior**	**dissimillimus**
gracilis	thin, slender	**gracilior**	**gracillimus**
humilis	low, humble	**humilior**	**humillimus**

§ 50. Adjectives ending in **-us** preceded by any vowel, except **-u**, form Comparative and Superlative Degrees by using the adverbs **magis,** more, and **maximē,** most, e.g. :

dubius, doubtful : **magis dubius,** more doubtful : **maximē dubius,** most doubtful.

idōneus, suitable : **magis idōneus,** more suitable : **maximē idōneus,** most suitable.

BUT

antīquus, ancient : **antīquior : antīquissimus.**

Note.—**Similis,** like, and **dissimilis,** unlike, are accompanied by the genitive, e.g. :

(*a*) **Puer similis patris est,** The boy is like his father.
(*b*) **Puella mātris dissimilis est,** The girl is unlike her mother.

EXERCISE 40

A

The First Foe from Overseas

[SEXTUS *leads—or, more accurately, compels—his father to tell of Rome's war with* PYRRHUS, *280–275 B.C.*]

SEXTUS : Pater ! (*There is no reply, so Sextus begins again.*)   Pater ! (*silence continues.*)   Pater ! Semper tōtus es in librō. Vae tibi, pater ! Ingentī in perīculō es, cum librō tuō. Nisi dīxeris, impetum in tē magnā vī faciam. Librum meum in tē coniciam, deinde sellam, mēnsam, statuam——

PATER (*in mild astonishment at the volley of threats*) : Ō ! . . . Quid est, Sexte ?

SEXTUS : Quis Pyrrhus fuit ? Nōmen Pyrrhī in librō meō videō, sed dē Pyrrhō nihil.

PATER : Vir Graecus erat, rēx Ēpīrī. Prīmus hostis trānsmarīnus (*from over the sea*) populī Rōmānī fuit.

SEXTUS (*in a tone of contempt*) : Ō ! hostis fuit populī Rōmānī. Satis est. Mehercule, scelestus homō fuit, Tarquiniī et Lartis Porsinnae similis.

PATER : Minimē vērō, Sexte. Fortissimus erat et iūstissimus. Rōmānī semper Pyrrhum laudant.

SEXTUS : Quid dīcis ? hostemne laudant ? Cūr ?

PATER : Audiēs. Tarentīnī, ubi bellum cum Rōmānīs gerēbant, perīculō sollicitī, auxilium Pyrrhī rogāvērunt. Ad Ītaliam igitur cum

magnō exercitū et multīs elephantīs nāvigāvit.
Prīmō proeliō paene superātus est. Tandem
auxiliō elephantōrum Rōmānōs superāvit.
Nostrī enim elephantōs numquam viderant;
timēbant igitur ingentia corpora elephantōrum.
Post proelium tamen, Pyrrhus propter virtūtem
nostrōrum captīvōs imperātōrī reddidit, necā-
tōs sepelīvit. Ubi corpora necātōrum vīdit,
attonitus, "Quam fortēs," inquit, "virī fuērunt!
Impetūs enim nostrōrum diū sustinuērunt.
Ecce! vulnera sunt adversa omnia (*all in front*).
Etiam in morte trucēs vultūs sunt. Sī auxilium
Rōmānōrum comparāverō, dominus orbis terrārum ōlim erō. Quis enim virōs Rōmānōs
sustinēbit? Quot enim mīlitum nostrōrum
Rōmānī hodiē necāvērunt? Mehercule, sī
Rōmānōs sīc iterum superāverō, cum nūllō
exercitū in Ēpīrum ex Ītaliā nāvigābō."

B

1. With a word chosen from the following list, complete each
   of the sentences given below :

*truciōrem, dissimillimus, pulchrior, breviōrem, humiliōrem,
altum, difficilius, altius, simillimus.*

(a) Quis togam —— habet?
(b) Domum —— numquam vīdī.
(c) Quis est —— quam māter tua?
(d) Frāter meus —— est fīliī tuī.
(e) Elephantus —— est equī.
(f) Īrātus est dominus : vultum —— numquam vīdī.
(g) Quid facis? Labōrō. Estne facile? Nihil —— vīdī.
(h) Flūmen est ——. Mare tamen —— est.

2. I was delighted by the ambassador's talk.
3. The poet is very just and brave.
4. The Greeks were astounded by the valour of Hector.
5. The little boy was terrified by the soldier's grim face.
6. The shepherd's house was very low. The shepherd was very poor.
7. Yesterday we remained at home and told stories.
8. To-day we shall walk in the fields. It isn't raining.
9. After the battle the soldiers buried the slain.
10. Why were the Romans terrified by the elephants ?
11. No race was bolder than the Romans.
12. Quintus is very like his father.
13. Good day, Marcus ! What a short toga you have !
14. What huge shoes the boy has ! Yes, indeed ; for he has big feet.
15. Valerius has a very beautiful country house. Upon my word, Valerius is a very happy man.

WORD STUDY

The phrase **bellum gerere** will perhaps stick better in your memory if you realise that it has given us the English word *belligerent* which means " one who is carrying on a war " ; in short, a combatant.

Trux gives us *truculence*, which means a harsh, bullying, overbearing style of behaviour ; and *truculent*, which is the adjective to apply to a fierce, grim-looking bully of a fellow.

Similis and **dissimilis** give us quite a crop of English words. There are our familiar friends *similar* and *dissimilar*, *similarity* and *dissimilarity*, and there is the very interesting word *simile*. What is a *simile* ?

XLI

COMPARISON OF ADJECTIVES—*continued*

§ 51. Some Adjectives are irregularly compared, e.g. :

bŏnus	good	**melior**	**optimus**
mălus	bad	**peior**	**pessimus**
magnus	great	**māior**	**maximus**
parvus	small	**minor**	**minimus**
multus	much	**plūs**	**plūrimus**
multī	many	**plūrēs**	**plūrimī**

Note.—In singular **plūs** is used as a noun and occurs only in Nominative (**plūs**), Accusative (**plūs**), and Genitive (**plūris**), e.g. **plūs pecūniae**, more (of) money.

In the plural it is used as an adjective, and is declined as follows :

	Masc.	Fem.	Neut.
Nom.	**plūrēs**	**plūrēs**	**plūră**
Acc.	**plūrēs**	**plūrēs**	**plūră**
Gen.	**plūrium**	**plūrium**	**plūrium**
Dat.	**plūribus**	**plūribus**	**plūribus**
Abl.	**plūribus**	**plūribus**	**plūribus**

EXERCISE 41

A

More about Pyrrhus

Pater : Pyrrhus tandem, ubi Rōmānōs iam saepe superāvit, in agrōs eōrum (*their*) iter fēcit.

Sextus : Ēheu ! quid tum Rōmāni fēcērunt ? Pācemne rogāvērunt ? Urbemne trādidērunt ?

Pater : Minimē vērō, Sexte. Maxima semper maximō in perīculō virtūs est Rōmānōrum.

Māiōre vī impetum in hostēs parāvērunt. Paucīs diēbus magnus exercitus contrā Pyrrhum festīnāvit. Pyrrhus tamen impetum nostrōrum nōn sustinuit, sed exercitum in Campāniam dūxit.

SEXTUS : Mehercule, fortūna, sīcut semper dīcis, fortēs amat.

PATER : Ita vērō. Deinde veniunt ad Pyrrhum ā Rōmānīs lēgātī. Sīc nūntiant : " Sī captīvōs, Pyrrhe, līberāveritis, pretium ā populō Rōmānō maximum accipiēs." Sed Pyrrhus, " Sine pretiō," inquit, " captīvōs, virōs fortissimōs, reddō. Ferrō, nōn aurō, bellum gerēmus : virtūte, nōn pretiō aut (either) ego vōs superābō, aut (or) vōs mē superābitis."

SEXTUS : Quam laudō Pyrrhum, virum bonum et iūstum !

PATER : Erat inter lēgātōs Fabricius, vir pauperrimus sed honestus et bellō cōnsiliōque ācerrimus. Fabriciō Pyrrhus, " Sī amīcus," inquit, " meus eris, dīvitissimum tē faciam. Aurum enim dabō, et quārtam partem rēgnī, sī auxiliō tuō mē cōnsiliōque adiūveris." Fabricius sermōnem rēgis rīsit. " Nōn mōs est," inquit, " Rōmānōrum contrā patriam hostem adiuvāre." Deinde Pyrrhus, mīrāculō honestātis paene attonitus, lēgātōs dē pāce ad Senātum mīsit. Appius Claudius Cēnsor, senex et iam caecus, ubi lēgātōs audīvit, trucī vultū, " Senātus," inquit,

APPIUS CLAUDIUS DISSUADES THE SENATE FROM MAKING
PEACE WITH PYRRHUS

"populusque Rōmānus dē pāce non agit dum
hostis in Ītaliā est." Et Cīneās, ūnus lēgā-
tōrum, ubi ad Pyrrhum vēnit, " Rēgum,"
inquit, " patriam vīdī : rēgum enim similēs
Senātōrēs Rōmānōrum sunt."

Proximō annō medicus Pyrrhī nocte vēnit
ad castra Rōmānōrum, et Fabriciō, " Quid
dīcis," inquit, " Fabricī! Sī satis aurī dederis,
Pyrrhum venēnō necābō." Sed Fabricius
hominem scelestum nōn laudāvit : statim
medicum ad Pyrrhum mīsit et omnia nārrāvit. Tum rēx, " Difficilius est," inquit,
" Fabricium ab honestāte quam sōlem ā
cursū āvertere."

B

1. Iron is often more useful than gold.
2. Honour is better than much gold.
3. Fabricius sent the wicked doctor to the king.
4. If you will set free the prisoners, we shall give you a great price.
5. The senator is old and blind, but very brave.
6. The Romans have been advised by the old man. They will not make an attack to-day.
7. There were more soldiers in the camp yesterday.
8. Very many of the Romans were terrified by the elephants.
9. Yes, indeed; for the elephants were very large and fierce.
10. The danger was very great, but the young man feared nothing.
11. He sat at home, engrossed in a book.
12. On the tenth day more ambassadors came from the barbarians.
13. Marcus is the best soldier of the legion, but Balbus is the worst.
14. The doctor was a very bad man. He had conspired against his master.
15. The inn is very small, but very beautiful.

C

1. Give the Latin for: Of a very big dog: for the bigger boys: he is like his brother: for many days: what will be better? : in three days: for a most honourable man: she is more beautiful than her beautiful mother: in a very small country house: into the smaller camp.
2. Give the English for: Plūrimīs perīculīs sollicitus sum : sellam māiōrem comparāvī: plūrium sacerdōtum : in māiōra maria : nihil pulchrius vīdī: servum pessimum verberāvī: pēiōra timēbam: optimus poēta : rosās habēbam pulcherrimās : optima dīcis.

3. Give the English for : Inter fēminās : ē sellā dēsilueram :
dextram in ignem iniēcit : terrēbāmur omnēs :
omnēs terrēbāmus : rēgnum occupābit : pilam in
ignem coniēcit : flammīs attonitī sunt : mīrāculum
virtūtis : urbs dēlēta est.

REVISION EXERCISES

A

1. The pupils were delighted by the master's talk.
2. They had been frightened by many things.
3. The brave soldier had leapt down into the sea.
4. The customs of the ancient Romans are often praised.
5. The boys had been taught by a wicked master.
6. The senators were warned by the blind old man.
7. The general was overcome by the tears of his wife and mother.
8. Our plans have often been changed.
9. Poison was given to the king by the doctor.
10. All the world has been overcome by the Romans.

B

1. Monuerās : monitus eris : territī estis : vāstātum erat :
mūtābitur : docēbiminī : timuerāmus : datur : obsidē-
bantur : habētur.
2. Humiliōris domūs : meliōrem hominem : maximō elephantō :
proximō diē : puer est simillimus patris : senātor
honestissimus : plūrima vulnera : rēgis fēlīciōris : pessi-
mus medicus : liber ūtilissimus.
3. Plūrimī senātōrēs in sellīs sedent.
4. Nihil cīvibus ūtilius est quam pāx.
5. Quis est melior homō quam magister noster ?
6. Pretiumne māius mīlitibus dabitur ?
7. Quandō māiōrēs elephantōs vīdistī ?
8. Cūr sunt mīlitum vultūs trīstissimī ?
9. Quis plūra vulnera accēpit quam imperātor ?
10. Proximō diē necātōs sepelīvimus.

C

1. Of greater burdens : for most honourable citizens : of very low houses : by larger weapons : of better fortune : for a very good doctor : of a fiercer attack : by more wounds : by better fortune : sadder faces (*subj.*).
2. We had never heard a louder (greater) crash.
3. Who is more noble than Veturia ?
4. Nothing is more useful than iron.
5. In the battle the general has received very many wounds.
6. The old man is very sad, for he is blind.
7. We shall hand over a very great price to the farmer.
8. In the city there is very great scarcity of all things.
9. We shall not withstand a fiercer attack.
10. Very many citizens have conspired against the Senate.

D

1. Turn the following sentences into passive form, and translate :
   (a) Sermō senātōrum mē dēlectāvit.
   (b) Sacerdōs miserōs cīvēs monēbat.
   (c) Ingentēs elephantī Rōmānōs terruerant.
   (d) Omnēs mōrēs Rōmānōrum nōn laudant.
   (e) Optimus magister discipulōs docuerat.
   (f) Plūrimī hominēs iūstitiam laudant.
   (g) Imperātōrem lacrimae fēminārum superābant.
   (h) Scaevola rēgem īgnōrābat.

2. Translate :
   (a) In three days : on the fourth day : for many days : on the next day : in ten days.
   (b) In nine days we shall receive the price.
   (c) We had awaited the ambassadors for five days.
   (d) When will you (s.) come ?   I shall come in a few days.
   (e) Nothing is harder than iron.
   (f) There was very great scarcity of all things.
   (g) It rained for three days.
   (h) The farmer had thrust the iron into the fire.

ROMAN BOOKS

Every time we use the word " volume " we are using a word which exactly describes a Roman book, but does not really suggest a modern one. For " volume " is just the old Latin word **volūmen,** which means " a roll." And that is what a Roman book was—a roll of material anything up to twenty or thirty feet in length and, on the average, about a foot broad. On the inner side of this roll appeared the contents of the book, not printed—for the Romans never hit upon the art of printing— but written by hand in narrow columns or pages (**pāginae**), three or four inches wide, so arranged that the lines of writing were parallel to the sides of the roll, thus :

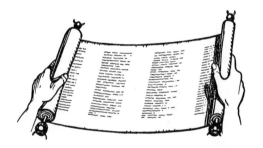

The material of which the book was made was usually papyrus —from which is derived our word " paper." The pith of the papyrus reed was cut up into strips, a number of which were laid together horizontally so as to form a sheet of writing material. They were pasted together, and then the sheet was strengthened by pasting over the first strips a second layer consisting of strips laid at right angles to the first lot. Then the whole sheet was pressed, carefully smoothed, and, in some cases at least, ruled off for writing.

The book consisted of a large number of such sheets gummed together, thus :

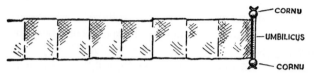

The right hand edge of the last sheet was regularly attached to a stick, called the **umbilicus**. The end of this stick had knobs, also called **umbilicī**, or sometimes ornaments called **cornua**. One is reminded of the roller of a modern wall-map. Round the **umbilicus** the whole length of papyrus was rolled up. The ends of the wound roll (**frontēs**) were frequently smoothed and coloured. To one of the ends of the **umbilicus** a label (**titulus**) was attached, bearing the author's name and the name of the work. In expensive copies of a work the first page of the roll might be occupied by a portrait of the author. The writing was done in ink (**ātrāmentum**). Usually this was compounded of soot and gum, but sometimes a natural dye was used, obtained from cuttle-fish.

The reader held the roll in his right hand, and, as he read, rolled up the read portion with his left. Thus, when he had read the book through, he would need to re-wind it, so that it would be correctly rolled for the next reader when he began his reading.

The writing of copies of books was done by educated slaves. There were booksellers, who were also publishers, employing staffs of slaves to produce a number of copies of a work. The Romans, however, had no law of copyright. If a man bought a book from a bookseller and liked it, he could set his own slave to make as many copies of it as he liked. Similarly with a book received on loan. If the reader liked it, there was nothing to prevent him from having a copy made for his library, or even to give to a friend.

XLII

THE THIRD CONJUGATION—*continued*

§ 52. Present, Future, Imperfect Indicative Passive of **regĕre**, to rule.

Tense	Pers.	Singular	Plural
Present	1	rég-or I am ruled	rég-ĭmur we are ruled
	2	rég-ĕris you are ruled	reg-ĭminī you are ruled
	3	rég-ĭtur he, she, it is ruled	reg-untur they are ruled
Future	1	reg-ar I shall be ruled	reg-ēmur we shall be ruled
	2	reg-ēris you will be ruled	reg-ēminī you will be ruled
	3	reg-ētur he, she, it will be ruled	reg-entur they will be ruled
Imperfect	1	reg-ēbar I was being ruled	reg-ēbāmur we were being ruled
	2	reg-ēbāris you were being ruled	reg-ēbāminī you were being ruled
	3	reg-ēbātur he, she, it was being ruled	reg-ēbantur they were being ruled

§ 53. Perfect, Future Perfect and Pluperfect Indicative Passive of **regĕre**, to rule.

Tense	Pers.	Singular	Plural
Perfect	1	**rēctus sum** I have been ruled, etc.	**rēctī sumus** we have been ruled, etc.
	2	**rēctus es** you have been ruled, etc.	**rēctī estis** you have been ruled, etc.
	3	**rēctus est** he has been ruled, etc.	**rēctī sunt** they have been ruled, etc.
Future Perfect	1	**rēctus erō** I shall have been ruled	**rēctī erimus** we shall have been ruled
	2	**rēctus eris** you will have been ruled	**rēctī eritis** you will have been ruled
	3	**rēctus erit** he will have been ruled	**rēctī erunt** they will have been ruled
Pluperfect	1	**rēctus eram** I had been ruled	**rēctī erāmus** we had been ruled
	2	**rēctus erās** you had been ruled	**rēctī erātis** you had been ruled
	3	**rēctus erat** he had been ruled	**rēctī erant** they had been ruled

Note.—See § 41, note.

EXERCISE 42

A

THE EMBASSY OF REGULUS

[*A story of the First Carthaginian War*, 264–242 *B.C.*]

M. Atīlius Rēgulus, imperātor Rōmānus, ā Carthāginiēnsibus captus est. Tandem Carthāginiēnsēs, ubi saepe ā Rōmānīs superātī sunt, pācem et captīvōrum permūtātiōnem dēsīderābant. Rēgulō, igitur, sīc dīxērunt : " Iam ad senātum, Rēgule, tē mittēmus. Sī pācem et permūtātiōnem captīvōrum Carthāginiēnsibus faciēs, līber eris et in patriā manēbis : sī nōn, statim ad nōs veniēs, et necāberis. Quid dīcis, Rēgule ? Accipisne condiciōnēs nostrās ? " Tum Rēgulus, " Accipiō," inquit, et ad Ītaliam nāvigāvit.

In urbem vēnit ; in senātum festīnāvit ; omnia patribus nūntiāvit. Patrēs dē rē agēbant ; tandem, ubi nūllum cōnsilium cēperunt, cōnsul Rēgulō, " Quid dīcis," inquit, " Rēgule ? Age, senātor enim es, quid faciēmus ? " Sed trucī vultū Rēgulus, " Nōn senātor," inquit, " nōn cīvis Rōmānus iam sum, sed miser captīvus Carthāginiēnsium. Tamen, sī cōnsilium meum audiētis, pācem cum Carthāginiēnsibus numquam faciētis. Bellō enim dēfessī spem nūllam iam habent. Captīvōs reddētis numquam : iuvenēs enim sunt et bonī dūcēs. Sed Rōmānōrum paucōs hostēs cēperunt, senēs, hominēs īgnāvissimōs."

Patrēs cōnsilium Rēgulī laudant : pācem nōn faciunt : captīvōs nōn reddunt. Quid Rēgulus facit ? Manetne cum uxōre, cum līberīs, cum amīcīs ? Minimē vērō. Fidem servat. " Nōn manēbō," inquit, " sīc enim dīgnitātem honestī cīvis numquam habēbō." Amplexum igitur uxōris nōn accipiēbat : lacrimīs amīcōrum nōn superātus est. Ō mīrāculum honestātis ! Ad Carthāginiēnsēs, ad mortem, festīnāvit.

B

1. A very great war is being waged by land and sea.
2. For many years the Romans were masters of the world.
3. The doctor will be handed over to the king by Fabricius.
4. Alas ! we have no hope. Our city will be burned by the enemy.
5. The Romans had more prisoners than the Carthaginians.
6. The Senators therefore did not make an exchange of prisoners.
7. Regulus, however, kept faith and hastened from the city.
8. Good morning, Valerius ! What is the Senate doing to-day ?
9. The Senators are discussing the conditions of peace.
10. Why had Regulus been sent to Italy by the Carthaginians ?
11. The Roman Senators are like kings.
12. Upon my word, they have more dignity than many kings.
13. See ! the river has been turned away from its course.
14. Honour, my son, is better than gold.
15. Next day, the enemy made an attack on the bridge.
16. The approach to (in Latin, *of*) the bridge was defended by Horatius.
17. What a lazy pupil Marcus is ! He'll be sent home by the master.

C

A Bad Poet is Suitably Rewarded

VALERIUS : Salvē, mī fīlī, optime discipule optimī magistrī !
Quid hodiē in lūdō fēcistī ?

MARCUS : Diū dē poētīs Rōmānīs ēgimus.

VALERIUS : Optima nārrās, mī fīlī. Multī enim poētārum
nostrōrum virī bonī et honestissimī fuērunt.

MARCUS : Quid ? tūne omnia dē poētīs Rōmānīs scīs ?

VALERIUS : Ita vērō, Marce. Quis enim dē Enniō, Vergiliō,
Horātiō nōn audīvit ?

MARCUS : Audīvistīne umquam dē imperātōre Rōmānō,
quī (who) magnam pecūniam propter carmen poētae
dedit ?

VALERIUS : Saepe, mī fīlī. Enniō enim ā Scīpiōne multa
data sunt ; Vergilius et Horātius ā Caesare Augustō
plūrima accēpērunt.

MARCUS : Sed dē malō poētā quid ? Deditne umquam
imperātor Rōmānus malō poētae praemium ?

VALERIUS : Ha ! ha ! ha ! Minimē vērō, mī fīlī. Quis
umquam malum poētam laudāvit ?

MARCUS : Audiēs, pater. Ego enim plūra quam tū dē
poētīs Rōmānīs sciō. Hodiē dē malō poētā magister
fābulam nārrāvit. Carmen dē Sullā, maximō imperātōre, scrīpserat. Dī immortālēs ! quam rīdiculum
carmen fuit. Versūs enim plūrimī breviōrēs (too short)
erant, plūrimī longiōrēs (too long). Et verba ? Ō
pater, verba mīrābilia erant ; plūrima enim vix Latīna
erant. Poēta tamen, " Mehercule," inquit, " fēlīx
homō erō. Ad Sullam enim festīnābō ; carmen reci-
tābō : praemium maximum accipiam."

VALERIUS : Ō quam audāx cōnsilium ! Quid Sulla fēcit ?
Trādiditne poētam mīlitibus ? Virgīsne poētam ver-
berāvērunt et ex castrīs traxērunt ?

MARCUS : Minimē vērō, pater. Poēta ad Sullam ductus est ; carmen recitāvit. Tum Sulla, cum maximō rīsū mīlitum, " Vae tibi," inquit, " pessime poētārum ! Praemium tibi dō. Audīsne tamen condiciōnem ? Carmen posthac nūllum scrībēs ! " Et statim ē praedā, bonam et magnam partem poētae dedit ; incolumem ē castrīs mīsit.

Note :

sciō, scīre, scīvī, scītum, to know.
carmen, -inis, *n.,* poem, song.
umquam, *adv.,* ever.
praemium, -iī, *n.,* reward.
rīdiculus, -a, -um, ridiculous.
versus, -ūs, *m.,* verse.
verbum, -ī, *n.,* a word.

mīrābilis, -is, -e, wonderful.
vix, hardly, scarcely.
Latīnus, -a, -um, Latin.
posthac, *adv.,* hereafter.
scrībō, -ere, scrīpsī, scrīptum, to write.
incolumis, -is, -e, unharmed.

WORD STUDY

When you say that you feel an *aversion* to anything do you mean that you feel drawn to, or somehow turned from, it ? Your Latin will guide you to the right answer.

In a famous passage Shakespeare calls the toad " ugly and *venomous.*" This big word is derived from **venēnum,** and means poisonous. There was a belief in the old days that the harmless toad was poisonous.

What is meant by the expression " Old *Sol,*" and what happens in a *solar* eclipse ? And what is *ferro*-concrete ?

Pretium appears in disguise in many English words. We have *price* itself, and *precious* and the verb *prize.* To *prize* anything is to set a high price or value on it. **Fidēs** figures in one of these genuine Latin phrases which have almost become English, so commonly are they employed. **Bonā fidē** means " in good faith," hence, a *bona fide* claimant, say to a fortune, is one who has a genuine claim to be considered, not a mere impostor. Lastly, you should note that **agere,** as well as meaning "to treat or negotiate about " or " to discuss," quite often means " to act " or " to do." Hence it has given us such words as *act, action, actor, agent* and *agenda.* The *agenda* of a committee are the items of business which it has to discuss and settle at its meeting.

XLIII

PERSONAL PRONOUNS

§ 54. The Pronoun **Ego**, I.

CASE	SINGULAR		PLURAL	
Nom.	**ego**	I	**nōs**	we
Acc.	**mē**	me	**nōs**	us
Gen.	**meī**	of me	**nostrī** **nostrum**	of us
Dat.	**mihi**	to, for me	**nōbīs**	to, for us
Abl.	**mē**	by, with, from me	**nōbīs**	by, with, from us

§ 55. The Pronoun **Tū**, you (thou).

CASE	SINGULAR		PLURAL	
Nom.	**tū**	you, thou	**vōs**	you, ye
Acc.	**tē**	you, thee	**vōs**	you, ye
Gen.	**tuī**	of you, of thee	**vestrī** **vestrum**	of you
Dat.	**tibi**	to, for you, thee	**vōbīs**	to, for you
Abl.	**tē**	by, with, from you, thee	**vōbīs**	by, with, from you

Notes.—(1) With the ablative of the above a preposition is always required, e.g. :

ā mē, by me ; ā tē, by you (*s.*) ; ā nōbīs, by us ; ā vōbīs, by you (*pl.*).

mēcum, with me ; tēcum, with you (*s.*) ; nōbīscum, with us ; vōbīscum, with you (*pl.*).

(2) the forms **nostrum, vestrum** are used as Partitive Genitives, e.g. :

multī nostrum, many of us ; multī vestrum, many of you.

plūrēs nostrum, more of us ; plūrēs vestrum, more of you.

7

EXERCISE 43

Note.—The pronouns **ego, tū, nōs, vōs** are not usually expressed in Latin. They must, however, be inserted when it is desired to indicate emphasis, especially emphasis by contrast, e.g.: **Ego regō, tū regeris,** I rule, (but) you are ruled.

A

THE DARKEST HOUR

[*After the first Carthaginian war, the Carthaginian general* HAMILCAR *built up a Carthaginian empire in Spain. In* 221 *B.C. his son,* HANNIBAL, *became commander. Almost his first act was to attack Saguntum, a city allied to Rome, thus provoking war with the Romans. In* 218 HANNIBAL *marched across Gaul and over the Alps into Italy. Again and again he defeated the Romans—at the river Ticinus, in the great battle of the Trebia, next year at the Trasimene lake, finally in* 216 *B.C. at Cannae. This was the darkest hour in Roman history. Rome seemed at* HANNIBAL'S *mercy. Yet, by sheer courage she gradually wore* HANNIBAL *down. The end came in* 202 *B.C.* HANNIBAL *was defeated in the great battle of Zama.*]

Quandō maximō in perīculō erat rēs pūblica Rōmāna ? Post pugnam Cannēnsem. Exercitus enim Rōmānus paene dēlētus erat : cōnsulum Aemilius ab hostibus necātus erat, Varrō cum paucīs mīlitibus ē pugnā fūgerat. Maxima tamen cōnstantia Varrōnis erat. Clādem accēperat ingentem ; spem iam vidēbat nūllam. Nōn tamen dēspērāvit, sed mīlitibus arma, vestīmenta, omnia comparābat ; animōs cōnfirmābat ; deinde ad oppidum Canusium dūxit. " Moenia enim," inquit, " Canusiī nōs intereā dēfendent."

VARRO'S RETURN FROM CANNAE

Nōn minor erat cōnstantia senātōrum. Animōs cīvium cōnfirmābant : intrā urbem omnia ad pugnam parābant : arma senibus, puerīs, servīs dedērunt. Ubi satis armōrum nōn erat, ex templīs cēpērunt. Sīc paucīs diēbus novus exercitus parātus est. Veniunt intereā lēgātī ab Hannibale. Sīc nūntiant : " Hannibal, sī pretium dederitis, cap-tīvōs līberābit." Sed senātus, " Condiciōnēs," inquit, " nōn accipimus. Sine auxiliō hominum ignāvōrum nōs patriam dēfendēmus."

Ubi Varrō ad urbem iam festīnābat, cīvēs, propter clādem īrātī, exclāmābant, " Ō scelus ! Varrōnemne in urbem accipiēmus ? Varrōnemne laudābimus ? Minimē vērō. Sī in urbem intrāverit, hominem scelestum necābimus. Cōnsiliō enim Varrōnis nostrī pugnāvērunt et superātī sunt : propter Varrōnem patria paene dēlēta est." Sed Q. Fabius Maximus, " Quid dīcitis," inquit, " cīvēs ? Nōn mōs est Rōmānōrum propter clādem imperātōrem necāre. Quid ? Reddetne nōbīs mors Varrōnis patrēs, frātrēs, fīliōs, amīcōs necātōs ? Minimē vērō. Agite, ex urbe festīnābimus : Varrōnem accipiēmus : propter cōnstantiam laudābimus et omnī honōre in urbem dūcēmus." Cōnsilium Fabiī cīvēs capiunt ; omnī honōre Varrōnem salūtant ; virtūtem cōnstantiamque laudant. Et Fabius, " Grātiās tibi maximās," inquit, " senātus populusque Rōmānus agit, quod dē rē publicā nōn dēspērāvistī."

A Carthaginian Helmet found at Cannae

B

1. To me : for us : with you (*s.*) : I see you (*pl.*) : he came
   with me : why do you praise us ? : I have nothing for
   you, my son : many of us were wounded : there were
   more of you in the camp : he was ruled for many years
   by me : they had been seen by us.

2. The danger is great, citizens, but we shall never despair.

3. You (*pl.*) have reassured the minds of the citizens : we have
   praised the constancy of the senators.

4. We have restored your friends to you, (but) you have not
   thanked us.

5. You (*s.*) blame Varro : I shall receive him with all honour.

6. We thank you because you have helped us in a very great
   danger.

7. We shall not accept the terms, for we do not despair of
   (*dē*) the state.

8. A messenger will be sent to you by us in a few days.

9. Many honours will be given to you by the citizens.

10. Alas ! the citizens will not receive us into the city.

11. We have sustained a very great defeat.

12. The prisoners will never be restored to you (*pl.*) by us.

13. The senate will never discuss terms of peace with you,
    Pyrrhus.

14. The allies have kept faith ; the minds of our men are re-
    assured.

15. Honour and dignity are loved by us ; gold is praised
    by you.

16. Why are the wretched citizens despairing of victory ?

17. Because the army has been almost destroyed by Hannibal.

18. Alas ! the danger is greater to-day than it was yesterday.

19. I am bigger than you, Marcus. Yes, indeed, Sextus ; but
    I am braver than you.

20. Nothing will terrify the king. In the greatest danger he
    never despaired of the kingdom.

C

Another cross-word !

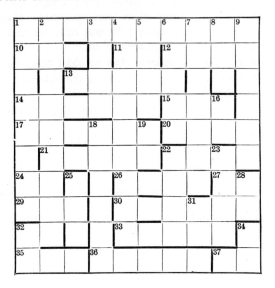

CLUES ACROSS

1. Unlike.
10. No. 5 is possessive of this.
11. Acc. or abl. sing. of 10.
12. A Latin word used in English for part of a cathedral.
13. You put a *petasus* on this.
14. Horatius defended one of these.
15. I shall be.
17. To wander.
20. If I did this long enough I would shed 7.
21. This adjective would describe Horatius.

22. You love.
24. 1st declension acc. sing. ending.
26. Missiles.
27. Abl. sing. of " thing."
29. " Your " (abl. sing. masc.).
30. " Best " (abl. sing. masc.).
32. 3rd declension genitive sing. ending.
33. A ruin.
35. Abl. sing. of a 5th declension noun.
36. The world (accus.).
37. " About " or " concerning."

CLUES DOWN

1. Describes a man who has none of 35 across.

2. This Latin verb is also an English noun meaning an ignorant person.

3. He stands.

4. Julius Caesar was a good one.

5. Not *yours* nor *his.*

6. Prep. gov. acc.

7. Don't shed any over this puzzle.

8. Perf. indic. active of the 4th conj. ends in this.

9. Life was not very pleasant for these.

16. Many a dog would like one.

18. I help.

19. Out of.

22. Describes the Alps.

23. Roman soldiers carried them.

25. Soon.

28. 2nd conjug. pres. ind. active ends in this.

31. This prep. can govern acc. or abl.

32. The same as 32 across.

34. This pronoun is the same in Latin and English.

WORD STUDY

Captīvus gives us *captive,* meaning a prisoner ; and it also gives us *caitiff,* which means a low, contemptible fellow. How do these two words, which look different and have quite different shades of meaning, both come from the same Latin parent ? The answer is that they came into our language at different times and by different ways. *Captive* came straight from Latin and has kept its Latin meaning and appearance fairly well, while *caitiff* came through the French, which was brought by the Norman invaders. Pairs of words like these, where one word has come directly from Latin and the other has come from the same original Latin word, but by way of French, are called doublets. Here are some more doublets for you to study—*regal* and *royal* ; *legal* and *loyal* ; *fidelity* and *fealty.*

XLIV

THIRD CONJUGATION: VERBS ENDING IN -iō, PASSIVE VOICE, INDICATIVE MOOD

§ 56. Passive voice of :
căpĭō, căpĕrĕ, cēpī, captum, to take, to capture.

1. The Perfect, Future Perfect and Pluperfect Tenses are perfectly regular, viz. :

Perfect   .   .   . **captus sum,** etc.
Future Perfect   .   . **captus erō,** etc.
Pluperfect .   .   . **captus eram,** etc.

2. The Present, Future and Imperfect Tenses are as follows :

PRESENT TENSE

1 **capior**	**capĭmur**
2 **capĕris**	**capĭminī**
3 **capĭtur**	**capiuntur**

FUTURE TENSE

1 **capiar**	**capiēmur**
2 **capiēris**	**capiēminī**
3 **capiĕtur**	**capientur**

IMPERFECT TENSE

1 **capiēbar**	**capiēbāmur**
2 **capiēbāris**	**capiēbāminī**
3 **capiēbātur**	**capiēbantur**

EXERCISE 44

A

A Chivalrous Commander

[*One reason for* Hannibal's *failure in Italy was* Scipio's *presence in Spain.* Scipio *was a great gentleman as well as a great general. To-day we read how he treated* Allucius, *a Celtiberian chief, and his betrothed. The girl was taken prisoner.* Scipio *treated her with all honour, summoned her parents and her lover, then restored her without ransom.*]

Captīva ōlim ā mīlitibus ad Scīpiōnem dūcitur, virgō nōbilis et pulcherrima. Scīpiō multa dē patriā virginis et parentibus rogat : nārrat omnia virgō, et tandem, " Spōnsa sum," inquit, " prīncipis Celtibērōrum. Allucius nōmen iuvenis est." Statim, igitur, Scīpiō ad parentēs virginis et ad Allucium nūntium mīsit. Ad castra festīnāvērunt. Ubi vēnērunt, Scīpiō Alluciō, " Ego iuvenis," inquit, " iuvenī tibi dīcō : sīc enim līberrimus inter nōs sermō erit. Ubi spōnsa tua ā mīlitibus nostrīs capta est et ad mē ducta est, dē amōre tuō audīvī. Ego numquam amōre virginis captus sum ; rēs pūblica enim animum meum semper occupāvit. Sed nōn ego tē, quod virginem amās, culpō. Laudō enim ; et spōnsam tuam tibi servāvī. In castrīs meīs nūllam iniūriam accēpit. Maximō honōre semper tractāta est. Ecce, spōnsam tuam in manūs tuās iam reddō."

Tum iuvenis, mīrāculō honestātis paene attonitus, dextram Scīpiōnis cēpit, et " Grātiās tibi maximās," inquit, " vir optime, agō. Sed quid dabō, quid

SCIPIO AND ALLUCIUS

faciam prō beneficiō tuō ? " Sed Scīpiō, " Satis,"
inquit, " faciēs, sī amīcus Rōmānōrum eris. Sī ego,
sīcut pater meus semper erat, vir bonus sum, sunt
inter Rōmānōs multī nostrī similēs. In orbe terrārum nōn hostem ācriōrem, nōn meliōrem amīcum
quam populum Rōmānum comparābis."

Parentēs virginis prō beneficiō grātiās Scīpiōnī
agunt, et pater, " Age, Scīpiō," inquit, " quod
fīliam sine pretiō nōbīs reddidistī, hōc (*this*) aurum
ā nōbīs dōnum accipiēs." Scīpiō accēpit, sed statim
Alluciō, " Dōtī," inquit, " quam (*which*) ā patre
spōnsae tuae accipiēs, hōc (*this*) dōnum ā mē
addētur."

B

1. I was always very poor : you were once very rich.
2. Many beautiful cities were taken by us in Gaul.
3. After the battle many prisoners will be taken by the soldiers of the second legion.
4. The general's plan is very good : it will be adopted by all.
5. No injury has been received by the maiden in the camp.
6. If we remain at home, we shall not be taken by the enemy.
7. Gifts will be sent to Scipio by the chiefs of the barbarians.
8. Tired by the long war, the citizens long for peace.
9. You are tired, friend ; I am not tired.
10. A very great defeat has been sustained by the Roman army.
11. The guards are standing at the gate ; they will lead us to Scipio.
12. A dowry will be given to the young man by the father of his betrothed.
13. A gift will be added to the dowry by the Roman general.
14. The old man's joy was very great : he was delighted by the kindness of Scipio.
15. By the kindness of Caesar (*Caesar, Caesaris*) many noble citizens were restored to their native land.
16. When will the Senate discuss the general's plan ?
17. In the morning we shall see you all at home.

WORD STUDY

Dēspērō has not only given us the word *despair* itself, but also *desperate, desperation* and the rather interesting *desperado*.

You have no difficulty now in realising that to *confirm* a statement is to back it up, to strengthen it, to set it beyond doubt ; that *constancy* of purpose means firmness, unchangeableness ; and that our everyday word *constant* means, first of all, firm, fixed, unchangeable ; and secondly, is naturally applied to something that is, so to speak, " always there." We use the word in this sense when we speak of *constant* interruptions, or *constant* trouble.

XLV

DEMONSTRATIVE PRONOUNS

§ 57. Is, ĕă, id.

This word may be either Pronoun or Adjective. As a pronoun it means *he, she, it*. As an adjective it means *that*, e.g. :

  is puer, that boy.
  ĕă bellă, those wars.

Its declension is as follows :

Number	Case	Masculine	Feminine	Neuter
Singular	*Nom.*	**is**	**ĕă**	**id**
	Acc.	**ĕum**	**ĕam**	**id**
	Gen.	**eius**	**eius**	**eius**
	Dat.	**ĕī**	**ĕī**	**ĕī**
	Abl.	**ĕō**	**ĕā**	**ĕō**
Plural	*Nom.*	**ĭī, or ĕī**	**ĕae**	**ĕă**
	Acc.	**ĕōs**	**ĕās**	**ĕă**
	Gen.	**ĕōrum**	**ĕārum**	**ĕōrum**
	Dat.	**ĭīs, or ĕīs**	**ĭīs, or ĕīs**	**ĭīs, or ĕīs**
	Abl.	**ĭīs, or ĕīs**	**ĭīs, or ĕīs**	**ĭīs, or ĕīs**

Note.—**ēius,** the Genitive Singular of **is, ĕă, id** means *his, her* or *its*.
  ĕōrum, ĕārum, the Genitive Plural of **is, ĕă, id** means *their*.

EXERCISE 45

A

THE MAGIC OF A GREAT NAME

[*In the century before the birth of Christ, the Roman State was torn by a number of civil wars. The first of these was between rival generals, C. MARIUS and L. SULLA. Our reading lesson describes two incidents which illustrate the power of the name of the grim old soldier who had saved Italy in his day and had held six consulships.*]

Ubi Sulla in urbem intrāvit, Marius iam fūgerat. Īrātus, Sulla amīcīs " Quid ? " inquit, " Vīvetne C. Marius ? Minimē vērō. Eius enim cōnsiliīs multī ex amīcīs nostrīs necātī sunt. Propter eum patria paene dēlēta est. Sī is vīvet, numquam ā perīculō līberābimur. Mīlitēs igitur statim mittam : Marium capient ; ubi eum cēperint, necābunt."

Intereā ad flūmen Līrim Marius festīnāverat. Dēfessus itinere perīculōque sollicitus, ē viā errābat. Tandem pauper senex eum vīdit ; ad rīpam flūminis eum dūxit ; in occultō locō collocāvit. Deinde magnus clāmor audītur. Mīlitēs Sullae veniunt. Senem capiunt ; dē Mariō rogant. " Vae tibi, sceleste ! " exclāmant, " Hostem populī Rōmānī accēpistī. Ubi eum collocāvistī ? Ubi est ? " Festīnat Marius intereā in flūmen. " Undae flūminis," inquit, " ab hostibus mē dēfendent." Vident tamen eum hostēs : ex undīs eum trahunt ; ad oppidum Minturnās dūcunt ; deinde in carcerem coniciunt.

Eā nocte Minturnēnsēs mīlitem ad carcerem mittunt. Strictō gladiō (*with drawn sword*) intrat. Parātus est Marium necāre. Prīmō Marium nōn videt ; sedet enim in tenebrīs. Deinde flammae ex oculīs Mariī coruscant (*flash*), et vōcem eius mīles audit, " Vae tibi, homō īgnāvissime ! Gāium Marium necābis ? " Territus est mīles : statim ex carcere fūgit.

Deinde Marius ad urbem Carthāginem nāvigāvit. In Āfricā, enim, spēs erat auxiliī. Sed ubi Marius vēnit, Sextilius—is tum prōvinciam regēbat—servum ad eum mīsit. Sīc nūntiat : " Dominus meus," inquit, " nisi ē prōvinciā festīnāveris, tē, sīcut iūssit senātus populusque Rōmānus, necābit." Sed trucī vultū Marius, " Audīsne ? " inquit. " Ad dominum tuum festīnābis et sīc nārrābis : ' Vīdī Gāium Marium in ruīnīs Carthāginis sedentem (*sitting*).' "

B

1. That king was driven out by the citizens.
2. That river is very wide. We used to sail on it.
3. Those burdens were carried home by those slaves.
4. To-day we see the ruins of ancient Rome.
5. I shall thank Marcus, because he has given the children many books.
6. Why are the girls sad ? Alas ! their father has been led to prison.
7. He has conspired against the Roman Senate and people.
8. Where are you, Sextus ? I don't see you in the darkness.
9. Those slaves work on the farm. How active they are !
10. The slave did not see the face of Marius, but he feared his voice.

11. The soldiers of that legion were in those ships.
12. Very small boys often fear the darkness of night.
13. For many days the Senators discussed an exchange of prisoners.
14. The children's mother is very beautiful. Their father is very brave.
15. Very many wars have been waged by us on behalf of our native land.

WORD STUDY

A whole battery of questions is awaiting you to-day. Can you say or find out what is meant by a **vīvā-vōce** examination, by an *undulating* line, by the well-known Latin phrase **lūx in tenebrīs,** by the term **locum tenēns,** by the long word *incarceration* ?

Prīnceps has given us many valuable words. Thus from it we have *prince, principal, principality* and even *principle,* which means a great ruling thought or truth or belief.

Vīvō is, as you would expect, a lively word, which has left many traces on our language. *Vivid* means life-like ; *vivacious* means lively ; to *revive* something is to bring it back into life again. With the help of your dictionary explore the meanings of *vivacity, revival, revivify.* And every boy and girl should know the meaning of **Vīvat rēx, Vīvat rēgīna !**

By courtesy of the British Museum

SLAVE'S BADGE. The inscription reads : " Hold me lest I escape, and take me back to my master VIVENTIUS on the estate of Callistus."

XLVI

THE FOURTH CONJUGATION—*continued*

§ 58. Present, Future and Imperfect Indicative Passive of **audīre,** to hear.

TENSE	PERS.	SINGULAR	PLURAL
PRESENT	1	**aúdi-or** I am heard	**audī-mur** we are heard
	2	**audī-ris** you are heard	**audī-minī** you are heard
	3	**audī-tur** he, she, it is heard	**audi-untur** they are heard
FUTURE	1	**audi-ar** I shall be heard	**audi-ēmur** we shall be heard
	2	**audi-ēris** you will be heard	**audi-ēminī** you will be heard
	3	**audi-ētur** he, she, it will be heard	**audi-entur** they will be heard
IMPERFECT	1	**audi-ēbar** I was being heard	**audi-ēbāmur** we were being heard
	2	**audi-ēbāris** you were being heard	**audi-ēbāminī** you were being heard
	3	**audi-ēbātur** he, she, it was being heard	**audi-ēbantur** they were being heard

§ 59. Perfect, Future Perfect, Pluperfect Indicative Passive of **audīre,** to hear.

Tense	Pers.	Singular	Plural
Perfect	1	**audītus sum** I have been heard, etc.	**audītī sumus** we have been heard, etc.
	2	**audītus es** you have been heard, etc.	**audītī estis** you have been heard, etc.
	3	**audītus est** he has been heard, etc.	**audītī sunt** they have been heard, etc.
Future Perfect	1	**audītus erō** I shall have been heard	**audītī erimus** we shall have been heard
	2	**audītus eris** you will have been heard	**audītī eritis** you will have been heard
	3	**audītus erit** he will have been heard	**audītī erunt** they will have been heard
Pluperfect	1	**audītus eram** I had been heard	**audītī erāmus** we had been heard
	2	**audītus erās** you had been heard	**audītī erātis** you had been heard
	3	**audītus erat** he had been heard	**audītī erant** they had been heard

Note.—See § 41, note.

EXERCISE 46

A

AN ARMY OF ARCHÆOLOGISTS !

[Shortly after the death of MARIUS, CN. POMPEIUS *rose to great fame as a general. To-day we read an amusing incident in one of Pompey's earlier campaigns. He had been sent to Africa to stamp out a rebellion. He pitched camp near Carthage. One of the soldiers while digging chanced upon a buried treasure. The cry arose that the place was full of gold, buried in the time of the Carthaginian war, and for several days on end the whole army gave itself up to digging for hidden gold !]*

Initiō eius bellī Pompēius in agrīs Carthāginiēnsibus castra posuit. Dum (*while*) legiōnēs castra mūniunt, vōx ūnīus ex mīlitibus audītur. " Dī immortālēs ! " inquit, " Quid videō ? " Clāmōre eius attonitī, sociī ad locum festīnant. Tum mīles, " Ecce ! " inquit, " dum fodiō, aurum invēnī." Et statim ē terrā ingēns aurī pondus traxit. Maximus est in castrīs clāmor. Omnēs mīlitem laudant ; fēlīcem dīvitemque appellant. Mīrāculō attonitī, dē rē agunt. Exclāmant " Quid ? Unde vēnit tam ingēns aurī pondus ? Quis in eō locō collocāvit ? " Tandem ūnus, " Mehercule ! " inquit, " Cīvis Carthāginiēnsis id in occultō locō ōlim sepelīvit, ubi mīlitēs Rōmānī moenia Carthāginis oppugnābant et Carthāginiēnsēs perīculum omnēs timēbant. Agite, sociī, sī meō cōnsiliō dūcēminī, hodiē castra

THE ARMY OF ARCHÆOLOGISTS

nōn mūniēmus. Plūrimī enim Carthāginiēnsium
aurum argentumque habēbant. Multī igitur in iīs
agrīs id sepelīvērunt. Mehercule, omnibus in locīs
fodiēmus! Nisi deōs īrātōs habēmus, nisi hostēs
impetum facient, multum aurum et argentum brevī
tempore inveniēmus. Sīcut rēgēs, dīvitēs fēlīcēsque
erimus." Omnēs cōnsilium laudant: arma abiciunt:
omnēs fodiunt. Vōcēs centuriōnum nōn audiuntur:
spēs aurī animōs omnium occupāverat.

Rēs intereā ā Pompēiō audīta erat. Nōn sollicitus inter mīlitēs ambulābat. Rīdet ubi labōrēs
mīlitum videt. Multōs diēs fodiunt, labōrant,
terram vertunt. Aurum tamen inventum est

nūllum. Omnēs tandem spem abiciunt : ad
Pompēium festīnant. Exclāmant : " Stultī fuimus,
imperātor. Spēs enim aurī nōs ab officiō āvertit.
Poenās tamen stultitiae dedimus ; labōribus enim
dēfessī sumus." Pompēius rīsit : mīlitibus veniam
dedit.

B

1. We shall be heard : it has been found : it has been fortified :
   you (*pl.*) will be heard : you (*pl.*) were being heard : they
   are being heard : they will have been heard : you (*s.*) will
   be heard : you (*s.*) are being heard : it will have been
   found.
2. In a few days that camp will have been fortified by the
   soldiers.
3. Why do I hear the shouts of the soldiers ? Why are they
   not working ?
4. A great mass of gold has been found by one of the soldiers.
5. In the hope of gold all are now digging in the fields.
6. What do I hear ? upon my word, it is the general's
   voice.
7. He is angry, because the camp is not being fortified.
8. That wretched boy came late to school yesterday.
9. Nevertheless he paid the penalty for (*of*) his folly ; for the
   master sent him home.
10. The foolish old man has buried the silver : to-morrow he
    will not find it.
11. The master has given pardon to the idle pupil.
12. In the army the centurions have great glory and dignity.
13. The poet has read a very beautiful story to the queen's
    sons.
14. In the darkness the shouts of men and women were heard.
15. The name of Marius was often heard in that city.
16. In a short time the camp had been pitched on the bank of
    the river.

REVISION EXERCISES

A

1. We shall be ruled : it is being taken : we have been heard : you (s.) were ruling : he had been taken : you (pl.) were heard : he is heard : she will have been taken : we were being ruled.
2. For me : that plan (subj.) : of you (pl.) : for them : by those gifts : at that time : in those places : of that maiden : of you (s.) : by those honours.
3. We have done as the Senators had ordered.
4. Many wars will be waged by land and sea.
5. The house has been restored to me.
6. Therefore I shall thank the Senators.
7. The silver had been found by the lucky soldier.
8. At that time Marius and Sulla were living.
9. Very beautiful gifts have been received by the maiden.
10. On the next day the camp was pitched.

B

1. Inveniētur : audiēbāminī : vīvent : geritur : pōnentur : mūnītum erat : mūniēbāmus : pōnitur : audīminī : mūnītum erit.
2. Eā spē : eius captīvae : ā vōbīs : eōrum castrōrum : eā clāde : tibi : eīs prīncipibus : id beneficium : eī mīlitī : in eō locō.
3. Eō tempore iuvenis animus amōre reī pūblicae occupātus est.
4. Multae captīvae ad imperātōrem ductae sunt.
5. Ego bellum geram ; tū dē pāce agēs.
6. Dēspērantne cīvēs ? Animōs eōrum cōnfirmābō.
7. Vīvuntne parentēs tuī ? Ita vērō, et prō mē magnum pretium dabunt.
8. Castra hodiē ā nōbīs mūnientur.
9. Quandō ā vōbīs stīpendium mīlitibus trādētur ?
10. Dōna nōbīs ā parentibus data sunt.

C

1. Put into passive form and translate :
    (*a*) The citizens have heard the shouts of the enemy.
    (*b*) The messenger has reported the disaster to us.
    (*c*) Love of his native country occupied the soldier's mind
    (*d*) At that time we were pitching camp in the plain.
    (*e*) On the next day the soldiers found Marius in a secret place.

2. Translate :
    (*a*) The silver had been found by us.
    (*b*) A disaster has been sustained by them.
    (*c*) All attacks will be withstood by those soldiers.
    (*d*) The minds of the citizens will be reassured by you.
    (*e*) Many kindnesses have been received by us.

D

A VOCABULARY TEST

(1) by love	(6) we are waging
(2) of dignity	(7) by exchanges
(3) without hope	(8) for the state
(4) with many gifts	(9) in return for a kindness
(5) by the death of Regulus	(10) without life
(11) we have thanked	(16) in secret places
(12) it had been fortified	(17) into prison
(13) we shall place	(18) of injuries
(14) they are living	(19) meanwhile
(15) at those times	(20) by folly
(21) they have ordered	(26) by hope of victory
(22) you (*s.*) are waging	(27) in those provinces
(23) they had lived	(28) for us
(24) by great disasters	(29) by them
(25) of the foolish maiden	(30) my parents (*obj.*).

XLVII

REFLEXIVE PRONOUNS

§ 60. Pronouns which refer back to the subject of the sentence,
e.g. : I praise *myself* ; you hurt *yourself* ; they bought
the book for *themselves* ;

are called *Reflexive Pronouns* because through them the action
expressed by the verb is *reflected* (i.e. bent) back upon the doer.

Latin has three reflexive pronouns, *mē*, myself ; *tē*, yourself ; *sē*, himself, herself, itself, themselves.

These are declined as follows :

(*a*) The reflexive pronoun of the first person : **mē**, myself.

CASE	SINGULAR		PLURAL	
Acc.	**mē**	myself	**nōs**	ourselves
Gen.	**meī**	of myself	**nostrī** **nostrum** }	of ourselves
Dat.	**mihi**	to, for myself	**nōbīs**	to, for ourselves
Abl.	**mē**	by, with, from my-self	**nōbīs**	by, with, from ourselves

(*b*) The Reflexive Pronoun of the second person : **tē**, yourself.

CASE	SINGULAR		PLURAL	
Acc.	**tē**	yourself	**vōs**	yourselves
Gen.	**tuī**	of yourself	**vestrī** **vestrum** }	of yourselves
Dat.	**tibi**	to, for yourself	**vōbīs**	to, for your-selves
Abl.	**tē**	by, with, from yourself	**vōbīs**	by, with, from yourselves

(c) The Reflexive Pronoun of the third person : **sē**, himself, etc.

CASE	SINGULAR AND PLURAL	
Acc.	**sē**	himself, herself, itself, themselves
Gen.	**suī**	of himself, etc.
Dat.	**sibi**	to, for himself, etc.
Abl.	**sē**	by, with, from himself, etc.

Notes.—(1) With the ablative of the above pronouns a preposition is necessary. Note the form **sēcum**, with himself, etc.

(2) The forms **nostrum, vestrum** are used as partitive genitives.

EXERCISE 47

A

RENOWN HAS ITS LIMITS !

[*To the age of* POMPEY *belongs* CICERO, *the greatest Roman orator and one of the world's greatest prose writers. Our reading lesson tells how, after serving with great brilliance as quaestor at Lilybaeum in Sicily, he returned to Italy to find men quite ignorant about his wonderful quaestorship ! Cicero played a considerable part in politics, but his real glory lies in the services he rendered to literature.*]

Multā spē laudis Cicerō ex Siciliā in Ītaliam nāvigābat. Quandō enim quaestor fuerat honestior ? Quis in omnī officiō fuerat dīligentior ? Quid ? Quis in prōvinciā omnēs hominēs tam inaudītā iūstitiā tractāverat ? Honōrēs eī plūrimōs Siculī

dederant, mīrāculō honestātis paene attonitī. Propter quaestūram ēius magnum erat in Siciliā nōmen
Rōmānum, magna auctōritās populī Rōmānī. Et
cīvēs Rōmānōs Cicerō in quaestūrā adiūverat.
Ubi ad Siciliam vēnit, erat in urbe Rōmā magna
inopia frūmentī. Statim igitur ex omnibus partibus
Siciliae frūmentum comparāverat et in urbem mīsit.
Iīs igitur diēbus quid ā populō Rōmānō nōn ex-
spectābat ? "Mehercule!" inquit, "Nihil nisi dē
quaestūrā meā cīvēs Rōmānī dīcunt. Ubi domum
vēnerō, honōrēs inaudītōs populus Rōmānus mihi
dabit."

Dum domum nāvigat, Cicerō ad urbem Puteolōs
vēnit. Magna urbs erat et pulcherrima. Hominēs
enim plūrimī et dīvitissimī in eā erant : ad aquās
enim multī semper veniēbant. Dum Cicerō in forō
ambulat, homō, ubi eum vīdit, statim ad Cicerōnem
festīnāvit et, "Quid ?" inquit, "Quandō tū ex
urbe Rōmā vēnistī ? Age, in urbe quid novī est ?"
Attonitus Cicerō, "Sed ex prōvinciā," inquit, "vēnī."
Et homō, "Ita vērō," inquit, "ex Āfricā." Īrātus
quod quaestūra sīc ab homine īgnōrābātur, Cicerō
"Minimē vērō," inquit, "sed ex Siciliā." Intereā
plūrēs ad locum vēnerant et sermōnem audiēbant.
Tum ex eīs ūnus, "Quid ?" inquit, "Tū hunc
(this) virum īgnōrās ? Mehercule, quaestor in
urbe Syrācūsīs fuit." Quid multa ? Videt Cicerō
stultitiam suam, et cum rīsū, "Multī ad urbem
Puteolōs" inquit, "ad aquās veniunt. Ē multīs
ūnus ego."

26

THE APPROACH TO LATIN

B

1. The bad poet praises himself.
2. Why do you (s.) always blame yourself?
3. We shall hide ourselves in the wood.
4. The wretched girl blames herself.
5. The prisoners threw themselves into the river.
6. Why do you (*pl.*) always praise yourselves.
7. They had hidden themselves in a secret place.
8. The boys are training themselves in the field.
9. We shall build ourselves a beautiful country house.
10. You will never free yourselves, slaves.
11. The farmers had procured horses for themselves.
12. The soldier's son has made a wooden horse for himself.
13. The wretched boy has wounded himself with his father's sword.
14. Good day, Marcus? Where have you come from? What news is there?

C

Some of Cicero's Jests

Inter amīcōs Cicerōnis Lentulus erat, homō strenuus et bonus, sed minimae statūrae. Is ōlim, ubi sē pulcherrimīs vestīmentīs, gladiō longissimō ōrnāvit, maximā dignitāte in forum intrāvit. Dum in forō ambulat, Cicerō eum videt. Tum quasi attonitus Cicerō, " Dī immortālēs! " inquit, " Quis Lentulum ad gladium alligāvit? "

Salūtāvit ōlim Cicerōnem quīdam (*a certain man*) aeger pedibus. Is, ubi plūrima dē dolōribus nārrāvit, tandem, " Sed iam " inquit, " firmior sum. Iam enim duo mīlia passuum ūnō diē saepe ambulō." Et Cicerō, " Ita vērō " inquit, " Diēs enim iam longiōrēs sunt."

Iuvenis quī (*who*) venēnum in placentā patrī dederat ā

"Dī immortales, quis Lentulum ad gladium alligavit?"

Cicerōne ōlim accūsābātur. Ubi Cicerō multa dē scelestō homine dīxit, is, īrātus, plūrimīs et pessimīs probrīs Cicerōnem oppugnāvit. Cicerō tamen nōn sollicitus omnia audīvit : tum, " Probra tua " inquit, " nōn timeō. Melius enim est ā tē probra quam placentam accipere."

Note :

statūra, -ae, *f.*, stature.
alligō, -āre, -āvī, -ātum, bind,
    tie, tether.
aeger, -ra, -rum, ill, sick.
firmus, -a, -um, strong.
duo mīlia passuum, two miles.

placenta, -ae, *f.*, cake.
accūsō, -āre, -āvī, -ātum, accuse.
probrum, -ī, *n.*, reproach, libel,
    piece of abuse.
quasi, as if.

WORD STUDY

Officium is a most interesting word. It is the parent of our word *office*, which originally meant, and still often means, duty, employment, occupation; but which soon came to mean also the place where a duty or occupation was carried on. Hence the *office*, which plays such a part in the life of the business man. You can see for yourself how words like *officer*, *official*, *officious* are connected with **officium**. Watch *officious* carefully: it is the word to apply to the person who is rather too full of his duty, who becomes pompous and meddlesome in carrying it out.

Now here is something to try your mettle: why is a line of poetry sometimes called a *verse*; and what is *penal servitude*?

By courtesy of the British Museum

ROMAN PENS AND INKPOTS

The pens in the upper part of the picture were used for writing on wax tablets; note the flattened reverse end used for erasing mistakes. Those shown below were for use with ink.

XLVIII

THE EMPHASISING PRONOUN

§ 61. **Ipse, ipsa, ipsum,** self.

This word may be either Pronoun or Adjective, e.g. :

(a) As a Pronoun—**Ipse tē monuī,** I myself warned you.

Ipsa cīvēs regēbat, She herself ruled the citizens.

Ipsī mē audīvērunt, They themselves heard me.

(b) As an Adjective—**Rēgīna ipsa nōs regēbat,** The queen herself ruled us.

Cīvēs ipsōs culpāvit, He blamed the citizens themselves.

Number	Case	Masculine	Feminine	Neuter
Singular	*Nom.*	ipse	ipsa	ipsum
	Acc.	ipsum	ipsam	ipsum
	Gen.	ipsīus	ipsīus	ipsīus
	Dat.	ipsī	ipsī	ipsī
	Abl.	ipsō	ipsā	ipsō
Plural	*Nom.*	ipsī	ipsae	ipsă
	Acc.	ipsōs	ipsās	ipsă
	Gen.	ipsōrum	ipsārum	ipsōrum
	Dat.	ipsīs	ipsīs	ipsīs
	Abl.	ipsīs	ipsīs	ipsīs

EXERCISE 48

A

THE RUBICON

[*Between* 58 *B.C. and* 50 *B.C. a quarrel developed between the Senate and* POMPEY *on the one hand, and on the other,* C. JULIUS CAESAR, *the great Roman general who was at this time engaged in the conquest of Gaul. Early in January* 49 *B.C.* CAESAR *crossed the little river Rubicon which marked the frontier between his province and Italy. This was one of the great dramatic moments of history. It is the subject of the following lesson.*]

Caesar, ubi mandāta senātus audīvit, mīlitibus, "Novem annōs, mīlitēs," inquit, "semper in omni officiō dīligentissimī fuimus. Magnam glōriam comparāvimus. Germānōs superāvimus et ex Galliā expulimus. Gallia ipsa prōvincia Rōmāna iam est. Quid nōbīs prō tot labōribus perīculīsque dat senātus? Ō scelus! contrā nōs senātōrēs et amīcī arma capiunt. Nōs hostēs populī Rōmānī appellant." Ubi ea audīvērunt, ūnā vōce mīlitēs exclāmant: "Nōs tē, imperātor, adiuvābimus. Bellum prō tē cum Pompēiō, cum senātōribus gerēmus. Auxiliō nostrō Pompēium sīcut Gallōs, sīcut Germānōs, superābis." Caesar fidem mīlitum laudāvit. Deinde eōs occultissimīs itineribus praemīsit.

Eā nocte Caesar ipse ad Ītaliam festīnāvit. Multī hostēs Caesaris erant in prōvinciā. Caesar igitur, "Sī hostēs" inquit, "mē vīderint, statim ad senātum nūntium mittent. Senātōrēs, sī dē itinere nostrō audīverint, omnia ad bellum parābunt et

nōs diū sustinēbunt." In tenebrīs igitur iter fēcit.
Longa via erat, et propter tenebrās difficilior.
Tandem, prīmā lūce mīlitēs ad flūmen Rubicōnem
—is prōvinciae eius fīnis erat—invēnit. Tum
Caesar, plūrimīs rēbus sollicitus, inter sociōs diū
stābat. " Ēheu ! " inquit, " Egone patriam oppug-
nābō ? Ō mē miserum ! quam dūrum cōnsilium
capiō ! " Tum sociīs, " Quid faciēmus ? " inquit,
" Sī in prōvinciā manēbimus, pāx erit ; sī trāns eum
pontem iter faciēmus, vī et armīs omnia gerentur."

Ecce tamen, dum ea Caesar dīcit, vīsus est homō
harundine lūdēns (playing). Ad eum plūrimī ex
statiōnibus mīlitēs festīnant. Deinde homō, ubi
tubam ā mīlite cēpit, ad flūmen festīnāvit, et
ingentī spīritū tubae trāns pontem multōs mīlitēs
dūxit. Ubi id Caesar vīdit, " Iacta ālea est," [1]
inquit, et omnēs statim in Ītaliam dūxit.

B

1. In the following translate the words in italics only :
   (a) I shall teach you *myself.*
   (b) I have taught *myself.*
   (c) Caesar was struck by Brutus *himself.*
   (d) Caesar *himself* was struck by Brutus.
   (e) Brutus stabbed *himself* with a sword.
   (f) Did you see the ship *yourself* ?
   (g) Why did you throw *yourself* into the river ?
   (h) We *ourselves* have heard about the battle.
   (i) We blame *ourselves* for this disaster.
   (k) She told me this *herself.*
2. The master himself taught the new boys,

---

[1] The die is cast.

3. Our men will fortify a camp for themselves.
4. The shepherd will take (*dūcet*) the dogs with him to the hill.
5. The voice of the general himself was heard by the soldiers.
6. The State itself will always praise you, O consul.
7. Great is the glory of that race. Enemies themselves will praise it.
8. At dawn the general himself sent forward the centurion.
9. The prisoners have hidden themselves among the reeds.
10. The master himself was playing with the boys.

WORD STUDY

To-day, with the help of your Latin you can appreciate that fine word **lucid**. A *lucid* explanation is literally one that is full of light, dispelling the darkness of ignorance or uncertainty. *Translucent* is an adjective that you can apply to whatever allows light to pass through it without being *transparent*. A thing is not *transparent* unless it can be clearly seen through. *Lucifer* as a proper name is sometimes given to the morning star as being the light-bringer ; and the same word is applied to the humble match, because it too is in its way a light-bringer. Can you remember a line in a song often sung by our soldiers in the Great War where a match is called a *lucifer* ?

You have had **harundō** in the sense of a reed ; it is also a Latin word for a fishing-rod. No doubt you can guess why.

THE ROMAN ARMY

It is worth while to know something about the Roman army which our friend Titus was so anxious to join, for after all, the army was the instrument by which Rome won and guarded her great empire.

The army was organised in legions. A legion was something like a modern brigade. It contained anything from 3000 to

6000 men. From about 100 B.C. onwards these were professional soldiers serving for many years with the colours. The legion was divided into ten cohorts (**cohors, cohortis, f.**), each cohort into three maniples (**manipulī**), and each maniple into two centuries (**centuriae**). Under the general each legion was officered by six tribunes of soldiers (**tribūnī mīlitum**), and by the famous centurions. These were something like the sergeant-majors of a modern army. They were men who had risen from the ranks by sheer courage and merit, and in maintaining discipline and so on they were the real backbone of the army. Then every legion had attached to it a squadron of about 300 cavalry (**equitēs**), and a body of engineers (**fabrī**). In addition to the legions the Roman army had a lot of light armed troops called auxiliaries (**auxilia**). These were recruited from the provinces.

Legions were distinguished by their numbers and often by a special name. Thus the Sixth legion was called **Victrix**—the Victorious. Every legion had for its standard a silver eagle (**aquila**) and each cohort had its own standard (**signum**). It was considered a most terrible disgrace to lose the standards in battle.

The soldier of the legion was heavily armed. On his head he wore a metal helmet (**galea, -ae, f.**) on his breast a breast-plate (**lorīca, -ae, f.**) and on his legs, greaves (**ocreae**). Under the breast-plate he would have a sort of leather jerkin and a woollen tunic. On his feet he had heavy hob-nailed boots (**caligae**). In addition to this he carried a shield (**scūtum, -ī, n.**) and a sword (**gladius, -iī, m.**) On the march he had also his heavy pack (**sarcina, -ae, f.**).

Whenever the legion made a halt for any length of time, even if it were only a single night, it made itself a camp. Camps conformed to a fixed plan. They were rectangular, defended by a rampart (**vāllum, -ī, n.**) and ditch (**fossa, -ae, f.**). In a permanent camp the fortifications and buildings were very strong and elaborate. Britain is rich in sites of Roman camps. Try to visit one as soon as possible.

8

XLIX

POSSESSIVE PRONOUNS AND ADJECTIVES

§ 62. POSSESSIVE ADJECTIVES OF 1ST AND 2ND PERSONS.

(*a*) The Possessive Adjectives of the 1st Person are :

(1) **meus, mea, meum,** my, mine, declined like **bonus, bona, bonum,** except that the Vocative Singular Masculine is **mī,** e.g. :

mī amīce, O my friend !

mī fīlī, my son !

(2) **noster, nostra, nostrum,** our, ours, declined like **niger, nigra, nigrum.**

(*b*) The Possessive Adjectives of the 2nd Person are :

(1) **tuus, tua, tuum,** your, yours, thy, thine, declined like **bonus, bona, bonum.**

(2) **vester, vestra, vestrum,** your, yours, declined like **niger, nigra, nigrum.**

Note.—Use **tuus, tua, tuum,** when one person is addressed ;
vester, vestra, vestrum, when more than one is addressed, e.g. :

Dās mihi tuōs librōs puer, You give me your books, boy ;
Datis mihi vestrōs librōs, puerī, You give me your books, boys.

§ 63. POSSESSIVE PRONOUNS AND ADJECTIVES OF THE 3RD PERSON.

The translation of his, her, its, their, or theirs, varies according as the possessor is or is not the subject of the nearest verb.

1. When possessor is subject of nearest verb :

(*a*) When there is *no* emphasis on possession *no* word is used for *his, her, its, their,* e.g.:

He loves his father, **Patrem amat.**

They love their mother, **Mātrem amant.**

(*b*) When there is emphasis on possession the possessive adjective **suus, sua, suum,** is used, e.g. :

He loves his own father, **Patrem suum amat.**

They love their own mother, **Mātrem suam amant.**

2. When possessor is *not* subject of nearest verb, *his, her, its* is translated by **eius** (gen. sing. of **is, ea, id**), *their* is translated by **eōrum, eārum, eōrum** (gen. pl. of **is, ea, id**), e.g. :

I love his father, **Patrem eius amō.**

We love their mother, **Mātrem eōrum amāmus.**

EXERCISE 49

A

THE MURDER OF CAESAR

[BRUTUS *and* CASSIUS *headed a conspiracy against* CAESAR *and he was murdered in the Senate on the Ides* (i.e. *the 15th) of March, 44 B.C.*

And, in his mantle muffling up his face,
Even at the base of Pompey's statua,
Which all the while ran blood, great Caesar fell.

To-day's reading lesson deals with the tragedy of the murder.]

Dum Caesar ad cūriam festīnat, in itinere Arte-midōrus, amīcus eius, libellum eī dedit. In eō omnia cōnsilia coniūrātōrum Artemidōrus nārrā-verat, et nōmina eōrum dederat. Libellum Caesar accēpit, sed, multīs rēbus sollicitus, eum nōn lēgit. Mox ad cūriam vēnit. Ecce, inter cīvēs Spūrinnam videt. Is Caesarem dē perīculō iam monuerat, et saepe exclāmāverat, "Cavē Idūs Mārtiās!" Caesar igitur, ubi eum ad iānuam cūriae vīdit, cum rīsū, " Quid ? " inquit, " Ubi est perīculum, Spūrinna ? Vēnērunt enim Idūs Mārtiae, sine meā noxā." Sed trīstī vultū Spūrinna, " Vēnērunt, Caesar," inquit, " sed nōn praeteriērunt (*they have passed*)."

Ubi Caesar in cūriam intrāvit, coniūrātī circum eum stābant. Prīmō Tillius Cimber " Frātrem meum nōbīs, Caesar," inquit, " sī reddēs, grātiās maximās ego et omnēs senātōrēs agēmus." Caesar tamen, " Nōn reddam," inquit. Deinde Tillius togam Caesaris manū cēpit. Tum Caesar, " Quid ? " inquit, " Mehercule, ea vīs est." Statim Cāsca eum vulnerāvit. Tum omnēs coniūrātī in eum impetum faciunt. Ēheu ! nūlla spēs est. Caesar caput togā obvolvit : ad pedēs statuae Pompēiī cadit. Tria et vīgintī vulnera accēpit. Nōn nisi prīmō vulnere gemitum dedit. Tamen ubi Brūtus—eum enim Caesar semper amāverat—in eum impetum fēcit, exclāmāvit " Et tū, Brūte ? "

Ubi Caesar cecidit, omnēs ex cūriā festīnāvērunt. Tandem duo servī corpus domum portāvērunt.

B

1. Translate into English :

    (*a*) Nostrī bovēs sunt in vestrō agrō.

    (*b*) Meus frāter est amīcus tuus.

    (*c*) Tua vōx ā nostrō magistrō nōn audīta est.

    (*d*) Meum caput māius est quam tuum.

    (*e*) Vestra castra ā nostrīs sociīs dēfendentur.

    (*f*) Eōrum māter ā mē laudāta est.

    (*g*) Domus eārum antīqua est.

2. The idle boy is often blamed by his own father.
3. The old man does not hear his own voice.
4. The guard has wounded himself : his shouts were heard by us.
5. Artemidorus has given a pamphlet to Caesar, his friend.
6. The names of the conspirators are in his pamphlet.
7. See ! Caesar has wrapped his head in his toga.
8. What has his friend said to Caesar ?
9. Beware the Ides of March ; for your danger is very great.

L

DEMONSTRATIVE PRONOUNS—*continued*

§ 64. Hīc, haec, hōc, this (this of mine, this near me).

Number	Case	Masculine	Feminine	Neuter
Singular	*Nom.*	**hīc**	**haec**	**hōc**
	Acc.	**hunc**	**hanc**	**hōc**
	Gen.	**huius**	**huius**	**huius**
	Dat.	**huīc**	**huīc**	**huīc**
	Abl.	**hōc**	**hāc**	**hōc**
Plural	*Nom.*	**hī**	**hae**	**haec**
	Acc.	**hōs**	**hās**	**haec**
	Gen.	**hōrum**	**hārum**	**hōrum**
	Dat.	**hīs**	**hīs**	**hīs**
	Abl.	**hīs**	**hīs**	**hīs**

Note.—The above is used either as pronoun or as adjective, e.g. :
Hī pugnant, These men fight.
Haec laudō, I praise these things.
Hunc puerum laudō, I praise this boy.

EXERCISE 50

A

At Philippi

[*The murder of Caesar proved a terrible blunder. It did not bring about the restoration of the old Roman republic, but caused civil war to blaze out afresh. Caesar's friend, Mark Antony, and Octavius, Caesar's nephew and adopted son, defeated the leaders of the conspirators, Brutus and Cassius, at Philippi in Northern Greece in 42 B.C. To-day's reading lesson gives an account of the deaths of Brutus and Cassius.*]

Ubi Octāvius et Antōnius iam in Macedoniam exercitūs dūxērunt, ad urbem Philippōs Brūtum Cassiumque oppugnāvērunt. Brūtus cum suīs legiōnibus hostēs superāvit. Maxima enim virtūs eius erat : diū et fortiter pugnābat. Hostēs igitur ex castrīs tandem expulit, et ipsa castra cēpit.

Quid intereā Cassius fēcit ? Mīlitēs eius impetum hostium diū sustinēbant. Tandem superātī sunt ; et ex campō in altiōra loca fūgērunt. Tum perīculō sollicitus labōribusque dēfessus, Cassius spem omnem victōriae et vītae abiēcit. Ex suā fortūnā fortunam Brūtī aestimāvit. Ecce ! rēs nova animōs eius mīlitumque terret. Ingēns enim hominum multitūdō ad eōs iam festīnat. Ēheu ! quid est ? Hostēsne sunt, an (*or*) amīcī ? Propter pulverem nōn ipsī hominēs, nōn signa videntur. Tum mīlitī Cassius, " Cūr ad nōs " inquit " haec multitūdō festīnat ? Suntne mīlitēs Brūtī an (*or*) Antōniī ? "

Mīles ad eam multitūdinem festīnat : amīcōs invenit : magnō gaudiō dē victōriā Brūtī audit. Intereā, dum is multa audit, multa nārrat, Cassius, quod mīles nōn vēnerat sollicitus, " Ēheu ! " inquit, " Hostēs hī hominēs sunt. Iam dē victōriā, dē ipsā vītā dēspērō. Brūtus, sīcut ego, superātus est." Tum lacernā caput obvolvit : ad lībertum sē vertit, et, " Sī mē amās," inquit " ē miserā vītā mē līberābis." Lībertus Cassium necat : statim venit mīles : victoriam Brūtī nūntiat. Mox imperātōrem necātum videt. Tum, " Ō scelus ! " inquit, " ego tē, imperātor, tarditāte meā necāvī." Deinde miser homō gladiō sē necāvit. Post paucōs diēs Brūtus ab hostibus superātus est. Nocte ex proeliō fūgit, et auxiliō Stratōnis, amīcī sui, sē necāvit. Hunc exitum Brūtō fortūna dedit.

B

1. Give the proper part of **hīc** and **is** to agree with : Statuam ; lūcis ; pondere ; fidē ; sacerdōtibus ; condiciōnum ; senātōrēs (*acc.*) ; statiōnī ; clādem ; mōs.
2. We shall save ourselves by this stratagem, citizens.
3. In the morning Caesar himself came to this river.
4. Why is this man hurrying to the shop ?
5. Why are these boys playing in the street ?
6. Where are you carrying these roses to, girls ?
7. This soldier has killed his general by his slowness.
8. On account of the dust this multitude was not seen by our men.
9. Why did you give this book to my son ?
10. Are these the standards of our friends ?
11. Once upon a time this poet threw away his shield.

12. At last our men drove the enemy from the camp.
13. Why do you despair of (**dē**) victory ? This legion has never been defeated.
14. I do not praise this custom. The customs of the ancient Romans were better.
15. The conspirators had fled from the city by night.
16. This slave is troubled because his master has not come home.

WORD STUDY

You may have heard or read of an action for *libel*. You know that this means a prosecution for slander. But *libel* is a word that has gradually acquired that bad meaning. Originally it was an innocent little word, coming as it does from **libellus.** Step by step, however, it went downhill. It came to be applied particularly to a pamphlet that contained an accusation, then to the accusation itself and finally to a false accusation. It is strange how words, at first respectable, sometimes begin to make questionable associations and end up by becoming words of definitely shady meaning. *Pagan* is a good example. The Latin word **pāgānus** meant a dweller in a country village or district. When Christianity was introduced into the Roman empire it made most headway in the towns and cities ; the remote country villages and districts clung longest to the old religion. Hence the word **pāgānus** became a term of reproach and passed into English with the meaning of one who is a heathen.

You can now explain *pulverise, signet, tardy, exit, fortune* and *statue*. What about *noxious* ? To what kind of food or drink would you apply that term ?

There is an article of furniture in church called the *lectern*. What is it used for, and why does it get its name ?

LI

DEMONSTRATIVE PRONOUNS—*continued*

§ 65. **Ille, illa, illud,** that (that yonder).

NUMBER	CASE	MASCULINE	FEMININE	NEUTER
SINGULAR	*Nom.*	ille	illa	illud
	Acc.	illum	illam	illud
	Gen.	illīus	illīus	illīus
	Dat.	illī	illī	illī
	Abl.	illō	illā	illō
PLURAL	*Nom.*	illī	illae	illa
	Acc.	illōs	illās	illa
	Gen.	illōrum	illārum	illōrum
	Dat.	illīs	illīs	illīs
	Abl.	illīs	illīs	illīs

Note.—The above is used either as pronoun or as adjective, e.g. :

Illī pugnant, Those men fight.
Illa laudō, I praise those things.
Illum puerum laudō, I praise that boy.

EXERCISE 51

A

THE FOUNDER OF THE ROMAN PEACE

[*Our last reading-lesson tells how after Philippi there arose strife between Octavius and Antony. This ended in 31 B.C. when Antony was defeated at the naval battle of Actium. Antony and Cleopatra, queen of Egypt, whom he loved, committed suicide to avoid falling into the hands of Octavius. Octavius, under the name of Augustus which was given to him by the Senate, now proceeded to the founding of the Roman Empire. It was due to the Roman peace established by Augustus that Rome was able to give civilisation, laws and language to a great part of the world.*]

Brūtus et Cassius superātī sunt ; bellī tamen nōndum fīnis erat. Contrā Antōnium enim Octāvius mox novum bellum gerēbat. Antōnius enim, dum Āfricam et Asiam occupat, Cleopātram vīdit, Aegyptī rēgīnam. Mox illam amat. Cum illā vītam agit, glōriae nōminis Rōmānī immemor. Sollicitus est senātus : sollicitī sunt et cīvēs Rōmānī. Exclāmābant enim, " Quid ? Antōniusne rēx erit Rōmānōrum ? Cleopātramne rēgīnam in hāc urbe vidēbimus ? Minimē vērō ! Līberī in līberā rē pūblicā vītam agēmus : miserī servī dūrī rēgis numquam erimus. Auxiliō Octāviī patriam contrā tyrannum dēfendēmus." Bellum diū gestum est ; Tandem Octāvius cum classe classem Antōniī et Cleopātrae ad Actium oppugnāvit. Ācerrimum proelium erat ; nāvēs enim hostium plūrēs erant quam nāvēs Rōmānae. Virtūte tamen nautārum militumque Octāvius hostēs superāvit. Post

AUGUSTUS

multās hōrās enim Cleopātra, ubi iam dē victōriā dēspērāvit, ex proeliō cum omnibus nāvibus festīnāvit. Post paucōs diēs Antōnius cum classe suā ad Aegyptum nāvigāvit. Proximō annō exercitūs Antōniī et Cleopātrae in Aegyptō ab Octāviō superātī sunt. Antōnius et ipsa rēgīna, quod nūlla iam via fugae erat, sē necāvērunt.

Octāvius hostēs iam vīcerat omnēs; populum

Rōmānum ingentī perīculō līberāverat. Omnibus prōvinciīs et ipsī Ītaliae pācem reddidit. Augustus igitur ā senātū appellātus est, et multōs annōs populum Rōmānum sociōsque imperiō bene regēbat. Omnibus in locīs hominēs fēlīcēs erant. Bellī immemorēs, pācis mōrem laudābant; agrōs colēbant; urbēs aedificābant. Quid multa? Augustum sīcut deum cīvēs laudābant; senātus eī honōrēs inaudītōs dedit; Vergilius et Horātius, poētae maximī, laudibus eum celebrābant.

B

1. Give the correct part of **hīc** and of **ille** to agree with: Mōribus; permūtātiōnem; īnsulārum; classium; tyrannōrum; petasīs; cērās; pāstōre; iuvenum; iuvenem; discipulōs.
2. We have not yet come to the end of the way.
3. Who was ever more diligent in every duty than Augustus?
4. The greatest poets have celebrated Augustus with praises.
5. Why is the farmer now cultivating more fields?
6. Augustus has restored peace to Italy.
7. Now we do not fear the dangers of war.
8. Therefore we are cultivating more fields and building cities.
9. Who will ever be forgetful of Augustus?
10. When he despaired of (**dē**) escape, Hannibal killed himself by poison.
11. That was the end of the life of Hannibal.
12. That boy is walking in the dust.
13. If his mother sees him, she will be angry.
14. On that day Brutus and Cassius were defeated by Octavius and Antony.
15. How hard that centurion is! All the soldiers fear him.

Alinari

THE ROMAN PEACE SYMBOLISED IN STONE

One of the sculptured slabs of the ARA PACIS (Altar of Peace) which was erected in the Campus Martius to celebrate the return of Augustus from his campaigns. The altar has recently been reconstructed on nearly its original site by the Italian Government.

C

And now for a cross-word !

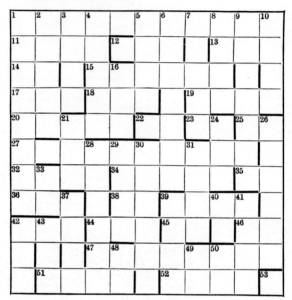

CLUES ACROSS

1. What news is there ?
11. Whence ?
12. Present infin. ending.
13. Same as 24 down.
14. To, towards.
15. The Romans were defeated here.
17. " Them " (fem.).
18. A personal pronoun.
19. Missile weapons.
20. Talk.
22. A preposition both in English and Latin.
23. He.
25. Accusative of 50 down.
27. This is how the Roman soldiers looked to Pyrrhus.
32. Bones.
34. I fear.
35. A little word that often makes a big difference.
36. A thing (acc.).
38. Another form of 53 across.
39. Second pers. sing. of 16 down.
42. This with the truth and the life makes a famous phrase.
44. This is to the fourth conjugation what 12 across is to the second or third.
45. I give.
46. Nominative of 25 across.
47. This is what killed Cassius.
51. Possessive pronoun, accus. sing. fem.
52. A heavy one is hard to bear.
53. Another form of 38 across.

CLUES DOWN

1. A Roman magistrate.
2. Waves.
3. Caesar was warned to beware of them.
4. A number.
5. I adorn.
6. Poison.
7. A beginning without an end.
8. To be.
9. Foolish.
10. A Roman wore one.
16. "I thank" without the "thanks."
21. Opposite of "the city."
24. I usually do this on my feet, not on my head.
26. An end of life.
28. Two of these are better than one.

29. This word increases by two syllables in the genitive singular.
30. I shall have lived.
31. I read.
33. Reflexive pronoun of third person.
37. By hand.
39. I add.
40. It.
41. Second pers. sing. of 24 down.
42. Woe!
43. A right.
48. Accusative sing. ending of first declension.
49. Same as 22 across.
50. Same as 46 across.

AQUILA—THE STANDARD OF THE LEGION

REVISION EXERCISES

A

1. Of this crime : at dawn : by that fleet : of that multitude : what news ? : a more diligent quaestor (*obj.*) : by our crimes : of Caesar himself : by my slowness : for Augustus himself.
2. It will be cultivated : we shall read : they are playing : it will have been sent forward : they had been hidden.
3. The general estimated the multitude by the dust.
4. Cicero has been most diligent in his quaestorship.
5. My sword is longer than yours.
6. The quaestor has sent very much corn to the city.
7. Alas ! The general has been killed by my slowness.
8. Many boys are playing in our street.
9. The camp has been well fortified by those soldiers.
10. At dawn the horse was found in the field.

B

1. Cēlātum erat : gerētur : castra mūniuntur : praemissa est : dēspērābāmus : castra pōnentur : librī lēctī erunt : inveniuntur : mūniēmus : lūditis.
2. In eōrum castrīs : mihi ipsī : ā meā mātre : hōc gladiō : huīc quaestōrī : illōrum dōna : ipsī cōnsulī : hōc cōnsiliō : Cleopātrae ipsīus : hāc laude.
3. Nōndum dē rēbus nostrīs dēspērāmus.
4. Magna multitūdō hominum in viā vīsa erat.
5. Ego in silvā mē cēlābō ; tū domī manēbis.
6. Hodiē mēcum ad urbem festīnābis.
7. Herī mēcum domō festīnāvistī.
8. Immemor nostrī erat.
9. Vōs auctōritāte vestrā nōs dēfendētis.
10. Quis scelestior fuit quam ille magister ?

C

1. In the following, translate words in italics only :

    (a) I told you that *myself*.
    (b) He won the battle *by his own stratagem*.
    (c) Brutus *himself* was one of the conspirators.
    (d) I hid *myself* under the table.
    (e) That plan was adopted by Pompey *himself*.
    (f) Why did you not do this *yourself* ?
    (g) You had hidden *yourselves* for a long time.
    (h) *Our men themselves* despaired.

2. Translate :
    (a) Tibi ipsī grātiās aget.
    (b) Nōs ipsōs terruērunt.
    (c) Ipsīus vōcem timēmus.
    (d) Vōcem ipsam hominis timent.
    (e) Eōrum auctōritās magna est in urbe.
    (f) Ipsī terrā marīque bellum gerēmus.
    (g) Tandem Brūtus sē necāvit.
    (h) Ego in urbe labōrō ; tū agrum colis.

D

1. The standards will not be taken by the enemy.
2. For we ourselves will defend them.
3. Cassius himself was killed by the slowness of the soldier.
4. The soldier was killed by his own sword.
5. Because of his own crimes the quaestor was not praised.
6. We shall thank Caesar himself.
7. The mind of Scipio himself was occupied by the state.
8. We ourselves are not forgetful of you (*pl.*).
9. Why have you not hidden yourselves, citizens ?
10. Our minds have been reassured by Caesar himself.

THE ROMAN DAY

Summer or winter, spring or autumn, the Roman day was one of twelve hours measured from sunrise to sunset. The length of an hour varied with the seasons, and so did the length of the day, but the number of hours was always the same.

The Roman rose early—at dawn, or even before it. As soon as he was up, washed and dressed, he would find—if he were a man of property and position—quite a number of poor friends or dependants waiting in his atrium to pay their respects, and escort him by and by to the Forum. For this attention he gave rewards in the form of a gift of food or a small sum of money, or, in some cases, in the form of an invitation to dinner. During the first or second morning hour, according as was most suitable, our Roman had breakfast (**ientāculum, -ī,** *n.*) which was a very light repast, consisting frequently of nothing more than a piece of bread dipped in wine. Doubtless you have heard of the extremely light continental breakfasts of the present day !

In those first two hours or so of the day, the Roman gentleman might have to transact quite an amount of business. His dependants might ask his advice on problems or even solicit his help in difficulties : he would have to see that instructions for the day were issued to the slaves : he would have important letters to write or dictate to a secretary : there might be some domestic matters to talk over with his wife. At length, about the third hour of the day he would set out for the Forum.

On his journey to the Forum he liked to be escorted by a retinue of his dependants. The size of his retinue was considered a mark of a man's social standing. Once arrived at the Forum, the Roman would find several exceedingly busy hours ahead. He might have friends to meet, or appointments to keep with business men. He might have to go to the law courts as a pleader, or a witness, or a juryman. He might have a meeting of the Senate to attend. If he held a magistracy, he would have government business to attend to, or might have to address the people from the Rostra.

In the early afternoon our Roman would take lunch (**prandium, -iī,** *n.*) which would be followed by a short siesta. Then came a visit to one or other of the great and magnificent public baths. These establishments not only comprised splendid buildings with every appointment for luxurious bathing, but were laid out with recreation grounds, gardens, and equipped with halls and colonnades for lectures and recitations. Our Roman friend would have no lack of companions with whom to join in a game of ball. After the bath, he would have opportunities of hearing a lecture by a distinguished philosopher, if he wished, or of listening to some poet or man of letters giving a reading from his works.

The remaining hours of the afternoon might be spent at home in reading, writing or study. Presently came at about the tenth hour the chief meal of the day. Dinner (**cēna, -ae,** *f.*) consisted of three main stages. The first was a course of hors-d'oeuvres, eggs, olives, tit-bits to whet the appetite. In the second stage there were served courses of meat and fish. Lastly came the dessert—pastry and fruit. After the dessert, guests usually lingered on for an hour or two, discussing, over their wine, all kinds of topics connected with politics, the events of the day, art, literature, science, philosophy.

With sunset and the coming of darkness the activities of the day ended. The Romans had no electric light, no incandescent gas, nothing in the way of artificial lighting but small oil lamps which must have shed a very poor light. We do hear of studious people " burning the midnight oil," and there are tales of the idle rich revelling till far into the night, but the average Roman went off to bed soon after dark. Thanks to this healthy practice he was able to begin his day at dawn or before it.

EPILOGUE

In Praise of Rome

In the year A.D. 410, centuries after the establishment of the Roman Empire, a poet called Namatianus was called away from Rome to his native country, which was Gaul. The following are among the noblest lines in the noble poem in which he bade farewell to the Imperial City. Compare the Latin with the translation given below, and ask your teacher to help you with anything you do not understand.

Exaudī, rēgīna tuī pulcherrima mundī,
   inter sīdereōs Rōma recepta polōs,
exaudī, genetrix hominum genetrixque deōrum,
   nōn procul ā caelō per tua templa sumus :
tē canimus semperque, sinent dum fāta, canēmus :
   hospes nēmo potest immemor esse tuī.

Hearken, most beautiful queen of a world that is thine, O Rome, received amid the starry skies, hearken, mother of men and mother of gods, we are not far from heaven thanks to thy temples ; thee we sing, and shall ever sing, while the fates permit ; no guest of thine can be forgetful of thee.

APPENDIX I

SONGS IN LATIN

O ANGLIAE NAUTAE

Tune : " Ye Mariners of England "

Ō Angliae nautae quī
   Servātis hās ōrās,
Vexilla vestra prōvocant
   Et pugnās et aurās !
Refulgēns signum tollite
   In hostem dēnuō ;
Refulgēns signum tollite
   In hostem dēnuō,
Fluctibus trucibus
   Superātīs et ventīs,
Fluctibus trucibus
   Superātīs et ventīs,
Dumque pugna dēsaevit diū,
Dumque pugna dēsaevit diū,
   Atque fervet tempestās
   Atque fervet tempestās.

SODALITATIS VETERIS

Tune : " Auld Lang Syne "

Sodālitātis veteris
  Cūr immemor erō ?
Cūr temporis praeteritī
  Fiet oblīviō ?

Ob aevum iam praeteritum,
  Praeteritum diū,
Nōs pōculum plēnissimum
  Sūmēmus nunc manū.

Tum dextra dextram implicet,
  Ō vōs fīdissimī ;
Prōlixē prōluāmus nōs
  Flūminibus vīnī.

Ob aevum iam praeteritum,
  Praeteritum diū,
Nōs pōculum plēnissimum
  Sūmēmus nunc manū.

Servet regem Deus

Tune : " God Save the King "

Servet rēgem Deus :
Vīvat rēx optimus :
  Servet Deus.
Compos victōriae
  Plēnusque glōriae
Sit fēlīx atque flōreat;
  Servet Deus.

Dā, Deus, munera
Ampla, pulcherrima.
  Rēgnet diū.
Legēs sustineat,
  Causamque praebeat
Ut cor et lingua concinant
  " Servet Deus."

APPENDIX II

A PLAY IN LATIN

THE YOUNG DIPLOMATIST

Dramatis Personae

THE MOTHER OF PAPIRIUS, a Roman Lady.
PAPIRIUS, a Roman Boy.
CONSUL.
SENATORS.
CROWD OF WOMEN.

SCENE 1

[*After dinner in the house of* PAPIRIUS SENIOR.]

MĀTER PAPĪRIĪ (*fussily*) : Quid est, mī Papīrī ?
Cūr tē tam trīstem videō ? Quid ? Nihil dīcis ?
nihil facis ? Edepol, labōribus dēfessus es !

PAPĪRIUS : Minimē vērō, māter. Tōtus sum in rē
gravī (*serious*).

MĀTER (*wheedling*) : Age, mī fīlī, rem omnem mātrī
nārrā (*tell*).

PAPĪRIUS : Dūxit mē pater hodiē, sīcut audīvistī,
ad senātum. Ō quam nōbilēs senātorēs sunt
quam rēgum similēs ! Nihil nisi dē senātū
cōgitō (*I think*).

MĀTER (*very sweetly and persuasively*) : Sed quid
hodiē in senātū āctum est ? Age, Papīrī, fīlī mī
dulcissime, omnia mihi nārrā. Ō quam cupiō
omnia audīre !

PAPĪRIUS (*not a little shocked at the suggestion*) : Ō
māter ! quam scelestus sermō tuus est ! Egone
cōnsilia senātōrum nārrābō ? Numquam id
faciam. Patrēs enim maximā dē rē agēbant ;
multī cōnsilia dabant ; nūllum tamen cōnsilium
hodiē cēpit senātus. Crās igitur, prīmā lūce ad
cūriam senātōrēs omnēs festīnābunt ; iterum
(*again*) dē illā ipsā rē dēlīberābunt. Intereā
tamen nihil dē cōnsiliīs senātōrum extrā cūriam
dīcētur.

MĀTER (*impatiently*) : Similēs estis, tū et pater tuus.
Sī dē senātū rogō, ea ipsa ille semper dīcit. Ō
mē miseram ! domī sedeō semper ; nihil umquam
audiō magnīs dē rēbus. (*Changing her tone*) : Sed,
mī Papīrī, tū nōn dūrus eris, sīcut pater tuus ;
tū mātrī dīcēs. Ecce, Papīrī, sī dīxeris, plūrima
tibi dōna dabō, novam tunicam, calceōs novōs,
pilam magnam et pulcherrimam. Quid iam
dīcis, mī fīlī ?

PAPĪRIUS : Audiēs. Senātōrēs enim mōrem cīvium
Rōmānōrum mūtant. Nunc enim ūnus vir
ūnam uxōrem habet ; sed dehinc (*henceforth*)
ūnus vir duās uxōrēs habēbit, aut ūna uxor duōs
virōs. Ecce, māter, omnia audīvistī. Crās senātōrēs cōnstituent (*will decide*).

MĀTER (*speechless*) : Dī immortālēs !

Scene 2

[*Next morning. The door of* Papirius's *house. His wife watches husband and son set out for the Senate. She shakes her fist behind their backs, then speaks.*]

Tandem ad senātum festīnātis. Ō mē miseram ! per omnem noctem vigilāvī (*I lay awake*). Numquam dormiēbam ; nihil nisi dē scelestō senātūs cōnsiliō cōgitāvī. Ō scelus ! Ō mīrāculum audāciae ! (*She falls silent, ponders some course of action and resumes.*) Ita vērō ; sīc, sīc faciam. (*She calls the slaves.*) Geta ! Galle ! Syre ! ad vīcīnās domūs festīnāte (*hasten*) et sīc fēminīs nūntiāte (*announce*), " Ad cūriam festīnāte ; ad portās cūriae uxōrem Papīriī exspectāte ; ubi vēnerit, omnia vōbīs dīcet."

Scene 3

[*The Senate The wife of* Papirius *has told her son's tale to the assembled women. They burst into the Senate.*

Fēminae : Ō hominēs dūrī et scelestī ! Ō quid facitis ? Cūr tam inaudītum cōnsilium capitis ? Sī nōn verba nostra, nōn lacrimae, nōn precēs (*prayers*) vōs superābunt, saltem (*at least*) ūnam uxōrem duōbus virīs date, potius (*rather*) quam ūnum virum duābus uxōribus.

Cōnsul : Quid est, patrēs ? Cūr uxōrēs nostrae in cūriam intrāvērunt ? Quid dēsīderant ?

[*The Senators look at one another helplessly, shake their heads and converse in whispers. They cannot understand the situation. At last a diminutive figure arises—* PAPIRIUS MINOR.]

PAPĪRIUS : Ego vōbīs, patrēs, omnia nārrābō. Herī, ubi domum vēnī, post cēnam māter multa dē senātōrum cōnsiliīs rogāvit. Prīmō nihil dīcēbam, tandem, ubi precibus eius dēfessus sum, sīc nārrāvī ; " Dē magnā rē patrēs agunt ; mōrem antīquum mūtant ; dehinc ūnus vir duās uxōrēs habēbit aut ūna uxor duōs virōs."

SENĀTŌRĒS : Ha ! ha ! ha !

CŌNSUL : Mehercule, tē laudāmus, Papīrī, quod cōnsilia nostra nōn nārrāvistī. Est tamen in hāc rē perīculum. Multī puerī cum patribus ad senātum veniunt ; in cūriā sedent ; omnia audiunt. Quid sī ūnus ex eīs cōnsilia nostra prōdet (*shall betray*) ? Dehinc, igitur, puerī in senātum nōn venient, praeter . . . (*he pauses dramatically*) . . . Papīrium sōlum (*alone*).

FINIS

SUMMARY OF GRAMMAR

I. NOUNS

1. THE FIRST DECLENSION

mēnsă, mēnsae, *f.,* a table.

	SINGULAR	PLURAL
Nom.	mēns-ă	mēns-ae
Voc.	mēns-ă	mēns-ae
Acc.	mēns-am	mēns-ās
Gen.	mēns-ae	mēns-ārum
Dat.	mēns-ae	mēns-īs
Abl.	mēns-ā	mēns-īs

Notes.—(1) Nouns of the First Declension are feminine, except names of males and nouns denoting male occupations, as **nauta,** a sailor; **agricola,** a farmer; **poēta,** a poet.

(2) The dative and ablative plural of **dea,** a goddess, and of **fīlia,** a daughter, are **deābus, fīliābus.**

2. THE SECOND DECLENSION

	dominus, -ī, *m.,* master	**ager, -rī,** *m.,* field	**puer, -ī,** *m.,* boy	**bellum, -ī,** *n.,* war
Nom.	domin-us	ager	puer	bell-um
Voc.	domin-ĕ	ager	puer	bell-um
Acc.	domin-um	agr-um	puer-um	bell-um
Gen.	domin-ī	agr-ī	puer-ī	bell-ī
Dat.	domin-ō	agr-ō	puer-ō	bell-ō
Abl.	domin-ō	agr-ō	puer-ō	bell-ō
Nom.	domin-ī	agr-ī	puer-ī	bell-ă
Voc.	domin-ī	agr-ī	puer-ī	bell-ă
Acc.	domin-ōs	agr-ōs	puer-ōs	bell-ă
Gen.	domin-ōrum	agr-ōrum	puer-ōrum	bell-ōrum
Dat.	domin-īs	agr-īs	puer-īs	bell-īs
Abl.	domin-īs	agr-īs	puer-īs	bell-īs

Notes.—(1) Nouns ending in **-us** and **-er** are mostly masculine ; nouns ending in **-um** are neuter.

(2) **Fīlius,** a son, has vocative sing. **fīlī,** and gen. sing. **fīliī** or **fīlī.**

(3) Proper names ending in **-ius** are declined like **fīlius.**

(4) **Deus,** a god, has vocative **deus** ; nom. and voc. plural **dī** or **dĕī** ; dat. and abl. plural **dīs** or **dĕīs.**

(5) **Vir, virī,** *m.,* a man, is declined like **puer.**

3. THE THIRD DECLENSION

(a) Increasing nouns, masculine, feminine, neuter.

	rēx, rēgĭs, m., king	legiō, -iōnĭs, f., legion	nōmen, -inĭs, n., name	ŏnus, -erĭs, n., burden
Nom.	rēx	legiō	nōmen	ŏnus
Voc.	rēx	legiō	nōmen	ŏnus
Acc.	rēg-em	legiōn-em	nōmen	ŏnus
Gen.	rēg-is	legiōn-is	nōmin-is	ŏner-ĭs
Dat.	rēg-ī	legiōn-ī	nōmin-ī	ŏner-ī
Abl.	rēg-ĕ	legiōn-ĕ	nōmin-ĕ	ŏner-ĕ
Nom.	rēg-ēs	legiōn-ēs	nōmin-ă	ŏner-ă
Voc.	rēg-ēs	legiōn-ēs	nōmin-ă	ŏner-ă
Acc.	rēg-ēs	legiōn-ēs	nōmin-ă	ŏner-ă
Gen.	rēg-um	legiōn-um	nōmin-um	ŏner-um
Dat.	rēg-ibus	legiōn-ibus	nōmín-ibus	ŏnér-ibus
Abl.	rēg-ibus	legiōn-ibus	nōmín-ibus	ŏnér-ibus

(b) Non-increasing nouns, masc., fem., neuter.

	cīvĭs, -ĭs, m., citizen	nāvĭs, -ĭs, f., ship	cubīlĕ, -ĭs, n., bed
Nom.	cīvĭs	nāvĭs	cubīlĕ
Voc.	cīvĭs	nāvĭs	cubīlĕ
Acc.	cīv-em	nāv-em	cubīlĕ
Gen.	cīv-ĭs	nāv-ĭs	cubīl-ĭs
Dat.	cīv-ī	nāv-ī	cubīl-ī
Abl.	cīv-ĕ	nāv-ĕ	cubīl-ī
Nom.	cīv-ēs	nāv-ēs	cubīl-ĭă
Voc.	cīv-ēs	nāv-ēs	cubīl-ĭă
Acc.	cīv-ēs	nāv-ēs	cubīl-ĭă
Gen.	cīv-ium	nāv-ium	cubīl-ium
Dat.	cīv-ibus	nāv-ibus	cubīl-ibus
Abl.	cīv-ibus	nāv-ibus	cubīl-ibus

Note.—The genitive plural of non-increasing nouns regularly ends in -ium.

(c) Monosyllabic nouns ending in two consonants.

urbs, urbĭs, f., a city

	SINGULAR	PLURAL
Nom.	urbs	urb-ēs
Voc.	urbs	urb-ēs
Acc.	urb-em	urb-ēs
Gen.	urb-ĭs	urb-ium
Dat.	urb-ī	urb-ibus
Abl.	urb-ĕ	urb-ibus

Notes.—(1) The genitive plural of nouns of this class ends in -ium.
(2) Included in this class are nŏx, nŏctĭs, f., night ; ŏs, ossĭs, n., bone.

(d) Exceptional words of the Third Declension.

senex, senĭs, m., old man	bōs, bŏvĭs, c., ox, cow	vīs, f., s., force pl., strength	Iūppiter, Iŏvis, m., Jupiter

Nom.	senex	bōs	vīs	Iūppiter
Voc.	senex	bōs	—	Iūppiter
Acc.	sen-em	bŏv-em	vĭm	Iŏv-em
Gen.	sen-ĭs	bŏv-ĭs	—	Iŏv-ĭs
Dat.	sen-ī	bŏv-ī	—	Iŏv-ī
Abl.	sen-ĕ	bŏv-ĕ	vī	Iŏv-ĕ

Nom.	sen-ēs	bŏv-ēs	vīrēs
Voc.	sen-ēs	bŏv-ēs	vīrēs
Acc.	sen-ēs	bŏv-ēs	vīrēs
Gen.	sen-um	bŏum	vīrium
Dat.	sen-ibus	bōbus (būbus)	vīribus
Abl.	sen-ibus	bōbus (būbus)	vīribus

Notes.—(1) **Păter, pătrĭs,** m., father ; **māter, mātrĭs,** f., mother ; **frāter, frātrĭs,** m., brother ; **cănĭs, cănĭs,** m., dog ; **iuvenĭs, iuvenĭs,** m., young man, have **-um** in the genitive plural.

(2) **Moenia, moenium,** n., city walls, is used in plural only. Decline like plural of **cubīle.**

4. THE FOURTH DECLENSION

exercitus, -ūs, m., army　**cornū, -ūs,** n., horn, wing (of army)

	SINGULAR	PLURAL	SINGULAR	PLURAL
Nom.	exercit-us	exercit-ūs	corn-ū	corn-uă
Voc.	exercit-us	exercit-ūs	corn-ū	corn-uă
Acc.	exercit-um	exercit-ūs	corn-ū	corn-uă
Gen.	exercit-ūs	exercit-uum	corn-ūs	corn-uum
Dat.	exercit-uī	exercit-ibus	corn-ū	corn-ibus
Abl.	exercit-ū	exercit-ibus	corn-ū	corn-ibus

5. THE DECLENSION OF **dŏmus, dŏmūs,** f., a house

	SINGULAR	PLURAL
Nom.	dŏm-us	dŏm-ūs
Voc.	dŏm-us	dŏm-ūs
Acc.	dŏm-um	dŏm-ūs or dŏm-ōs
Gen.	dŏm-ūs	dŏm-uum or dŏm-ōrum
Dat.	dŏm-uī	dŏm-ibus
Abl.	dŏm-ō	dŏm-ibus

6. THE FIFTH DECLENSION

		diēs, diēī, m., day		rēs, rĕī, f., a thing	
	SINGULAR	PLURAL		SINGULAR	PLURAL
Nom.	dĭ-ēs	dĭ-ēs		r-ēs	r-ēs
Voc.	dĭ-ēs	dĭ-ēs		r-ēs	r-ēs
Acc.	dĭ-em	dĭ-ēs		r-em	r-ēs
Gen.	dĭ-ēī	dĭ-ērum		r-ĕī	r-ērum
Dat.	dĭ-ēī	dĭ-ēbus		r-ĕī	r-ēbus
Abl.	dĭ-ē	dĭ-ēbus		r-ē	r-ēbus

Notes.—(1) Fidēs, fidĕī, f., faith ; spēs, spĕī, f., hope, are declined like rēs.

(2) In the Fifth Declension diēs and rēs have complete plurals. Aciēs, aciēī, f., line of battle, and spēs have nominative and accusative plural only. Most other nouns of this declension have no plural.

II. ADJECTIVES

1. ADJECTIVES OF FIRST AND SECOND DECLENSIONS

(a) bŏnus, bŏna, bŏnum, good

	SINGULAR		
	Masc.	Fem.	Neuter
Nom.	bonus	bona	bonum
Voc.	bone	bona	bonum
Acc.	bonum	bonam	bonum
Gen.	bonī	bonae	bonī
Dat.	bonō	bonae	bonō
Abl.	bonō	bonā	bonō

	PLURAL		
	Masc.	Fem.	Neuter
Nom.	bonī	bonae	bonă
Voc.	bonī	bonae	bonă
Acc.	bonōs	bonās	bonă
Gen.	bonōrum	bonārum	bonōrum
Dat.	bonīs	bonīs	bonīs
Abl.	bonīs	bonīs	bonīs

(b) pulcher, pulchra, pulchrum, beautiful

Singular

	Masc.	Fem.	Neuter
Nom.	pulcher	pulchra	pulchrum
Voc.	pulcher	pulchra	pulchrum
Acc.	pulchrum	pulchram	pulchrum
Gen.	pulchrī	pulchrae	pulchrī
Dat.	pulchrō	pulchrae	pulchrō
Abl.	pulchrō	pulchrā	pulchrō

Plural

	Masc.	Fem.	Neuter
Nom.	pulchrī	pulchrae	pulchră
Voc.	pulchrī	pulchrae	pulchră
Acc.	pulchrōs	pulchrās	pulchră
Gen.	pulchrōrum	pulchrārum	pulchrōrum
Dat.	pulchrīs	pulchrīs	pulchrīs
Abl.	pulchrīs	pulchrīs	pulchrīs

(c) tener, tenera, tenerum, tender

Singular

	Masc.	Fem.	Neuter
Nom.	tener	tenera	tenerum
Voc.	tener	tenera	tenerum
Acc.	tenerum	teneram	tenerum
Gen.	tenerī	tenerae	tenerī
Dat.	tenerō	tenerae	tenerō
Abl.	tenerō	tenerā	tenerō

Plural

	Masc.	Fem.	Neuter
Nom.	tenerī	tenerae	teneră
Voc.	tenerī	tenerae	teneră
Acc.	tenerōs	tenerās	teneră
Gen.	tenerōrum	tenerārum	tenerōrum
Dat.	tenerīs	tenerīs	tenerīs
Abl.	tenerīs	tenerīs	tenerīs

2. ADJECTIVES OF THE THIRD DECLENSION

(a) audāx, audācis, bold

SINGULAR

	Masc.	Fem.	Neuter
Nom.	audāx	audāx	audāx
Voc.	audāx	audāx	audāx
Acc.	audācem	audācem	audāx
Gen.	audācis	audācis	audācis
Dat.	audācī	audācī	audācī
Abl.	audācī	audācī	audācī

PLURAL

	Masc.	Fem.	Neuter
Nom.	audācēs	audācēs	audāciă
Voc.	audācēs	audācēs	audāciă
Acc.	audācēs	audācēs	audāciă
Gen.	audācium	audācium	audācium
Dat.	audācibus	audācibus	audācibus
Abl.	audācibus	audācibus	audācibus

(b) ingēns, ingentis, huge

SINGULAR

	Masc.	Fem.	Neuter
Nom.	ingēns	ingēns	ingēns
Voc.	ingēns	ingēns	ingēns
Acc.	ingentem	ingentem	ingēns
Gen.	ingentis	ingentis	ingentis
Dat.	ingentī	ingentī	ingentī
Abl.	ingentī	ingentī	ingentī

PLURAL

	Masc.	Fem.	Neuter
Nom.	ingentēs	ingentēs	ingentiă
Voc.	ingentēs	ingentēs	ingentiă
Acc.	ingentēs	ingentēs	ingentiă
Gen.	ingentium	ingentium	ingentium
Dat.	ingentibus	ingentibus	ingentibus
Abl.	ingentibus	ingentibus	ingentibus

(c) **fortis, fortis, fortĕ,** brave

Singular

	Masc.	*Fem.*	*Neuter*
Nom.	fortis	fortis	fortĕ
Voc.	fortis	fortis	fortĕ
Acc.	fortem	fortem	fortĕ
Gen.	fortis	fortis	fortis
Dat.	fortī	fortī	fortī
Abl.	fortī	fortī	fortī

Plural

	Masc.	*Fem.*	*Neuter*
Nom.	fortēs	fortēs	fortiă
Voc.	fortēs	fortēs	fortiă
Acc.	fortēs	fortēs	fortiă
Gen.	fortium	fortium	fortium
Dat.	fortibus	fortibus	fortibus
Abl.	fortibus	fortibus	fortibus

(d) **ācer, ācris, ācrĕ,** keen, eager

Singular

	Masc.	*Fem.*	*Neuter*
Nom.	ācer	ācris	ācrĕ
Voc.	ācer	ācris	ācrĕ
Acc.	ācrem	ācrem	ācrĕ
Gen.	ācris	ācris	ācris
Dat.	ācrī	ācrī	ācrī
Abl.	ācrī	ācrī	ācrī

Plural

	Masc.	*Fem.*	*Neuter*
Nom.	ācrēs	ācrēs	ācriă
Voc.	ācrēs	ācrēs	ācriă
Acc.	ācrēs	ācrēs	ācriă
Gen.	ācrium	ācrium	ācrium
Dat.	ācribus	ācribus	ācribus
Abl.	ācribus	ācribus	ācribus

Note.—**Celer, celĕris, celĕrĕ,** swift, is declined like **ācer,** but keeps the **e** throughout.

(e) vetus, vetĕris, old

SINGULAR

	Masc.	Fem.	Neuter
Nom.	vetus	vetus	vetus
Voc.	vetus	vetus	vetus
Acc.	veterem	veterem	vetus
Gen.	veteris	veteris	veteris
Dat.	veterī	veterī	veterī
Abl.	vetere	vetere	vetere

PLURAL

	Masc.	Fem.	Neuter
Nom.	veterēs	veterēs	veteră
Voc.	veterēs	veterēs	veteră
Acc.	veterēs	veterēs	veteră
Gen.	veterum	veterum	veterum
Dat.	veteribus	veteribus	veteribus
Abl.	veteribus	veteribus	veteribus

(f) dīvĕs, dīvitis, rich

(g) pauper, paupĕris, poor

	SINGULAR Masc. Fem.	PLURAL Masc. Fem.	SINGULAR Masc. Fem.	PLURAL Masc. Fem.
Nom.	dīvĕs	dīvitēs	pauper	pauperēs
Voc.	dīves	dīvitēs	pauper	pauperēs
Acc.	dīvitem	dīvitēs	pauperem	pauperēs
Gen.	dīvitis	dīvitum	pauperis	pauperum
Dat.	dīvitī	dīvitibus	pauperī	pauperibus
Abl.	dīvite	dīvitibus	paupere	pauperibus

III. NUMERALS

(a) Cardinal Numbers, 1–10   (b) Ordinal Numbers, 1st to 10th

1	I	ūnus, -a, um	1st	prīmus, -a, -um
2	II	duŏ, -ae, -ŏ	2nd	secundus, -a, -um
3	III	trēs, trēs, trĭă	3rd	tertius, -a, -um
4	IV	quattuor	4th	quārtus, -a, -um
5	V	quīnque	5th	quīntus, -a, -um
6	VI	sex	6th	sextus, -a, -um
7	VII	septem	7th	septimus, -a, -um
8	VIII	octō	8th	octāvus, -a, -um
9	IX	nŏvem	9th	nōnus, -a, -um
10	X	dĕcem	10th	decimus, -a, -um

(c) Declension of **ūnus**

	Masc.	Fem.	Neuter
Nom.	ūnus	ūna	ūnum
Acc.	ūnum	ūnam	ūnum
Gen.	ūnīus	ūnīus	ūnīus
Dat.	ūnī	ūnī	ūnī
Abl.	ūnō	ūnā	ūnō

(d) Declension of **duŏ**

	Masc.	Fem.	Neuter
Nom.	duŏ	duae	duŏ
Acc.	duŏs	duās	duŏ
Gen.	duŏrum	duārum	duŏrum
Dat.	duŏbus	duābus	duŏbus
Abl.	duŏbus	duābus	duŏbus

(e) Declension of **trēs**

	Masc.	Fem.	Neuter
Nom.	trēs	trēs	trĭă
Acc.	trēs	trēs	trĭă
Gen.	trĭum	trĭum	trĭum
Dat.	trĭbus	trĭbus	trĭbus
Abl.	trĭbus	trĭbus	trĭbus

Note.—The other cardinal numbers are not declined.

IV. COMPARISON OF ADJECTIVES

1. To form the comparative, change **-ī** or **-is** of the genitive singular into **-ior.**

   To form the superlative, change **-ī** or **-is** of the genitive singular into **-issimus.**

   e.g. **altus,** high, deep   **altior**   **altissimus**

2. Adjectives ending in **-er** form their comparative according to the rule, but form the superlative by adding **-rimus** to the nom. sing. masc. of the positive.

   e.g. **mĭser**   **mĭserior**   **mĭserrimus**
   nĭger   **nĭgrior**   **nĭgerrimus**

3. Six adjectives ending in **-ilis** are compared thus :

facilis, easy	**facilior**	**facillimus**
difficilis, difficult	**difficilior**	**difficillimus**
similis, like	**similior**	**simillimus**
dissimilis, unlike	**dissimilior**	**dissimillimus**
gracilis, thin, slender	**gracilior**	**gracillimus**
humilis, low, humble	**humilior**	**humillimus**

4. Adjectives ending in **-us** preceded by any vowel except **-u** are compared by means of the adverbs **magis**, more, and **maximē**, most.

   e.g. **dubius**, doubtful   **magis dubius**   **maximē dubius**
       idōneus, suitable   **magis idōneus**   **maximē idōneus**

But **antīquus**, ancient, is compared according to rule.

   e.g. **antīquus**   **antīquior**   **antīquissimus**

5. The following are irregular :

bonus, good	**melior**	**optimus**
mǎlus, bad	**peior**	**pessimus**
magnus, great	**māior**	**maximus**
parvus, small	**mǐnor**	**mǐnimus**
multus, much	**plūs**	**plūrimus**
multī, many	**plūrēs**	**plūrimī**

6. A comparative adjective is declined thus :

SINGULAR

	Masc.	*Fem.*	*Neuter*
Nom.	**fortior**	**fortior**	**fortius**
Voc.	**fortior**	**fortior**	**fortius**
Acc.	**fortiōrem**	**fortiōrem**	**fortius**
Gen.	**fortiōris**	**fortiōris**	**fortiōris**
Dat.	**fortiōrī**	**fortiōrī**	**fortiōrī**
Abl.	**fortiōre**	**fortiōre**	**fortiōre**

PLURAL

	Masc.	*Fem.*	*Neuter*
Nom.	**fortiōrēs**	**fortiōrēs**	**fortiŏrǎ**
Voc.	**fortiōrēs**	**fortiōrēs**	**fortiŏrǎ**
Acc.	**fortiōrēs**	**fortiōrēs**	**fortiŏrǎ**
Gen.	**fortiōrum**	**fortiōrum**	**fortiōrum**
Dat.	**fortiōribus**	**fortiōribus**	**fortiōribus**
Abl.	**fortiōribus**	**fortiōribus**	**fortiōribus**

V. PRONOUNS

1. PERSONAL PRONOUNS

        ego, I   **tū,** you

	SINGULAR	PLURAL	SINGULAR	PLURAL
Nom.	**ego**	**nōs**	**tū**	**vōs**
Acc.	**mē**	**nōs**	**tē**	**vōs**
Gen.	**meī**	**nostrī, nostrum**	**tuī**	**vestrī, vestrum**
Dat.	**mihi**	**nōbīs**	**tibi**	**vōbīs**
Abl.	**mē**	**nōbīs**	**tē**	**vōbīs**

2. Demonstrative Pronouns

(a) is, ĕă, id (pron.), he, she, it ; (adj.) that

	SINGULAR			PLURAL		
	Masc.	Fem.	Neuter	Masc.	Fem.	Neuter
Nom.	is	ĕă	id	ĕī (īī)	ĕae	ĕă
Acc.	ĕum	ĕam	id	ĕōs	ĕās	ĕă
Gen.	eius	eius	eius	ĕōrum	ĕārum	ĕōrum
Dat.	ĕī	ĕī	ĕī	ĕīs (īīs)	ĕīs (īīs)	ĕīs (īīs)
Abl.	ĕō	ĕā	ĕō	ĕīs (īīs)	ĕīs (īīs)	ĕīs (īīs)

(b) hīc, haec, hōc, this

	SINGULAR			PLURAL		
	Masc.	Fem.	Neuter	Masc.	Fem.	Neuter
Nom.	hīc	haec	hōc	hī	hae	haec
Acc.	hunc	hanc	hōc	hōs	hās	haec
Gen.	huius	huius	huius	hōrum	hārum	hōrum
Dat.	huĭc	huĭc	huĭc	hīs	hīs	hīs
Abl.	hōc	hāc	hōc	hīs	hīs	hīs

(c) ille, illa, illud, that

	SINGULAR			PLURAL		
	Masc.	Fem.	Neuter	Masc.	Fem.	Neuter
Nom.	ille	illa	illud	illī	illae	illă
Acc.	illum	illam	illud	illōs	illās	illă
Gen.	illīus	illīus	illīus	illōrum	illārum	illōrum
Dat.	illī	illī	illī	illīs	illīs	illīs
Abl.	illō	illā	illō	illīs	illīs	illīs

3. Reflexive Pronouns

(a) mē, myself   (b) tē, yourself   (c) sē, himself, herself, itself, themselves

	SINGULAR	PLURAL	SINGULAR	PLURAL	SINGULAR AND PLURAL
Acc.	mē	nōs	tē	vōs	sē
Gen.	meī	nostrī, nostrum	tuī	vestrī, vestrum	suī
Dat.	mihi	nōbīs	tibi	vōbīs	sibi
Abl.	mē	nōbīs	tē	vōbīs	sē

4. The Emphasising Pronoun
ipse, ipsa, ipsum, self

SINGULAR

	Masc.	Fem.	Neuter
Nom.	ipse	ipsa	ipsum
Acc.	ipsum	ipsam	ipsum
Gen.	ipsīus	ipsīus	ipsīus
Dat.	ipsī	ipsī	ipsī
Abl.	ipsō	ipsā	ipsō

PLURAL

	Masc.	Fem.	Neuter
Nom.	ipsī	ipsae	ipsă
Acc.	ipsōs	ipsās	ipsă
Gen.	ipsōrum	ipsārum	ipsōrum
Dat.	ipsīs	ipsīs	ipsīs
Abl.	ipsīs	ipsīs	ipsīs

5. Possessive Adjectives and Pronouns

1st person   **meus, mea, meum,** my, mine (*voc. sing. masc.,* **mī**).
            noster, nostra, nostrum, our, ours.

2nd person   **tuus, tua, tuum,** your, yours (belonging to you, *sing.*).
            vester, vestra, vestrum, your, yours (belonging to you, *pl.*).

3rd person   **eius** (*gen. sing.* of **is, ea, id**), his, her, its.
            eōrum, eārum (*gen. pl.* of **is, ea, id**), their.
            suus, sua, suum, his own, her own, its own, their own
                (indicating that which belongs to subject of nearest
                verb).

VI. VERBS

1. The Irregular Verb sum, esse, fuī, to be

INDICATIVE MOOD

Present Tense		Perfect Tense	
sum	sumus	fú-ī	fú-imus
es	estis	fu-istī	fu-istis
est	sunt	fú-it	fu-ērunt

Future Tense		Future Perfect Tense	
érō	érimus	fú-erō	fu-erimus
éris	éritis	fú-eris	fu-eritis
érit	érunt	fú-erit	fú-erint

Imperfect Tense		Pluperfect Tense	
éram	erāmus	fú-eram	fu-erāmus
érās	erātis	fú-erās	fu-erātis
érat	erant	fú-erat	fú-erant

2. The First Conjugation

Indicative Mood Active and Passive of:

amō, amāre, amāvī, amātum, to love

ACTIVE		PASSIVE	
		Present Tense	
ám-ō	amā-mus	ám-or	amā-mur
ámā-s	amā-tis	amā-ris (-re)	amā-minī
áma-t	áma-nt	amā-tur	ama-ntur
		Future Tense	
ama-bō	amā-bimus	amā-bor	amā-bimur
amā-bis	amā-bitis	amā-bĕris	amā-biminī
amā-bit	amā-bunt	amā-bitur	amā-buntur
		Imperfect Tense	
amā-bam	amā-bāmus	amā-bar	amā-bāmur
amā-bās	amā-bātis	amā-bāris (-re)	amā-bāminī
amā-bat	amā-bant	amā-bātur	amā-bantur
		Perfect Tense	
amāv-ī	amāv-imus	amātus sum	amātī sumus
amāv-istī	amāv-istis	amātus es	amātī estis
amāv-it	amāv-ērunt	amātus est	amātī sunt
		Future Perfect Tense	
amāv-erō	amāv-erimus	amātus erō	amātī erimus
amāv-eris	amāv-eritis	amātus eris	amātī eritis
amāv-erit	amāv-erint	amātus erit	amātī erunt
		Pluperfect Tense	
amāv-eram	amāv-erāmus	amātus eram	amātī erāmus
amāv-erās	amāv-erātis	amātus erās	amātī erātis
amāv-erat	amāv-erant	amātus erat	amātī erant

3. The Second Conjugation

Indicative Mood Active and Passive of:

moneō, monēre, monuī, monitum, to advise, warn

ACTIVE		PASSIVE	
		Present Tense	
mónĕ-ō	monē-mus	mónĕ-or	monē-mur
mónĕ-s	monē-tis	monē-ris	monē-minī
móne-t	móne-nt	monē-tur	mone-ntur

ACTIVE			PASSIVE

Future Tense

monē-bŏ	monē-bimus	monē-bor	monē-bimur
monē-bis	monē-bitis	monē-bĕris	monē-biminī
monē-bit	monē-bunt	monē-bitur	monē-buntur

Imperfect Tense

monē-bam	monē-bāmus	monē-bar	monē-bāmur
monē-bās	monē-bātis	monē-bāris	monē-bāminī
monē-bat	monē-bant	monē-bātur	monē-bantur

Perfect Tense

monu-ī	monu-imus	monitus sum	monitī sumus
monu-istī	monu-istis	monitus es	monitī estis
monu-it	monu-ērunt	monitus est	monitī sunt

Future Perfect Tense

monu-erŏ	monu-erimus	monitus erŏ	monitī erimus
monu-eris	monu-eritis	monitus eris	monitī eritis
monu-erit	monu-erint	monitus erit	monitī erunt

Pluperfect Tense

monu-eram	monu-erāmus	monitus eram	monitī erāmus
monu-erās	monu-erātis	monitus erās	monitī erātis
monu-erat	monu-erant	monitus erat	monitī erant

4. THE THIRD CONJUGATION

Indicative Mood Active and Passive of:

regō, regere, rēxī, rēctum, to rule

ACTIVE		PASSIVE	

Present Tense

rég-ō	rég-imus	rég-or	rég-ĭmur
rég-is	rég-itis	rég-ĕris	rég-ĭminī
rég-it	rég-unt	rég-ĭtur	reg-untur

Future Tense

rég-am	reg-ēmus	reg-ar	reg-ēmur
rég-ēs	reg-ētis	reg-ēris	reg-ēminī
rég-et	rég-ent	reg-ētur	reg-entur

Imperfect Tense

reg-ēbam	reg-ēbāmus	reg-ēbar	reg-ēbāmur
reg-ēbās	reg-ēbātis	reg-ēbāris	reg-ēbāminī
reg-ēbat	reg-ēbant	reg-ēbātur	reg-ēbantur

	ACTIVE		PASSIVE

Perfect Tense

ACTIVE		PASSIVE	
rĕx-ī	rĕx-imus	rĕctus sum	rĕctī sumus
rĕx-istī	rĕx-istis	rĕctus es	rĕctī estis
rĕx-it	rĕx-ĕrunt	rĕctus est	rĕctī sunt

Future Perfect Tense

rĕx-erŏ	rĕx-erimus	rĕctus erŏ	rĕctī erimus
rĕx-eris	rĕx-eritis	rĕctus eris	rĕctī eritis
rĕx-erit	rĕx-erint	rĕctus erit	rĕctī erunt

Pluperfect Tense

rĕx-eram	rĕx-erāmus	rĕctus eram	rĕctī erāmus
rĕx-erās	rĕx-erātis	rĕctus erās	rĕctī erātis
rĕx-erat	rĕx-erant	rĕctus erat	rĕctī erant

5. VERBS OF THE THIRD CONJUGATION ENDING IN -iō

Indicative Mood Active and Passive of:

capiō, capere, cēpī, captum, to take, capture

ACTIVE		PASSIVE	

Present Tense

capiŏ	capĭmus	capior	capĭmur
capĭs	capĭtis	capĕris	capĭminī
capĭt	capiunt	capĭtur	capiuntur

Future Tense

capiam	capiēmus	capiar	capiēmur
capiēs	capiētis	capiēris	capiēminī
capiet	capient	capiētur	capientur

Imperfect Tense

capiēbam	capiēbāmus	capiēbar	capiēbāmur
capiēbās	capiēbātis	capiēbāris	capiēbāminī
capiēbat	capiēbant	capiēbātur	capiēbantur

Perfect Tense

cēpī	cēpimus	captus sum	captī sumus
cēpistī	cēpistis	captus es	captī estis
cēpit	cēpērunt	captus est	captī sunt

Future Perfect Tense

cēpĕrŏ	cēperĭmus	captus erŏ	captī erimus
cēperis	cēperĭtis	captus eris	captī eritis
cēperit	cēperint	captus erit	captī erunt

ACTIVE		PASSIVE	
Pluperfect Tense			
cēperam	cēperāmus	captus eram	captī erāmus
cēperās	cēperātis	captus erās	captī erātis
cēperat	cēperant	captus erat	captī erant

6. THE FOURTH CONJUGATION

Indicative Mood Active and Passive of:

audiō, audīre, audīvī, audītum, to hear

ACTIVE		PASSIVE	
Present Tense			
aúdi-ō	audī-mus	aúdi-or	audī-mur
aúdī-s	audī-tis	audī-ris	audī-minī
aúdi-t	aúdi-unt	audī-tur	audi-untur
Future Tense			
aúdi-am	audi-ēmus	audi-ar	audi-ēmur
aúdi-ēs	audi-ētis	audi-ēris	audi-ēminī
aúdi-et	aúdi-ent	audi-ētur	audi-ēntur
Imperfect Tense			
audi-ēbam	audi-ēbāmus	audi-ēbar	audi-ēbāmur
audi-ēbās	audi-ēbātis	audi-ēbāris	audi-ēbāminī
audi-ēbat	audi-ēbant	audi-ēbātur	audi-ēbantur
Perfect Tense			
audīv-ī	audīv-imus	audītus sum	audītī sumus
audīv-istī	audīv-istis	audītus es	audītī estis
audīv-it	audīv-ērunt	audītus est	audītī sunt
Future Perfect Tense			
audīv-erō	audīv-erimus	audītus erō	audītī erimus
audīv-eris	audīv-eritis	audītus eris	audītī eritis
audīv-erit	audīv-erint	audītus erit	audītī erunt
Pluperfect Tense			
audīv-eram	audīv-erāmus	audītus eram	audītī erāmus
audīv-erās	audīv-erātis	audītus erās	audītī erātis
audīv-erat	audīv-erant	audītus erat	audītī erant

SPECIAL VOCABULARIES

EXERCISE 1

amō, I love
laudō, I praise
superō, I overcome

salvē, salvēte, good morning !, good day !, hail !
valē, valēte, good-bye !, farewell !

EXERCISE 2

festīnō, I hasten, I hurry
habitō, I live, I dwell
parō, I prepare

portō, I carry
ubi ?, where ?

EXERCISE 3

nārrō, I tell (a story), I relate
vāstō, I lay waste

vulnerō, I wound
quō ?, whither ?, where . . . to ?

EXERCISE 4

fābula, -ae, *f.,* story
īnsula, -ae, *f.,* island
mēnsa, -ae, *f.,* table
puella, -ae, *f.,* girl
rēgīna, -ae, *f.,* queen

silva, -ae, *f.,* wood
ad (*prep. gov. acc.*), to, toward
in (*prep. gov. abl.*), in, on
unde ? whence ?, where . . . from ?

EXERCISE 5

dĕa, -ae, *f.,* goddess
hasta, -ae, *f.,* spear
fīlia, -ae, *f.,* daughter
nauta, -ae, *m.,* sailor
patria, -ae, *f.,* native land

rosa, -ae, *f.,* rose
taberna, -ae, *f.,* inn, shop
ōrnō, I adorn
cūr ?, why ?

EXERCISE 6

agricola, -ae, *m.*, farmer
poēta, -ae, *m.*, poet
sagitta, -ae, *f.*, arrow
ambulō, I walk
oppugnō, I attack
servo, I save, I protect

et, and
ex, ē (*prep. gov. abl.*), from, out of
nōn, not
quandō? when?

EXERCISE 7

pugna, -ae, *f.*, battle, fight
victōria, -ae, *f.*, victory
villa, -ae, *f.*, country house

nūntiō, I announce, I report
vītō, I avoid
ō! (*exclamation*), O!, oh!

EXERCISE 8

Britannia, -ae, *f.*, Britain
Gallia, -ae, *f.*, Gaul

sum, I am

EXERCISE 9

via, -ae, *f.*, way, road
bona (*fem. adj.*), good
longa (*fem. adj.*), long
magna (*fem. adj.*), large, big, great
multae (*fem. adj. pl.*), many

parva (*fem. adj.*), small, little
pugnō, I fight
crās, to-morrow
hĕrī, yesterday
hodiē, to-day

EXERCISE 10

captīvus, -ī, *m.*, captive, prisoner
dominus, -ī, *m.*, master, lord
mūrus, -ī, *m.*, wall
servus, -ī, *m.*, slave
bonus (*masc. adj.*), good
longus (*masc. adj.*), long

magnus (*masc. adj.*), large big, great
multī (*masc. adj. pl.*), many
parvus (*masc. adj.*), small, little
līberō, I free, I set free
saepe, often

EXERCISE 11

amicus, -ī, *m.*, friend
deus, dei, *m.*, god
fīlius, fīliī (or fīlī), *m.*, son
Valerius, -iī, *m.*, Valerius
appellō, I call

iam, now, already
ōlim, once, once upon a time, formerly, some day
semper, always

EXERCISE 12

ager, -rī, *m.,* field
Ĭtălia, -ae, *f.,* Italy
puer, -ī, *m.,* boy
vir, -ī *m.,* man
miser (*masc. adj.*), wretched, unhappy
misera (*fem. adj.*), wretched, unhappy

pulcher (*masc. adj.*), beautiful
pulchra (*fem. adj.*) beautiful
nāvigō, I sail
inter (*prep. gov. acc.*), among, between
enim (*conj. ; second word in clause*), for
sed (*conj.*), but

EXERCISE 13

Gallus, -i, *m.,* a Gaul
bellum, -i, *n.,* war
templum, -ī, *n.,* temple
comparō, I procure

magnum (*neut. adj.*), large, big, great
pulchrum (*neut. adj.*), beautiful

EXERCISE 14

fēmina, -ae, *f.,* woman
forum, -ī, *n.,* forum, market-place
Gallus, -ī, *m.,* Gallus
lībertus, -ī, *m.,* freedman
nostrī, -ōrum, *m. pl.,* our men
oppidum, -ī, *n.,* town
Quīntus, -ī, *m.,* Quintus
Rōmānus, -ī, *m.,* a Roman
Syrus, -ī, *m.,* Syrus

iūstus, -a, -um, just
līber, -a, -um, free
noster, -tra, -trum, our, ours
novus, -a, -um, new
labōrō, I work
dē (*prep. gov. abl.*), about, concerning
diū, for a long time
igitur (*second word in clause*), therefore

EXERCISE 15

discipulus, -ī, *m.,* pupil
liber, -brī, *m.,* book
lūdus, -ī, *m.,* school
magister, -trī, *m.,* master (of a school)
Orbilius, -iī, *m.,* Orbilius
vīcus, -ī, *m.,* street

īgnāvus, -a, -um, ĭdle, lazy
Rōmānus, -a, -um, Roman
culpō, I blame
intrō, I enter
salūtō, I greet, I salute
in (*prep. gov. acc.*), into
māne, in the morning

EXERCISE 16

iānua, -ae, *f.,* door
collocō, I place
doceō, I teach
exspectō, I await, I wait for

moneō, I advise, I warn
timeō, I fear
ad (*prep. gov. acc.*), at, near

EXERCISE 17

cēra, -ae, *f.*, writing-tablet
sella, -ae, *f.*, seat, chair
Sextus, -ī, *m.*, Sextus
stilus, -ī, *m.*, pen
Tullius, -iī, *m.*, Tullius
plāgōsus, -a, -um, full of blows
castīgō, I chide
numerō, I count
recitō, I read (aloud)
verberō, I beat
ita vērō, yes indeed
sērō, late

sī, if
ecce !, lo !, behold !, see !
edepol !, upon my word !, goodness gracious !
prīmum, firstly
deinde, afterwards, then, thereafter
ūnus, one (*full declension given later*)
duo, two (*full declension given later*)
quattuor, four (*indeclinable*)
litterae, -ārum, *f. pl.*, letters

EXERCISE 18

castra, -ōrum, *n. pl.*, camp
imperātor, -is, *m.*, general
legiō, -nis, *f.*, legion
nīles, -itis, *m.*, soldier
rēx, rēgis, *m.*, king
secundus, -a, -um, second

habeō, I have
terreō, I frighten, I terrify
quis ?, who ?
quem ?, whom ?
quid ?, what ?

EXERCISE 19

barbarus, -i, *m.*, barbarian
fundus, -ī., *m.*, farm
glōria, -ae, *f.*, glory
homō, -inis, *m.*, man
nōmen, -inis, *n.*, name
onus, -eris, *n.*, burden
perīculum, -ī, *n.*, danger
terra, -ae, *f.*, land
virtūs, -ūtis, *f.*, valour, courage

vīta, -ae, *f.*, life
dūrus, -a, -um, hard, harsh
nihil, nothing
numquam, never
contrā (*prep. gov. acc.*), against
cum (*prep. gov. abl.*), with
quam !, how !, what !
ō mē miserum !, woe is me !, hang it all ! (*Literally,* O wretched me !)

Proper Names

Marcus, -ī, *m.*, Marcus.
Lūcius, -iī, *m.*, Lucius.

Titus, -ī, *m.*, Titus.
Britannus, -ī, *m.*, a Briton.

EXERCISE 20

cīvis, -is, *m.*, citizen
corpus, -oris, *n.*, body
cubīle, -is, *n.*, bed
hostis, -is, *m.*, enemy
mare, -is, *n.*, sea

nāvis, -is, *f.*, ship; nāvis longa, warship
terrā marīque, by land and sea
dēsīderō, I long for

EXERCISE 21

calceus, -ī, *m.*, shoe
caput, capitis, *n.*, head
cūria, -ae, *f.*, senate house
gēns, gentis, *f.*, race
iter, itineris, *n.*, journey, march
pēs, pĕdis, *m.*, foot
petasus, -ī, *m.*, hat
sōl, sōlis, *m.*, sun
tŏga, -ae, *f.*, toga
tunica, -ae, *f.*, tunic
urbs, urbis, *f.*, city

vestīmentum, -ī, *n.*, garment
albus, -a, -um, white
meus, -a, -um, my, mine
nūdus, -a, -um, bare, naked
sordidus, -a, -um, dirty
togātus, -a, -um, clad in the toga
satis (*indeclinable*), enough
super (*prep. gov. acc.*), above, over
modo, only

EXERCISE 22

arma, -ōrum, *n. pl.*, arms
bōs, bŏvis, *c.*, ox, cow
canis, -is, *c.*, dog
frāter, -ris, *m.*, brother
Iŭppiter, Iŏvĭs, *m.*, Jupiter
iuvenis, -is, *m.*, youth, young man
māter, -tris, *f.*, mother
moenia, -ium, *n. pl.*, walls (of a city)

pars, -tis, *f.*, part
pater, -tris, *m.*, father
senex, senis, *m.*, old man
vīs, *f. sing.*, force, violence; *pl.*, strength
post (*prep. gov. acc.*), after
nusquam, nowhere
mē, me (*accusative case*)
videō, I see

EXERCISE 23

aedificium, -iī, *n.*, building

cēna, -ae, *f.*, dinner

flūmen, -inis, *n.*, river

mōns, -tis, *m.*, mountain

pōns, -tis, *m.*, bridge

porta, -ae, *f.*, gate

rīpa, -ae, *f.*, bank (of a river)

Rōma, -ae, *f.*, Rome

Tiberis, -is, *m.*, Tiber

antīquus, -a, -um, ancient

lātus, -a, -um, wide, broad

ligneus, -a, -um, wooden, of wood

prīmus, -a, -um, first

aedificō, -āre, -āvī, -ātum, to build

dō, dăre, dĕdī, dătum, to give

maneō, -ēre, mānsī, mānsum, to remain, to stay

stō, stāre, stĕtī, stātum, to stand

videō, -ēre, vīdī, vīsum, to see

FURTHER PROPER NAMES

Horātius, -iī, *m.*, Horatius (hero who defended the Pons Sublicius).

Mōns Capitōlīnus, *m.*, The Mons Capitolinus, Capitoline Hill.

Pōns Aemilius, *m.*, The Aemilian Bridge (179 B.C.).

Pōns Cestius, *m.*, The Cestian Bridge (46 B.C.).

Pōns Sublicius, *m.*, The Sublician Bridge.

Via Appia, *f.*, The Appian Way (Ran South).

Via Flāminia, *f.*, The Flaminian Way (Ran North).

EXERCISE 24

campus, -ī, *m.*, plain

collis, -is, *m.*, hill

lūdus, -ī, *m.*, game

negōtium, -iī, *n.*, business

pĭla, -ae, *f.*, ball

exerceō, -ēre, -uī, -itum, to exercise, to train

sedeō, -ēre, sēdī, sessum, to sit

quot ? (*indeclinable*), how many ?

sacer, sacra, sacrum, sacred

septem (*indeclinable*), seven

extrā (*prep. gov. acc.*), outside

intrā (*prep. gov. acc.*), within, inside

etiam, also

Proper Names

Campus Mārtius, *m.*, The Campus Martius, a meadow about 120 hectares in extent, between the city wall and the Tiber on the N.-W. side.

Circus Maximus, *m.*, The Circus Maximus, an oval racecourse between the Aventine and Palatine. It was surrounded by galleries three stories high, and could hold over 100,000 spectators.

Cūria, *f.*, The Curia Hostilia, the senate-house, situated in the N.-W. corner of the Forum.

Rōstra, *n.pl.*, The Rostra, a platform in the Forum for speakers. It was decorated with the beaks (**rōstra**) of warships captured in 338 B.C.

Vesta, *f.*, Vesta, the goddess of the hearth. She had a temple in the Forum, in which the sacred fire was kept constantly burning and was tended by maidens of noble birth called the Vestal Virgins.

EXERCISE 25

arx, arcis, *f.*, citadel

rēgia, -ae, *f.*, palace

dēfendō, -ere, -fendī, -fēn-sum, to defend

dūcō, -ere, dūxī, ductum, to lead, to take

mittō, -ere, mīsī, missum, to send

necō, -āre, -āvī, -ātum, to kill

regō, -ere, rēxī, rēctum, to rule

fortiter, bravely

EXERCISE 26

Asia, -ae, *f.*, Asia

dolor, -ōris, *m.*, grief

equus, -ī, *m.*, horse

Graecia, -ae, *f.*, Greece

Graecus, -ī, *m.*, a Greek

initium, -iī, *n.*, beginning

mortālis, -is, *c.*, a mortal

proelium, -iī, *n.*, battle

Sparta, -ae, *f.*, Sparta

Trōia, -ae, *f.*, Troy

Trōiānus, -ī, *m.*, a Trojan

Trōiānus, -a, -um, Trojan

uxor, -ōris, *f.*, wife

ēheu !, alas !

tamen, however, nevertheless

ā, ab (*prep. gov. abl.*), from, by

Further Proper Names

Aenēās, Aenēae, *m.*, Aeneas, a great Trojan hero.

Dīdō, Dīdōnis, *f.*, Dido, queen of Carthage.

Hector, -oris, *m.*, Hector, bravest of the Trojans.

Helena, -ae, *f.*, Helen, beautiful wife of Menelaus.

Menelāus, -ī, *m.*, Menelaus, king of Sparta.

Paris, Paridis, *m.*, Paris, son of Priam.

Priamus, -ī, *m.*, Priam, the aged king of Troy.

EXERCISE 27

auxilium, -iī, *n.*, help
cōnsilium, -iī, *n.*, plan, device, stratagem
gaudium, -iī, *n.*, joy
pāstor, -ōris, *m.*, shepherd
dēfessus, -a, -um, tired, weary
paucī, -ae, -a, few
capiō, -ere, cēpī, captum, to take, to capture
cōnsilium capere, to adopt a plan

exclāmō, -āre, -āvī, -ātum, to exclaim, to shout aloud
faciō, -ere, fēcī, factum, to make, to do
iter facere, to march, to journey
trahō, -ere, traxī, tractum, to drag
tandem, at length
tum, then
statim, at once, immediately

Proper Names

Achillēs, -is, *m.*, Achilles, the bravest of the Greeks.
Sinōn, -ōnis, *m.*, Sinon, a Greek who deceived the Trojans.

EXERCISE 28

dux, ducis, *m.*, leader
praeda, -ae, *f.*, booty
sanguis, sanguinis, *m.*, blood
fēlīx, -īcis, happy, fortunate, successful, lucky
Graecus, -a, -um, Greek

ingēns, -entis, huge
dēleō, -ēre, -ēvī, -ētum, to destroy
inquit, says, *or* said he, she, it
mox, soon, presently
audāx, -ācis, bold

Proper Name

Palamēdes, -is, *m.*, Palamedes, friend of Sinon.

EXERCISE 29

clāmor, -ōris, *m.*, shout
cūstōs, -ōdis, *m.*, guard
nox, noctis, *f.*, night
signum, -ī, *n.*, signal
socius, -iī, *m.*, ally, companion

ācer, ācris, ācre, keen, fierce, spirited
celer, celeris, celere, swift
fortis, -is, -e, brave
omnis, -is, -e, all, every
per (*prep. gov. acc.*), through, throughout, over

Proper Name

Hecuba, -ae, *f.*, Hecuba, the wife of Priam.

EXERCISE 30

nūntius, -iī, *m.,* messenger
sōl occidēns, the West
aeternus, -a, -um, eternal
dīves, -itis, rich
immortālis, -is, -e, immortal
īgnāvus, -a, -um, cowardly

pauper, -is, poor
vetus, -eris, old
errō, -āre, -āvī, -ātum, to
wander
incendō, -ere, -ī, incēnsum,
to burn

EXERCISE 31

audiō, -īre, -īvī, -ītum, to
hear
**coniciō, -ere, coniēcī, coni-
ectum,** to throw

occupō, -āre, -āvī, -ātum,
to seize
veniō, -īre, vēnī, ventum,
to come

PROPER NAMES

Laurentum, -ī, *n.,* Laurentum, a city in Italy occupied by the Trojans
under Aeneas.

Alba Longa, *f.* Alba Longa, a city in Italy occupied by the descendants
of Aeneas.

Numitor, -ōris, *m.,* Numitor, a king of Alba Longa.

Amūlius, -iī, Amulius, brother of King Numitor.

Rhea Silvia, *f.,* Rhea Silvia, daughter of Numitor.

Rōmulus, -ī, *m.,* Romulus, son of Mars and Rhea Silvia.

Remus, -ī, *m.* Remus, the twin brother of Romulus.

Mārs, Mārtis *m.,* Mars, the god of war.

EXERCISE 32

cornū, -ūs, *n.,* horn, wing
(of an army)
exercitus, -ūs, *m.,* army
lupa, -ae, *f.,* she-wolf
manus, -ūs, *f.,* hand
rīsus, -ūs, *m.,* smile

rīdeō, -ēre, rīsī, rīsum, to
laugh, to laugh at
tendō, -ere, tetendī, to
stretch, to stretch out
trīstis, -is, -e, sad
tam, so

PROPER NAME

Faustulus, -ī, *m.,* Faustulus, the shepherd who rescued the infants
Romulus and Remus.

EXERCISE 33

domus, -ūs, *f.,* house, home
gladius, -iī, *m.,* sword
labor, -ōris, *m.,* work
rēgnum, -ī, *n.,* kingdom
age !, agite !, come !
reddō, -ere, reddidī, redditum, to restore, to give back

īrātus, -a, -um, angry
scelestus, -a, -um, wicked
strenuus, -a, -um, active, energetic
et, also, even
-que, and
vae tibi !, woe to you !

EXERCISE 34

pāx, pācis, *f.,* peace
pluit, it rains
quārtus, -a, -um, fourth
quīntus, -a, -um, fifth

minimē vērō, no, no indeed, not at all
os, ossis, *n.,* bone

PROPER NAMES

Iūppiter Pluvius, *m.,* Jupiter Pluvius, the god who sends rain.
Rōmulus, -ī, *m.,* Romulus, son of Mars and Rhea Silvia, twin brother of Remus ; founder and first king of Rome.
Numa Pompilius, *m.,* Numa Pompilius, second king of Rome, founder of the state religion.
Tullus Hostīlius, *m.,* Tullus Hostilius, third king of Rome ; great warrior, destroyed Alba Longa and transferred its people to Rome.
Ancus Mārtius, *m.,* Ancus Martius, fourth king, extended Roman territory as far as the sea and built Ostia, the port of Rome at mouth of the Tiber.
Tarquinius Prīscus *m.,* Tarquinius Priscus, the fifth king ; responsible for great public buildings.
Servius Tullius, *m.,* Servius Tullius, sixth king ; reorganised the Roman people.
Tarquinius Superbus, *m.,* Tarquinius Superbus, or, Tarquin the Proud ; seventh and last king of Rome; harsh tyrant who was finally expelled in 510 B.C.
Brūtus, *m.,* Lucius Iunius Brutus, at whose instigation the Romans expelled Tarquin the Proud.

EXERCISE 35

aditus, ūs, *m.,* an approach
fragor, -ōris, *m.,* crash
impetus, -ūs, *m.,* attack
tēlum, -ī, *n.,* weapon
dēsiliō, -īre, -uī, -ultum, to leap down
expellō, -ere, -pulī, -pulsum, to drive out
attonitus, -a, -um, astounded

fugiō, -ere, -fūgī, -fugitum, to flee
sustineō, -ēre, -uī, -tentum, to withstand
septimus, -a, -um, seventh
ego, *acc.,* **mē,** *dat.,* **mihi,** I
paene, almost
ubi, when

Proper Names

Clūsīnus, -a, -um, of, or belonging to, Clusium, one of the chief towns of Etruria and capital of Lars Porsena.
Horātius Cocles, *m.,* Horatius Cocles, Roman hero who defended the Pons Sublicius against the Etruscans.
Lārs Porsinna, *m.,* Lars Porsena, king of Clusium, who tried to restore Tarquin to Rome.
Spurius Larcius, *m.,* Spurius Larcius, comrade of Horatius.
Titus Herminius, *m.,* Titus Herminius, comrade of Horatius.
Tiberīnus, of, or belonging to, the Tiber. **Pater Tiberīnus** is the god of the river Tiber—" Father Tiber."

EXERCISE 36

alius, -a, -ud, other, another
inopia, -ae, *f.,* lack, scarcity, want
patrēs, -um, *m. pl.,* senators
rēs, reī, *f.,* thing, business, affair, matter
scrība, -ae, *m.,* clerk, secretary
senātor, -ōris, *m.,* senator

stīpendium, -iī, *n.,* pay
īgnōrō, -āre, -āvī, -ātum, not to know
obsideō, -ēre, -sēdī, -sessum, to besiege
nōbilis, -is, -e, noble
tē (*acc. sing.*), you
trāns (*prep. gov. acc.*), across
diēs, diēī, *m.,* day

Proper Name

C. Mūcius, *m.,* Gaius Mucius, Roman youth who entered the Etruscan camp and tried to kill Lars Porsena.

EXERCISE 37

dextra, -ae, *f.*, right hand

dolor, -ōris, *m.*, pain

flamma, -ae, *f.*, flame

ignis, -is, *m.*, fire

mīrāculum, -ī, *n.*, marvel

mors, -tis, *f.*, death

sacrificium, -iī, *n.*, sacrifice

coniūrō, -āre, -āvī, -ātum, to conspire

dīcō, -ere, dīxī, dictum, to say

iniciō, -ere, iniēcī, iniectum, to thrust

rogō, -āre, -āvī, -ātum, to ask, ask for

parātus, -a, -um, prepared, ready

sollicitus, -a, -um, anxious, troubled

trecentī, -ae, -a, three hundred

vīlis, -is, -e, cheap

circum (*prep. gov. acc.*), around, round

propter (*prep. gov. acc.*), on account of

tibi (*dat. sing. of tū*), to, for you

Proper Name

Scaevola, -ae, *m.*, Scaevola, " the Left-handed," an additional name given to C. Mucius after he had destroyed his right hand in the fire.

EXERCISE 38

annus, -ī, *m.*, year

cōnsul, -is, *m.*, consul

lacrima, ae, *f.*, tear

lēgātus, -ī, *m.*, ambassador

populus, -ī, *m.*, people

sacerdōs, -dōtis, *m.*, priest

tuus, -a, -um, your

accipiō, -ere, -cēpī, -ceptum, to receive

mūtō, -āre, -āvī, -ātum, to change

proximus, -a, -um, next

iterum, again, for a second time

mehercule !, upon my word !

Proper Names

Coriolī, -ōrum, *m. pl.*, Corioli, town in Latium destroyed by Cn. Marcius.

Cn. Marcius, Gnaeus Marcius, the Roman general who destroyed Corioli.

Coriolānus, of, or belonging to, Corioli, surname given to Cn. Marcius after he destroyed Corioli.

Veturia, -ae, *f.*, Veturia, mother of Coriolanus.

Volumnia, -ae, *f.* Volumnia, wife of Coriolanus.

Volscī, -ōrum, *m. pl.*, the Volsci.

EXERCISE 39

factum, -ī, n., deed

iūs, iūris, n., right

iūstitia, -ae, f., justice

mōs, mōris, m., custom

sermō, -ōnis, m., talk

spatium, -iī, n., space, interval

statiō, -ōnis, f., outpost

virga, -ae, f., rod

addō, -ere, addidī, additum, to add

prō (*prep. gov. abl.*), for, on behalf of

dēlectō, -āre, -āvī, -ātum, to delight

gerō, -ere, gessī, gestum, to wage (war)

trādō, -ere, trādidī, trāditum, to hand over

brevis, -is, -e, short

ita, so, thus

iūstē, justly

nōn modo . . . sed etiam, not only . . . but also

sīcut, just as

Proper Names

Camillus, -ī, m., Marcus Furius Camillus, great Roman hero who, among many victories, took Falerii.

Falēriī, -ōrum, m., Falerii, an important city in Etruria.

Faliscī, -ōrum, m., the Falisci, the people of Falerii.

EXERCISE 40

elephantus, -ī, m., elephant

necātī, -ōrum, m. pl., the slain

orbis terrārum, m., world

statua, -ae, f., statue

vulnus, -eris, n., wound

vultus, -ūs, m., expression, countenance, face

sepeliō, -īre, -īvī, sepultum, to bury

altus, -a, -um, high, deep

difficilis, -is, -e, difficult

humilis, -is, -e, humble, low, lowly

nūllus, -a, -um, no, none

similis, -is, -e, like

tōtus sum in (*with abl.*), I am engrossed in

trux, trucis, grim

etiam, even

nisi, unless

Proper Names

Ēpīrus, -ī, f., Epirus, a country in N.-W. of Greece.

Pyrrhus, -ī, m., Pyrrhus, king of Epirus.

Tarentīnī, -ōrum, m. pl., the Tarentines, the people of Tarentum, a city and port in S. Italy.

EXERCISE 41

aurum, -ī, *n.*, gold
cursus, -ūs, *m.*, course
ferrum, -ī, *n.*, iron
fortūna, -ae, *f.*, fortune
honestās, -ātis, *f.*, honour
medicus, -ī, *m.*, doctor
pretium, -iī, *n.*, price
senātus, -ūs, *m.*, senate
venēnum, -ī, *n.*, poison
vōs (*n., v., acc. pl.*), you
caecus, -a, -um, blind

honestus, -a, -um, honourable
ūtilis, -is, -e, useful
adiuvō, -āre, -iūvī, -iūtum, to help
agō, -ere, ēgī, āctum, to discuss
āvertō, -ere, -ī, āversum, to turn away
dum, while
sine (*prep. gov. abl.*), without
sīc, thus, so

Proper Names

Campānia, -ae, *f.*, Campania, district south of Latium.
Appius Claudius, *m.*, Appius Claudius, famous Roman who, during his tenure of the office of Censor, built the great Appian aqueduct and began the construction of the Via Appia. In his old age he induced the Senate to reject the peace terms offered by Pyrrhus.
Cīneās, -ae, *m.*, Cineas, the minister of Pyrrhus.

EXERCISE 42

amplexus, -ūs, *m.*, embrace
condiciō, -iōnis, *f.*, condition
dignitās, -ātis, *f.*, dignity
fidēs, -eī, *f.*, faith

līberī, -ōrum, *m. pl.*, children
permūtātiō, -iōnis, *f.*, exchange
spēs, -eī, *f.*, hope

Proper Names

M. Atīlius Rēgulus, *m.*, Regulus, Roman commander in the First Carthaginian war; failed in attempt to capture Carthage, and taken prisoner by the enemy.
Carthāginiēnsēs, -ium, *m. pl.*, the Carthaginians.

EXERCISE 43

animus, -ī, *m.*, mind

clādēs, -is, *f.*, disaster, defeat

clādem accipere, to sustain a disaster, defeat

condiciōnēs, -um, *f. pl.*, terms

cōnstantia, -ae, *f.*, constancy

honor, -ōris, *m.*, honour

rēs pūblica, reī pūblicae, *f.*, state, republic

agite ! (*pl.* of age !), come !

cōnfirmō, -āre, -āvī, -ātum, to reassure

dēspērō, -āre, -āvī, -ātum, to despair

grātiās agere, to thank

intereā, meanwhile

ego, I

tū, you (*sing.*)

quod, because

PROPER NAMES

Cannēnsis, -is, -e, of, or belonging to, Cannae a village in Apulia, scene of Hannibal's victory over the Romans in 216 B.C.

Canusium, -iī, *n.*, Canusium, town near Cannae.

Varrō, -ōnis, *m.*, Varro, the Roman general in command at Cannae.

Q. Fabius Māximus, *m.*, Quintus Fabius Maximus, Roman general who, by his harassing tactics and skilful avoidance of a pitched battle, wore down the strength of Hannibal.

EXERCISE 44

amor, -ōris, *m.*, love

beneficium, -iī, *n.*, kindness

captīva, -ae, *f.*, captive woman

dōnum, -ī, *n.*, gift

dōs, dōtis, *f.*, dowry

iniūria, -ae, *f.*, injury, wrong

parēns, -entis, *c.*, parent

prīnceps, -ipis, *m.*, chief

spōnsa, -ae, *f.*, betrothed

virgō, -inis, *f.*, maiden

occupō, -āre, -āvī, -ātum, to seize

tracto, -āre, -āvī, -ātum, to treat

prō (*prep. gov. abl.*), on behalf of, in return for

PROPER NAMES

Allucius, -iī, *m.*, Allucius, young Spanish chief.

Celtibērī, -ōrum, *m. pl.*, the Celtiberi, a Spanish tribe.

Scīpiō, -iōnis, *m.*, Scipio, great Roman general, who finally defeated Hannibal at battle of Zama, 202 B.C.

EXERCISE 45

carcer, -eris, *m.,* prison
locus, -ī, *m.,* place
oculus, -ī, *m.,* eye
prōvincia, -ae, *f.,* province
ruīna, -ae, *f.,* ruin
tenebrae, -ārum, *f. pl.,* darkness
unda, -ae, *f.,* wave
vōx, vōcis, *f.,* voice

coruscō, -āre, -āvī, -ātum, to flash
iubeō, -ēre, iūssī, iūssum, to order
vīvō, -ere, vīxī, vīctum, to live
occultus, -a, -um, secret
is, ea, id, that; he, she, it
prīmō, at first

Proper Names

Carthāgō, -inis, *f.,* Carthage, great city on N. coast of Africa.
Līris, -is, *m.,* the Liris, a river between Latium and Campania.
Marius, -iī, *m.,* Marius, famous Roman general whose strife with Sulla led to the first civil war at Rome.
Minturnae, -ārum, *f. pl.,* Minturnae, a town on the borders of Latium and Campania.
Minturnēnsēs, -ium, *m. pl.,* the people of Minturnae.
Sulla, -ae, *m.,* Sulla, the great rival of Marius.

EXERCISE 46

argentum, -ī, *n.,* silver
centuriō, -iōnis, *m.,* centurion
officium, -iī, *n.,* duty
pondus, -eris, *n.,* weight, mass
stultitia, -ae, *f.,* folly
tempus, -oris, *n.,* time
venia, -ae, *f.,* pardon
stultus, -a, -um, foolish
abiciō, -ere, abiēcī, abiectum, to throw away

fodiō, -ere, fōdī, fossum, to dig
inveniō, -īre, -vēnī, -ventum, to find
mūniō, -īre, -īvī, -ītum, to fortify
poenās dăre, to be punished, pay the penalty
pōnō, -ere, posuī, positum, to place, to pitch
vertō, -ere, vertī, versum, to turn

Proper Name

Pompēius, -iī, *m.,* Pompey, great Roman general who in later life was the champion of the Senate against Julius Caesar.

EXERCISE 47

aqua, -ae, *f.*, water

auctōritās, -ātis, *f.*, authority, influence

frūmentum, -ī, *n.*, corn

gladius, -iī, *m.*, sword

laus, laudis, *f.*, praise

quaestor, -ōris, *m.*, quaestor

quaestūra, -ae, *f.*, quaestorship

dīligēns, -entis, diligent

inaudītus, -a, -um, unheard
of

quid multa ?, to cut a long
story short

quid novī ?, what news ?

cēlō, -āre, -āvī, -ātum, to
hide, to conceal

PROPER NAMES

Cicerō, -ōnis, *m.*, Cicero, great Roman statesman and orator.

Puteolī, -ōrum, *m. pl.*, Puteoli, a fashionable watering-place on the coast
of Campania.

Sicilia, -ae, *f.*, Sicily.

Siculī, -ōrum, *m. pl.*, the Sicilians.

Syrācūsae, -ārum, *f. pl.*, Syracuse, the largest city of Sicily.

EXERCISE 48

fīnis, -is, *m.*, end, limit,
boundary

harundō, -inis, *f.*, reed

lūx, lūcis, *f.*, light

mandāta, -ōrum, *n. pl.*, instructions

prīma lūx, *f.*, dawn

scelus, -eris, *n.*, crime

spīritus, -ūs, *m.*, blast

tuba, -ae, *f.*, bugle

lūdō, -ere, lūsī, lūsum, to
play

praemittō, -ere, -mīsī,
-missum, to send forward

tot, so many

PROPER NAMES

Caesar, -aris, *m.*, C. Julius Caesar, the greatest of the Romans ; con-
quered Gaul, invaded Britain, fought and defeated Pompey in the
civil war ; murdered in the Senate, March 15th, 44 B.C.

Germānī, -ōrum, *m. pl.*, the Germans.

EXERCISE 49

coniūrātus, -ī, *m.*, conspirator

ġemitus, -ūs, *m.*, groan

libellus, -ī, *m.*, pamphlet

noxa, -ae, *f.*, hurt

cadō, -ere, cecidī, cāsum, to fall

cavē Īdūs Mārtiās, beware the Ides of March

legō, -ere, lēgī, lēctum, to read

obvolvō, -ere, -ī, -volūtum, to wrap

meus, mea, meum, my, mine

noster, -tra, -trum, our, ours

tuus, -a, -um, your

vester, -tra, -trum, your

vīgintī, twenty

Proper Names

Artemidōrus, -ī, *m.*, Artemidorus, a soothsayer who warned Caesar to beware of the Ides of March.

Brūtus, -ī, *m.*, Brutus, friend of Caesar who joined the conspiracy against him.

Cāsca, -ae, *m.*, Casca, one of the murderers of Caesar.

Spūrinna, -ae, *m.*, Spurinna, also a conspirator.

Tillius Cimber, *m.*, Tillius Cimber, whose petition was the beginning of the attack on Caesar.

EXERCISE 50

cōnsilium, -iī, *n.*, stratagem

exitus, -ūs, *m.*, end

lacerna, -ae, *f.*, cloak

multitūdō, -inis, *f.*, multitude, crowd

pulvis, -eris, *m.*, dust

signum, -ī, *n.*, standard

tarditās, -ātis, *f.*, slowness

aestimō, -āre, -āvī, -ātum, reckon, estimate

hīc, haec, hōc, this

scūtum, -ī, *n.*, shield

Proper Names

Antōnius, -iī, *m.*, Antony, friend and avenger of Caesar.

Cassius, -iī, *m.*, Cassius, one of the murderers of Caesar, who afterwards aided Brutus against Antony and Octavius.

Macedonia, -ae, *f.*, Macedonia, a district in Greece.

Octāvius, -iī, *m.*, nephew and adopted son of Caesar.

Philippī, -ōrum, *m. pl.*, Philippi, town in Macedonia.

Stratō, -ōnis, *m.*, Strato.

EXERCISE 51

clāssis, -is, *f.*, fleet

fuga, -ae, *f.*, flight

hōra, -ae, *f.*, hour

imperium, -iī, *n.*, power, command, authority

tyrannus, -ī, *m.*, tyrant

immemor, -ŏris, forgetful of

celebrō, -āre, -āvī, -ātum, to celebrate

colō, -ere, coluī, cultum, to till, to cultivate

vincō, -ere, vīcī, victum, to conquer

vītam agere, to spend one's life

bene, well

nōndum, not yet

ille, illa, illud, that ; he, she, it

PROPER NAMES

Actium, -iī, *n.*, Actium, promontory in W. Greece, scene of defeat of fleets of Antony and Cleopatra by Octavius in 31 B.C.

Aegyptus, -ī, *f.*, Egypt.

Āfrica, -ae, *f.*, Africa.

Augustus, -ī, *m.*, Augustus, name conferred on Octavius by the Senate after his pacification of the Roman world.

Cleopātra, -ae, *f.*, Cleopatra, the beautiful queen of Egypt.

GENERAL VOCABULARIES

1. LATIN-ENGLISH

ā, ab (*prep. gov. abl.*), from, by

abiciō, -ere, -iēcī, -iectum, throw away

accipiō, -ere, -cēpī, -ceptum, receive, accept ; **clādem accipere,** to sustain a disaster

ācer, ācris, ācre, fierce, keen, spirited

Achillēs, -is, *m.,* Achilles

Actium, -iī, *n.,* Actium

ad (*prep. gov. acc.*), to, towards, at, near.

addō, -ere, -didī, -ditum, add

aditus, -ūs, *m.,* approach

adiuvō, -āre, -iūvī, -iūtum, help, assist

aedificium, -iī, *n.,* building

aedificō, -āre, -āvī, -ātum, build

Aegyptus, -ī, *f.,* Egypt

Aenēās, -ēae, *m.,* Aeneas

aestimō, -āre, -āvī, -ātum, reckon, estimate

aeternus, -a, -um, eternal

Āfrica, -ae, *f.,* Africa

age !, agite !, come !

ager, -rī, *m.,* field

agō, -ere, ēgī, āctum, do, act ; **agere dē,** to discuss ; **grātiās agere,** to thank ; **vītam agere,** to spend *or* pass one's life

agricola, -ae, *m.,* farmer

Alba Longa, Albae Longae, *f.,* Alba Longa

albus, -a, -um, white

alius, -a, -ud, other, another

Allucius, -iī, *m.,* Allucius

altus, -a, -um, high, deep

ambulō, -āre, -āvī, -ātum, to walk

amīcus, -ī, *m.,* friend

amō, -āre, -āvī, -ātum, to love

amor, -ōris, *m.,* love

amplexus, -ūs, *m.,* embrace

Ancus Mārtius, Ancī Mārtiī, *m.,* Ancus Martius

animus, -ī, *m.,* mind

annus, -ī, *m.,* year

antīquus, -a, -um, ancient

Antōnius, -iī, *m.,* Antony

appellō, -āre, -āvī, -ātum, call

Appius Claudius, Appiī Claudiī, *m.,* Appius Claudius

aqua, -ae, *f.,* water

argentum, -ī, *n.,* silver

arma, -ōrum, *n. pl.,* arms

Artemidōrus, -ī, *m.,* Artemidorus

arx, arcis, *f.,* citadel

Asia, -ae, *f.,* Asia

attonitus, -a, -um, astounded, astonished

auctōritās, -ātis, *f.,* authority, influence

audāx, -ācis, bold

audiō, -īre, -īvī, -ītum, hear

Augustus, -i, *m.,* Augustus

aurum, -ī, *n.,* gold

auxilium, -iī, *n.*, help

āvertō, -ere, āvertī, āversum, turn away

barbarus, -ī, *m.*, barbarian, native

barbarus, -a, -um (*adj.*), barbarian, uncivilised

bellum, -ī, *n.*, war

bene (*adv.*), well

beneficium, -iī, *n.*, kindness

bonus, -a, -um, good

bōs, bŏvis, *c.*, ox, cow

brevis, -is, -e, short

Britannia, -ae, *f.*, Britain

Britannus, -ī, *m.*, a Briton

Brūtus, -ī, *m.*, Brutus

C., contraction for Gāius

cadō, -ere, cecidī, cāsum, fall

caecus, -a, -um, blind

Caesar, -aris, *m.*, Caesar

calceus, -ī, *m.*, shoe

Camillus, -ī, *m.*, Camillus

Campānia, -ae, *f.*, Campania

campus, -ī *m.*, plain ; Campus Mārtius, Campī Mārtiī, the Campus Martius

canis, -is, *c.*, dog

Cannēnsis, -is, -e, of, or belonging to, Cannae

Canusium, -iī, *n.*, Canusium

capiō, -ere, cēpī, captum, take, capture ; cōnsilium capere, to adopt a plan

captīva, -ae, *f.*, captive woman

captīvus, -ī, *m.*, captive, prisoner

caput, -itis, *n.*, head

carcer, -eris, *m.*, prison

Carthāginiēnsis, -is, *m.*, a Carthaginian

Carthāginiēnsis, -is, -e, (*adj.*), Carthaginian

Carthāgŏ, -inis, *f.*, Carthage

Cāsca, -ae, *m.*, Casca

Cassius, -iī, *m.*, Cassius

castīgō, -āre, -āvī, -ātum, chide

castra, -ōrum, *n. pl.*, camp

cavē !, cavēte !, beware ! beware of !

cēlō, -āre, -āvī, -ātum, conceal, hide

celebrō, -āre, -āvī, -ātum, celebrate

celer, celeris, celere, swift

Celtibērī, -ōrum, *m. pl.*, Celtiberi

cēna, -ae, *f.*, dinner

cēnsor, -ōris, *m.*, censor

centuriō, -iōnis, *m.*, centurion

cērae, -ārum, *f. pl.*, writing tablets

Cicerō, -ōnis, *m.*, Cicero

Cīneās, -eae, *m.*, Cineas

circum (*prep. gov. acc.*), around, round

Circus Maximus, Circī Maximī, *m.*, the Circus Maximus

cīvis, -is, *m.*, citizen

clādēs, -is, *f.*, disaster ; clādem accipere, to sustain a disaster

clāmor, -ōris, *m.*, shout

clāssis, -is, *f.*, fleet

Cleopātra, -ae, *f.*, Cleopatra

Clūsīnus, -a, -um, of, or belonging to, Clusium

collis, -is, *m.*, hill

collocō, -āre, -āvī, -ātum, place

colō, -ere, coluī, cultum, till, cultivate

comparō, -āre, -āvī, -ātum, procure

condiciō, -iōnis, *f.*, condition ; *in pl.*, terms

cōnfirmō, -āre, -āvī, -ātum, reassure

coniciō, -ere, -iēcī, -iectum, throw, hurl

coniūrō, -āre, -āvī, -ātum, conspire

coniūrātus, -ī, m., conspirator

cōnsilium, -iī, n., plan, device, stratagem ; cōnsilium capere, to adopt a plan

cōnstantia, -ae, f., constancy

cōnsul, -is, m., consul

contrā (prep. gov. acc.), against

Coriolānus, -ī, m., Coriolanus

Coriolī, -ōrum, m. pl., Corioli

cornū, -ūs, n., horn, wing (of an army).

corpus, -oris, n., body

coruscō, -āre, -āvī, -ātum, flash

crās, to-morrow

cubīle, -is, n., bed

culpō, -āre, -āvī, -ātum, blame

cum (prep. gov. abl.), with

cūr ?, why ?

cūria, -ae, f., senate-house

cursus, -ūs, m., course

cūstōs, -ōdis, m., guard

dē (prep. gov. abl.),about,concerning

dea, -ae, f., goddess

dēfendō, -ere, -ī, dēfēnsum, defend

dēfessus, -a, -um, tired, weary

deinde, afterwards, then, thereafter

dēlectō, -āre, -āvī, -ātum, delight

dēleō, -ēre, -ēvī, -ētum, destroy

dēsīderō, -āre, -āvī, -ātum, long for

dēsiliō, -īre, -siluī, -sultum, leap down

dēspērō, -āre, -āvī, -ātum, despair

deus, -ī, m., god

dextra, -ae, f., right hand

dīcō, -ere, dīxī, dictum, say

Dīdō, -ōnis, f., Dido

diēs, -ēī, m., day

difficilis, -is, -e, difficult

dignitās, -ātis, f., dignity

dīligēns, -entis, diligent

discipulus, -ī, m., pupil

dīves, -itis (adj.), rich ; (noun), rich man

diū, for a long time

dō, dăre, dĕdī, dătum, give

doceō, -ēre, -uī, doctum, teach

dolor, -ōris, m., grief, pain

dominus, -ī, m., master, lord

domus, -ūs, f., house, home

dōnum, -ī, n., gift

dōs, dōtis, f., dowry

dūco, -ere, dūxī, ductum, lead

dum, while

duo, duae, duo, two

dūrus, -a, -um, hard, harsh

dux, ducis, m., leader

ē, ex (prep. gov. abl.), from, out of

ecce !, lo ! behold ! see !

edepol !, upon my word ! goodness gracious !

ego, meī, I

ēheu !, alas !

elephantus, -ī, m., elephant

enim (conj., second word in clause), for

Ēpīrus, -ī, f., Epirus

equus, -ī, m., horse

errō, -āre, -āvī, -ātum, wander

et, and, also, even

etiam, even, also

ex, ē (prep. gov. abl.), from, out of

exclāmō, -āre, -āvī, -ātum, exclaim, shout aloud

exerceō, -ēre, -uī, -itum, exercise, train

exercitus, -ūs, m., army

exitus, -ūs, m., end

expellō, -erə, -pulī, -pulsum, drive out

exspectō, -āre, -āvī, -ātum, await, wait for, look for

extrā (*prep. gov. acc.*), outside

Fabius, -iī, *m.,* Fabius

fābula, -ae, *f.,* story

faciō, -ere, fēcī, factum, make, do ; **iter facere,** to march, to journey

factum, -ī, *n.* deed

Falēriī, -ōrum, *m. pl.,* Falerii

Faliscī, -ōrum, *m. pl.,* the Falisci, the people of Falerii

Faustulus, -ī, *m.,* Faustulus

fēlīx, -īcis, happy, fortunate, successful, lucky

fēmina, -ae, *f.,* woman

ferrum, -ī, *n.,* iron

festīnō, -āre, -āvī, -ātum, hasten, hurry

fidēs, -eī, *f.,* faith

fīlia, -ae, *f.,* daughter

fīlius, -iī (-ī), *m.,* son

fīnis, -is, *m.,* end, limit, boundary

flamma, -ae, *f.,* flame

flūmen, -inis, *n.,* river

fodiō, -ere, fōdī, fossum, dig

fortis, -is, -e, brave

fortiter, bravely

fortūna, -ae, *f.,* fortune

forum, -ī, *n.,* Forum, marketplace

fragor, -ōris, *m.,* crash

frāter, -ris, *m.,* brother

frūmentum, -ī, *n.,* corn

fuga, -ae, *f.,* flight

fugiō, -ere, fūgī, fugitum, flee

fundus, -ī, *m.,* farm

Gallia, -ae, *f.,* Gaul

Gallus, -ī (*proper name*), *m.,* Gallus

Gallus, -ī, *m.,* a Gaul

gaudium, -iī, *n.,* joy

gemitus, -ūs, *m.,* groan

gēns, gentis, *f.,* race

Germānī, -ōrum, *m. pl.,* the Germans

gerō, -ere, gessī, gestum, carry on, wage (war)

gladius, -iī, *m.,* sword

glōria, -ae, *f.,* glory

Graecia, -ae, *f.,* Greece

Graecus, -a, -um, Greek

Graecus, -ī, *m.,* a Greek

grātiae, -ārum, *f. pl.,* thanks ; **grātiās agere,** to thank

habeō, -ēre, -uī, -itum, have

habitō, -āre, -āvī, -ātum, live, dwell

harundō, -inis, *f.,* reed

hasta, -ae, *f.,* spear

Hector, -oris, *m.,* Hector

Hecuba, -ae, *f.,* Hecuba

Helena, -ae, *f.,* Helen

herī, yesterday

hīc, haec, hōc, this

hodiē, to-day

homō, -inis, *m.,* man

honestās, -ātis, *f.,* honour

honestus, -a, -um, honourable

honor, -ōris, *m.,* honour

hōra, -ae, *f.,* hour

Horātius, -iī, *m.,* Horatius

hostis, -is, *m.,* enemy

humilis, -is, -e, humble, low, lowly

iam, now, already, by this time

iānua, -ae, *f.,* door

igitur (*second word in clause*), therefore

īgnāvus, -a, -um, idle, lazy, cowardly

ignis, -is, *m.,* fire

īgnōrō, -āre, -āvī, -ātum, not to know

ille, illa, illud, that ; he, she, it

immemor, -oris, forgetful of

immortālis, -is, -e, immortal

imperātor, -ōris, *m.,* general

imperium, -iī, *n.,* power, command, authority

impetus, -ūs, *m.,* attack

in (*prep. gov. abl.*), in, on ; (*gov. acc.*), into

inaudītus, -a, -um, unheard of

incendō, -ere, -cendī, -cēnsum, burn

ingēns, -entis, huge

iniciō, -ere, -iēcī, -iectum, thrust

initium, -iī, *n.,* beginning

iniūria, -ae, *f.,* injury, wrong

inopia, -ae, *f.,* lack, scarcity, want

inquit, says *or* said he, she, it

īnsula, -ae, *f.,* island

inter (*prep. gov. acc.*), among, between

intereā, meanwhile

intrā (*prep. gov. acc.*), within, inside

intrō, -āre, -āvī, -ātum, to enter

inveniō, -īre, -vēnī, -ventum, find

īrātus, -a, -um, angry

is, ea, id, that ; he, she, it

ita, thus, so ; **ita vērō,** yes indeed

Italia, -ae, *f.,* Italy

iter, itineris, *n.,* journey, march ; **iter facere,** to march, to journey

iterum, again, for a second time

iubeō, -ēre, iūssī, iūssum, order

Iūppiter, Iovis, *m.,* Jupiter ; **Iūppiter Pluvius,** Jupiter Pluvius, Jupiter the god of rain

iūs, iūris, *n.,* right

iūstitia, -ae, *f.,* justice

iūstē, justly

iūstus, -a, -um, just

iuvenis, -is, *m.,* youth, young man

labor, -ōris, *m.,* work

labōrō, -āre, -āvī, -ātum, to work

lacerna, -ae, *f.,* cloak

lacrima, -ae, *f.,* tear

Lārs Porsinna, Lārtis Porsinnae, *m.,* Lars Porsena

lātus, -a, -um, wide, broad

laudō, -āre, -āvī, -ātum, to praise

Laurentum, -ī, *n.,* Laurentum

laus, laudis, *f.,* praise

lēgātus, -ī, *m.,* ambassador

legiō, -iōnis, *f.,* legion

legō, -ere, lēgī, lēctum, to read

libellus, -ī, *m.,* pamphlet

liber, librī, *m.,* book

līber, lībera, līberum, free

līberī, -ōrum, *m. pl.,* children

līberō, -āre, -āvī, -ātum, to free, set free

lībertus, -ī, *m.,* freedman

ligneus, -a, -um, wooden, made of wood

Līris, -is, *m.,* the Liris

littera, -ae, *f.,* letter

locus, -ī, *m.,* place, position

longus, -a, -um, long

Lūcius, -iī, *m.,* Lucius

lūdō, -ere, lūsī, lūsum, to play

lūdus, -ī, *m.,* school, game ; **lūdī magister,** schoolmaster

lupa, -ae, *f.,* she-wolf

lūx, lūcis, *f.,* light ; **prīma lūx,** dawn

Macedonia, -ae, *f.,* Macedonia

magister, -trī, *m.,* master (of a school)

magnus, -a, -um, large, big, great

mandāta, -ōrum, *n. pl.,* instructions

māne, in the morning, early

maneō, -ēre, mānsī, mānsum, to remain, stay

manus, -ūs, *f.,* hand
Marcus, ī, *m.,* Marcus
mare, -is, *n.,* sea ; **terrā marī-que,** by land and sea
Marius, -iī, *m.,* Marius
Mārs, Mārtis, *m.,* Mars
māter, -tris, *f.,* mother
mē (*acc. of* **ego**), me
medicus, -ī, *m.,* doctor
mehercule !, upon my word !
Menelāus, -ī, *m.,* Menelaus
mēnsa, -ae, *f.,* table
meus, -a, -um, my, mine
mīles, -itis, *m.,* soldier
minimē vērō, no indeed, not at all
Minturnae, -ārum, *f. pl.,* Minturnae
Minturnēnsēs, -ium, *m. pl.,* the people of Minturnae
mīrāculum, -ī, *n.,* marvel
miser, misera, miserum, wretched, unhappy ; **ō mē miserum !,** woe is me !, hang it all !
mittō, -ere, mīsī, missum, to send
modo, only ; **nōn modo . . . sed etiam,** not only . . . but also
moenia, -ium, *n. pl.,* walls (of a city)
moneō, -ēre, -uī, -itum, to warn, advise
mōns, -tis, *m.,* mountain
mors, -tis, *f.,* death
mortālis, -is, *c.,* a mortal
mōs, mōris, *m.,* custom
mox, soon, presently
Mūcius, -iī, *m.,* Mucius
multitūdō, -inis, *f.,* multitude crowd
multus, -a, -um, much ; **multī, -ae, -a,** many ; **quid multa ?,** to cut a long story short

mūniō, -īre, -īvī, -ītum, to fortify
mūrus, -ī, *m.,* wall
mūtō, -āre, -āvī, -ātum, to change

nārrō, -āre, -āvī, -ātum, to tell (a story), to relate
nauta, -ae, *m.,* sailor
nāvigō, -āre, -āvī, -ātum, to sail
nāvis, -is, *f.,* ship
necātī, -ōrum, *m. pl.,* the slain
necō, -āre, -āvī, -ātum, to kill
negōtium, -iī, *n.,* business
nihil, nothing
nisi, unless ; if . . . not
nōbilis, -is, -e, noble
nōmen, -inis, *n.,* name
nōn, not ; **nōn modo . . . sed etiam,** not only . . . but also
nōndum, not yet
noster, -tra, -trum, our, ours ; **nostrī, -ōrum,** *m. pl.,* our men
novus, -a, -um, new
nox, noctis, *f.,* night
noxa, -ae, *f.,* hurt
nūdus, -a, -um, bare, naked
nūllus, -a, -um, no, none
Numa, -ae, *m.,* Numa
numerō, -āre, -āvī, -ātum, to count
Numitor, -ōris, *m.,* Numitor
numquam, never
nūntiō, -āre, -āvī, -ātum, to announce, report
nūntius, -iī, *m.,* messenger
nusquam, nowhere

ō (*exclamation*), O !, oh !
obsideō, -ēre, -sēdī, -sessum, to besiege
obvolvō, -ere, -ī, -volūtum, to wrap

occultus, -a, -um, secret
occupō, -āre, -āvī, -ātum, to seize
Octāvius, -iī, *m.*, Octavius
oculus, -ī, *m.*, eye
officium, -iī, *n.*, duty
ōlim, once, once upon a time, formerly, some day
omnis, -is, -e, all, every
onus, -eris, *n.*, burden
oppidum, -ī, *n.*, town
oppugnō, -āre, -āvī, -ātum, to attack
Orbilius, -iī, *m.*, Orbilius
orbis, -is, *m.*, circle ; orbis terrārum, the world
ōrnō, -āre, -āvī, -ātum, to adorn
os, ossis, *n.*, bone

paene, almost
Palamēdes, -is, *m.*, Palamedes
parātus, -a, -um, prepared, ready
parēns, -tis, *c.*, parent
Paris, -idis, *m.*, Paris (son of Priam)
parō, -āre, -āvī, -ātum, to prepare
pars, partis, *f.*, part
parvus, -a, -um, small, little
pāstor, -ōris, *m.*, shepherd
pater, -tris, *m.*, father ; patrēs, -trum, senators
patria, -ae, *f.*, native land
paucī, -ae, -a, few
pauper, -is, poor
pāx, pācis, *f.*, peace
per (*prep. gov. acc.*), through, throughout, over
perīculum, -ī, *n.*, danger
permūtātiō, -iōnis, *f.*, exchange
pēs, pedis, *m.*, foot
petasus, -ī, *m.*, hat

Philippī, -ōrum, *m. pl.*, Philippi
pila, -ae, *f.*, ball
plāgōsus, -a, -um, full of blows
pluit, it rains
Pluvius, see Iuppiter Pluvius
poenās dō, dare, dedī, datum, to be punished
poēta, -ae, *m.*, poet
Pompēius, -iī, *m.*, Pompey
pondus, -eris, *n.*, weight
pōnō, -ere, posuī, positum, to place, pitch
pōns, -tis, *m.*, bridge
populus, -ī, *m.*, people
Porsinna, -ae, *m.*, Porsena
porta, -ae, *f.*, gate
portō, -āre, -āvī, -ātum, carry
post (*prep. gov. acc.*), after
praeda, -ae, *f.*, booty
praemittō, -ere, -mīsī, -missum, to send forward
pretium, -iī, *n.*, price
Priamus, -ī, *m.*, Priam
prīmum, firstly, in the first place
prīmō, at first
prīmus, -a, -um, first ; prīma lūx, dawn
prīnceps, -cipis, *m.*, chief
prō (*prep. gov. abl.*), on behalf of, in return for
proelium, -iī, *n.*, battle
propter (*prep. gov. acc.*), on account of
prōvincia, -ae, *f.*, province
proximus, -a, -um, next
puella, -ae, *f.*, girl
puer, -ī, *m.*, boy
pugna, -ae, *f.*, battle, fight
pugnō, -āre, -āvī, -ātum, to fight
pulcher, -ra, -rum, beautiful
pulvis, pulveris, *m.*, dust
Puteolī, -ōrum, *m. pl.*, Puteoli
Pyrrhus, -ī, *m*, Pyrrhus

Q., abbreviation for **Quīntus**

quaestor, -ōris *m.*, quaestor

quaestūra, -ae, *f.*, quaestorship

quam !, how !, what !

quandō ? when ?

quārtus, -a, -um, fourth

quattuor, four

-que, and

quem? (*acc. sing. of* **quis ?**), whom?

quid ?, what ? ; **quid multa ?**, to cut a long story short ; **quid novī ?**, what news ?

Quīntus, -ī, *m.*, Quintus

quīntus, -a, -um, fifth

quis ?, who ?

quō ?, whither ?, where . . . to ?

quod, because

quot ?, how many ?

recitō, -āre, -āvī, -ātum, to read (aloud)

reddō, -ere, reddidī, redditum, to restore, give back

rēgia, -ae, *f.*, palace

rēgīna, -ae, *f.*, queen

rēgnum, -ī, *n.*, kingdom

regō, -ere, rēxī, rēctum, to rule

Remus, -ī, *m.*, Remus

reportō, -āre, -āvī, -ātum, to bring back

rēs, reī, *f.*, thing, business, affair, matter ; **rēs pūblica**, state, republic

rēx, rēgis, *m.*, king

rīdeō, -ēre, rīsī, rīsum, laugh, laugh at

rīpa, -ae, *f.*, bank (of a river)

rīsus, -ūs, *m.*, smile

rogō, -āre, -āvī, -ātum, ask, ask for

Rōma, -ae, *f.*, Rome

Rōmānus, -ī, *m.*, a Roman

Rōmānus, -a, -um, Roman

Rōmulus, -ī, *m.*, Romulus

rosa, -ae, *f.*, rose

Rōstra, -ōrum, *n. pl.*, the Rostra

ruīna, -ae, *f.*, ruin

sacer, -ra, -rum, sacred

sacerdōs, -dōtis, *m.*, priest

sacrificium, -iī, *n.*, sacrifice

saepe, often

sagitta, -ae, *f.*, arrow

salūtō, -āre, -āvī, -ātum, to greet, salute

salvē, salvēte, good morning, good day, hail !

sanguis, sanguinis, *m.*, blood

satis, enough

Scaevola, -ae, *m.*, Scaevola

scelestus, -a, -um, wicked

scelus, -eris, *n.*, crime

Scīpiō, -iōnis, *m.*, Scipio

scrība, -ae, *m.*, clerk, secretary

scrībō, -ere, scrīpsī, scrīptum, to write

scūtum, -ī, *n.*, shield

secundus, -a, -um, second

sed, but

sedeō, -ēre, sēdī, sessum, to sit

sella, -ae, *f.*, seat, chair

semper, always

senātor, -ōris, *m.*, senator

senātus, -ūs, *m.*, senate

senex, senis, *m.*, old man

sepeliō, -īre, -īvī, sepultum, to bury

septem, seven

septimus, -a, -um, seventh

sermō, -ōnis, *m.*, talk

sērō, late

servō, -āre, -āvī, -ātum, save, protect

servus, -ī, *m.*, slave

Sextus, -ī, *m.*, Sextus

sī, if

sīc, thus, so

Sicilia, -ae, *f.*, Sicily

Sĭculī, -ōrum, *m. pl.,* Sicilians

sīcut, just as

sĭgnum, -ī, *n.,* signal, standard

silva, -ae, *f.,* wood

similis, -is, -e, like

sine (*prep. gov. abl.*), without

Sinōn, -is, *m.,* Sinon

socius, -iī, *m.,* ally, companion

sōl, sōlis, *m.,* sun ; **sōl occĭdēns,** the West

sollicitus, -a, -um, anxious, troubled

sordidus, -a, -um, dirty

Sparta, -ae, *f.,* Sparta

spatium, -iī, *n.,* space, interval

spēs, speī, *f.,* hope

spīritus, -ūs, *m.,* blast

spōnsa, -ae, *f.,* betrothed

Spūrinna, -ae, *m.,* Spurinna

statim, at once, immediately

statiō, -iōnis, *f.,* outpost

statua, -ae, *f.,* statue

stilus, -ī, *m.,* pen

stīpendium, -iī, *n.,* pay

stō, stāre, stetī, stātum, to stand

Stratō, -ōnis, *m.,* Strato

strenuus, -a, -um, active, energetic

stultitia, -ae, *f.,* folly

stultus, -a, -um, foolish

Sulla, -ae, *m.,* Sulla

sum, esse, fuī, to be

super (*prep. gov. acc.*), above, over

superō, -āre, -āvī, -ātum, to overcome

sustineō, -ēre, -tinuī, -tentum, to withstand

Syrācūsae, -ārum, *f. pl.,* Syracuse

Syrus, -ī, *m.,* Syrus

taberna, -ae, *f.,* inn, shop

tam, so

tamen, however, nevertheless

tandem, at length

tardĭtās, -ātis, *f.,* slowness

Tarentīnī, -ōrum, *m. pl.,* the Tarentines

Tarquinius, -iī, *m.,* Tarquin

tēlum, -ī, *n.,* weapon

templum, -ī, *n.,* temple

tempus, -oris, *n.,* time

tendō, -ere, tetendī, stretch, stretch out

tenebrae, -ārum, *f. pl.,* darkness

terra, -ae, *f.,* land ; **terrā marīque,** by land and sea ; **orbis terrārum,** world

terreō, -ēre, -uī, -itum, frighten

tertius, -a, -um, third

Tiberīnus, -a, -um, of, or belonging to, the Tiber ; **Pater Tiberīnus,** the god of the river Tiber, " Father Tiber "

Tiberis, -is, *m.,* the Tiber

timeō, ēre, -uī, to fear

Titus, -ī, *m.,* Titus

toga, -ae, *f.,* toga

togātus, -a, -um, clad in the toga

tot, so many

tōtus, -a, -um, whole, entire ; **tōtus esse in,** to be engrossed in

tractō, -āre, -āvī, -ātum, to treat

trādō, -ere, -didī, -ditum, to hand over

trahō, -ere, traxī, tractum, to drag

trāns (*prep. gov. acc.*), across

trecentī, -ae, -a, three hundred

trīstis, -is, -e, sad

Trōia, -ae, *f.,* Troy

Trōiānus, -ī, *m.,* a Trojan

Trōiānus, -a, -um, Trojan

trux, trucis, grim

tū, tuī, you (*sing.*)

tuba, -ae, *f.,* bugle

Tullius, -iī, *m.,* Tullius
tum, then
tunica, -ae, *f.,* tunic
tuus, -a, -um, your
tyrannus, -ī, *m.,* tyrant

ubi ?, where ?
ubi, when
umquam, ever
unda, -ae, *f.,* wave
unde ? whence ?, where . . . from ?
ūnus, -a, -um, one
urbs, urbis, *f.,* city
ūtilis, -is, -e, useful
uxor, -ōris, *f.,* wife

Vae ! (*exclamation*), woe ! ; **vae tibi !,** woe to thee !
valē, valēte, good-bye, farewell
Valerius, -iī, *m.,* Valerius
Varrō, -ōnis, *m.,* Varro
vāstō, -āre, -āvī, -ātum, to lay waste
venēnum, -ī, *n.,* poison
venia, -ae, *f.,* pardon
veniō, -īre, vēnī, ventum, to come
verberō, -āre, -āvī, -ātum, to beat
vērō, indeed ; **ita vērō,** yes indeed
vertō, -ere, vertī, versum, to turn

Vesta, -ae, *f.,* Vesta
vester, -tra, -trum, your
vestīmentum, -ī, *n.,* garment ; **vestīmenta, -ōrum,** garments, clothes
Veturia, -ae, *f.,* Veturia
vetus, -eris, old
via, -ae, *f.,* way, road
victōria, -ae, *f.,* victory
vīcus, -ī, *m.,* street
videō, -ēre, vīdī, vīsum, to see
vīlis, -is, -e, cheap
vīlla, -ae, *f.,* country house
vir, -ī, *m.,* man
virga, -ae, *f.,* rod
virgō, -inis, *f.,* maiden
virtūs, -ūtis, *f.,* valour, courage
vīs, *f.* (*sing.*), force, violence ; (*pl.*), strength
vīta, -ae, *f.,* life ; **vītam agere,** to spend or pass one's life
vītō, -āre, -āvī, -ātum, to avoid
vīvō, -ere, vīxī, vīctum, to live
Volumnia, -ae, *f.,* Volumnia
vōs, vestrum (vestrī), you (*pl.*)
vōx, vōcis, *f.,* voice
vulnerō, -āre, -āvī, -ātum, to wound
vulnus, -eris, *n.,* a wound
vultus, -ūs, *m.,* expression, countenance

II. ENGLISH–LATIN

About, dē (*with abl.*)
above, super (*with acc.*)
accept, accipiŏ, -ere, accēpī, acceptum
active, strenuus, -a, -um
adopt a plan, cōnsilium capere
adorn, ŏrnō, -āre, -āvī, -ātum
advise, moneō, -ēre, -uī, monitum
after, post (*with acc.*)
again, iterum
against, contrā (*with acc.*)
alas !, ēheu !
all, omnis, -is, -e
ally, socius, -iī, *m.*
almost, paene
already, iam
also, et
always, semper
ambassador, lēgātus, -ī, *m.*
among, inter (*with acc.*)
ancient, antīquus, -a, -um
and, et, -que
angry, īrātus, -a, -um
announce, nūntiō, -āre, -āvī, -ātum
anxious, sollicitus, -a, -um
approach, aditus, -ūs, *m.*
army, exercitus, -ūs, *m.*
arrow, sagitta, -ae, *f.*
ask, ask for, rogō, -āre, -āvī, -ātum
astounded, attonitus, -a, -um
at last, tandem
attack, oppugnō, -āre, -āvī, -ātum
attack, impetus, -ūs, *m.*
avoid, vītō, -āre, -āvī, -ātum
await, exspectō, -āre, -āvī, -ātum
Augustus, Augustus, -ī, *m.*
authority, imperium, -iī, *n.*

Ball, pila, -ae, *f.*
bank (of a river), rīpa, -ae, *f.*

barbarian, barbarus, -ī, *m.*
bare, nūdus, -a, -um
battle, proelium, -iī, *n.*; pugna, -ae, *f.*
be, to, sum, esse, fuī
beat, verberō, -āre, -āvī, -ātum
beautiful, pulcher, pulchra, pulchrum
because, quod
bed, cubīle, -is, *n.*
beginning, initium, -iī, *n.*
behalf, on behalf of, prō (*with abl.*)
besiege, obsideō, -ēre, -sēdī, -sessum
betrothed, spōnsa, -ae, *f.*
between, inter (*with acc.*)
beware, cavē, cavetē
big, magnus, -a, -um
blame, culpō, -āre, -āvī, -ātum
blast, spīritus, -ūs, *m.*
blind, caecus, -a, -um
body, corpus, -oris, *n.*
bold, audāx, -ācis
bone, os, ossis, *n.*
book, līber, librī, *m.*
booty, praeda, -ae, *f.*
boundary, fīnis, -is, *m.*
boy, puer, -ī, *m.*
brave, fortis, -is, -e
bravely, fortiter
bridge, pōns, -tis, *m.*
Britain, Britannia, -ae, *f.*
broad, lātus, -a, -um
brother, frāter, -tris, *m.*
Brutus, Brūtus, -ī, *m.*
bugle, tŭba, -ae, *f.*
build, aedificō, -āre, -āvī, -ātum
building, aedificium, -iī, *n.*
burden, onus, -eris, *n.*
burn, incendō, -ere, -cendī, -cēnsum.

bury, sepeliō, -īre, -īvī, sepultum
business, negōtium, -iī, *n.*
but, sed
by, ā, ab (*with abl.*)
by land and sea, terrā marīque

Caesar, Caesar, -is, *m.*
call, appellō, -āre, -āvī, -ātum
camp, castra, -ōrum, *n. pl.*
captive, captīvus, -ī, *m.*
capture, capiō, -ere, cēpī, captum
carry, portō, -āre, -āvī, -ātum
Carthage, Carthāgō, -inis, *f.*
Carthaginian, Carthāginiēnsis, -is, *m.*
celebrate, celebrō, -āre, -āvī, -ātum
centurion, centuriō, -iōnis, *m.*
change, mūtō, -āre, -āvī, -ātum
chair, sella, -ae, *f.*
cheap, vīlis, -is, -e
chide, castīgō, -āre, -āvī, -ātum
chief, prīnceps, -cipis, *m.*
children, līberī, -ōrum, *m. pl.*
Cicero, Cicerō, -ōnis, *m.*
citadel, arx, arcis, *f.*
citizen, cīvis, -is, *m.*
city, urbs, -is, *f.*
city walls, moenia, -ium, *n. pl.*
cloak, lacerna, -ae, *f.*
clothes, vestīmenta, -ōrum, *n. pl.*
come, age, agite
come, to, veniō, -īre, vēni, ventum
command, imperium, iī, *n.*
companion, socius, -iī, *m.*
concerning, dē (*with abl.*)
condition, condiciō, -ōnis, *f.*
conspirator, coniūrātus, -ī, *m.*
conspire, coniūrō, -āre, -āvī, -ātum
constancy, cōnstantia, -ae, *f.*
consul, cōnsul, -is, *m.*
Coriolanus, Coriolānus, -ī, *m.*
corn, frūmentum, -ī, *n.*

count, numerō, -āre, -āvī, -ātum
country, native country, patria, -ae, *f.*
country house, vīlla, -ae, *f.*
courage, virtūs, -ūtis, *f.*
course, cursus, -ūs, *m.*
crash, fragor, -is, *m.*
crime, scelus, -eris, *n.*
cultivate, colō, -ere, -uī, cultum
custom, mōs, mōris, *m.*

Danger, perīculum, -ī, *n.*
darkness, tenebrae, -ārum, *f. pl.*
daughter, fīlia, -ae, *f.*
day, diēs, -ēī, *m.*
dawn, prīma lūx, *f.*
death, mors, mortis, *f.*
defeat, clādēs, -is, *f.*
defend, dēfendō, -ere, -ī, dēfēnsum
delight, dēlectō, -āre, -āvī, -ātum
despair, dēspērō, -āre, -āvī, -ātum
destroy, dēleō, -ēre, -ēvī, -ētum
difficult, difficilis, -is, -e
dig, fodiō, -ere, fōdī, fossum
dignity, dignitās, -ātis, *f.*
diligent, dīligēns, -entis
dinner, cēna, -ae, *f.*
dirty, sordidus, -a, -um
disaster, clādēs, -is, *f.*
discuss, agere dē (*with abl.*)
do, faciō, -ere, fēcī, factum
doctor, medicus, -ī, *m.*
dog, canis, -is, *c.*
door, iānua, -ae, *f.*
dowry, dōs, dōtis, .
drag, trahō, -ere, traxī, tractum *f.*
drive out, expellō, -ere, -pulī, -pulsum
dust, pulvis, -eris, *m.*
duty, officium, -iī, *n.*

Early (in the morning), māne
elephant, elephantus, -ī, *m.*

end, fīnis, -is, *m.* ; exitus, -ūs, *m.*

enemy, hostis, -is, *m.*

energetic, strenuus, -a, -um

engrossed in, tōtus sum in (*with abl.*)

enough, satis (*indeclinable*)

enter, intrō, -āre, -āvī, -ātum

eternal, aeternus, -a, -um

even, et, etiam

exchange, permūtātiō, -iōnis, *f.*

exercise, exerceō, -ēre, -uī, exercitum

Face, vultus, -ūs, *m.*

faith, fidēs, -eī, *f.*

farewell, valē, -ēte

farm, fundus, -ī, *m.*

farmer, agricola, -ae, *m.*

father, pater, -ris, *m.*

fear, timeō, -ēre, -uī

few, paucī, -ōrum, *m. pl.*

field, ager, -rī, *m.*

fierce, ācer, ācris, ācre

fifth, quīntus, -a, -um

fight, pugnō, -āre, -āvī, -ātum

find, inveniō, -īre, -vēnī, -ventum

fire, ignis, -is, *m.*

first, firstly, in the first place, prīmum; at first, prīmō

first (*adj.*), prīmus, -a, -um

flame, flamma, -ae, *f.*

flee, fugiō, -ere, fūgī, fugitum

fleet, clāssis, -is, *f.*

flight, fuga, -ae, *f.*

folly, stultitia, -ae, *f.*

foolish, stultus, -a, -um

foot, pēs, pedis, *m.*

for, enim (*second word in clause*)

for a long time, diū

force, vīs, vim, vī, *f.*

forgetful, immemor, -oris (*with gen.*)

fortify, mūniō, -īre, -īvī, -ītum

fortune, fortūna, -ae, *f.*

forum, forum, -ī, *n.*

four, quattuor (*indeclinable*)

fourth, quārtus, -a, -um

free (*adj.*), līber, lībera, līberum

free, to set free, līberō, -āre, -āvī, -ātum

freedman, lībertus, -ī, *m.*

friend, amīcus, -ī, *m.*

frighten, terreō, -ēre, -uī, -itum

from, ē, ex, ā, ab (*with abl.*)

Gallus, Gallus, -ī, *m.*

game, lūdus, -ī, *m.*

garment, vestīmentum, -ī, *n.*

gate, porta, -ae, *f.*

Gaul, Gallia, -ae, *f.*

general, imperātor, -ōris, *m.*

gift, dōnum, -ī, *n.*

girl, puella, -ae, *f.*

give, dō, dăre, dedī, datum

glory, glōria, -ae, *f.*

god, deus, deī, *m.*

goddess, dea, -ae, *f.*

gold, aurum, -ī, *n.*

good, bonus, -a, -um

good-bye, valē, valēte

good day, salvē, salvēte

good morning, salvē, salvēte

great, magnus, -a, -um

Greece, Graecia, -ae, *f.*

Greek (*noun*), Graecus, -ī, *m.*

Greek (*adj.*), Graecus, -a, -um

greet, salūtō, -āre, -āvī, -ātum

grief, dolor, -ōris, *m.*

grim, trux, trucis

groan, gemitus, -ūs, *m.*

guard, custōs, -ōdis, *m.*

Hail, salvē, salvēte

hand, manus, -ūs, *f.*

hand over, trādō, -ere, -didī, -ditum

hang it all, ō mē miserum !

happy, fēlīx, -īcis

hard, dūrus, -a, -um.
hasten, festīnō, -āre, -āvī, -ātum
hat, petasus, -ī, *m.*
have, habeō, -ēre, -uī, -itum
he, she, it, is, ea, id
head, caput, -itis, *n.*
hear, audiō, -īre, -īvī, -ītum
Hector, Hector, -oris, *m.*
help, auxilium, iī, *n.*
herself, sē (*reflexive*) ; ipsa (*emphasising*)
hide, cēlō, -āre, -āvī, -ātum
hill, collis, -is, *m.*
himself, sē (*reflexive*) ; ipse (*emphasising*)
hold out, tendō, -ere, tetendī, tentum (-sum)
honour, honor, -ōris, *m.*
honourable, honestus, -a, -um
hope, spēs, -eī, *f.*
Horatius, Horātius, -iī, *m.*
horn, cornū, -ūs, *n.*
horse, equus, -ī, *m.*
house, home, domus, -ūs, *f.*
house, country house, vīlla, -ae, *f.*
how !, quam !
however, tamen
how many ?, quot ? (*indeclinable*)
huge, ingēns, -entis
hurry, festīnō, -āre, -āvī, -ātum

I, ego
Ides of March, Īdūs Mārtiae, *f. pl.*
idle, īgnāvus, -a, -um
if, sī
immediately, statim
in, in (*with abl.*)
in the morning, māne
injury, iniūria -ae, *f.*
inn, taberna, -ae, *f.*
instructions, mandāta, -ōrum, *n. pl.*

into, in (*with acc.*)
iron, ferrum, -ī, *n.*
island, īnsula, -ae, *f*
Italy, Ītalia, -ae, *f.*
itself, sē (*reflexive*) ; ipse, ipsa, ipsum (*emphasising*)

Journey (*noun*), iter, itineris, *n.*
journey (*verb*), iter facere
joy, gaudium, -iī, *n.*
just, iūstus, -a, -um

Keen, ācer, -ācris, ācre
kill, necō, -āre, -āvī, -ātum
kindle, incendō, -ere, incendī, incēnsum
kindness, beneficium, -iī, *n.*
king, rēx, rēgis, *m.*
kingdom, rēgnum, -ī, *n.*
know, not to, īgnōrō, -āre, -āvī, -ātum

Lack, inopia, -ae, *f.*
land, terra, -ae, *f.*
land, native, patria, -ae, *f.*
large, magnus, -a, -um
late, sērō
laugh, laugh at, rīdeō, -ēre, rīsī, rīsum
lay waste, vāstō, -āre, -āvī, -ātum
lazy, īgnāvus, -a, um
lead, dūcō, -ere, dūxī, ductum
leader, dux, ducis, *m.*
leap down, dēsiliō, -īre, -uī, -sultum
legion, legiō, -iōnis, *f.*
letters, litterae, -ārum, *f. pl.*
life, vīta, -ae, *f.*
light, lūx, lūcis, *f.*
like, similis, -is, -e
little, parvus, -a, -um
live, dwell, habitō, -āre, -āvī, -ātum
live, exist, vīvō, -ere, vīxī, vīctum

lo ! look, !, ecce !

long, longus, -a, -um

long, for a long time, diū

long for, dēsīderō, -āre, -āvī, -ātum

look for, exspectō, -āre, -āvī,-ātum

love (*noun*), amor, -ōris, *m.*

love (*verb*), amō, -āre, -āvī, -ātum

low, humilis, -is, -e

Lucius, Lūcius, -iī, *m.*

lucky, fēlīx, -īcis

Maiden, virgō, -inis, *f.*

make, faciō, -ere, fēcī, factum

man, homō, -inis, *m.* ; vir, -ī, *m.*

many, multī, -ae, -a

mass, pondus, -eris, *n.*

master (who owns), dominus, -ī, *m.*

master (who teaches), magister, -trī, *m.*

marvel, mīrāculum, -ī, *n.*

me, mē

meanwhile, intereā

messenger, nūntius, -iī,*m.*

mind, animus, -ī, *m.*

morning, in the, māne

mortal, mortālis, -is, -e

mother, māter, -tris, *f.*

mountain, mōns, montis, *m.*

much, multus, -a, -um

multitude, multitūdō, -inis, *f.*

my, mine, meus, -a, -um

myself (*reflexive*), mē

Name, nōmen, -inis, *n.*

native land, patria, -ae, *f.*

never, numquam

new, novus, -a, -um

next, deinde

next (*adj.*), proximus, -a, -um

night, nox, noctis, *f.*

no, none, nūllus, -a, -um

no indeed, minimē vērō

noble, nōbilis, -is, -e

not, nōn

not to know, īgnorāre

nothing, nihil

now, iam

nowhere, nusquam

Occupy, occupō, -āre, -āvī, -ātum

often, saepe

old, vetus, -eris

old man, senex, senis, *m.*

on, in (*with abl.*)

on account of, propter (*with acc.*)

once, once upon a time, ōlim

one, ūnus, -a, -um

order, iubeō, -ēre, iūssī, iūssum

our, ours, noster, -tra, -trum

our men, nostrī, -ōrum, *m. pl.*

out of, ex, ē (*with abl.*)

outside, outside of, extrā (*with acc.*)

over, super (*with acc.*)

overcome, superō, -āre, -āvī, -ātum

ox, cow, bōs, bovis, *c.*

Pain, dolor, -ōris, *m.*

palace, rēgia, -ae, *f.*

pamphlet, libellus, -ī, *m.*

pardon, venia, -ae, *f.*

parent, parēns, -entis, *c.*

part, pars, partis, *f.*

pay, stīpendium, -iī, *n.*

pay the penalty, poenās dăre

peace, păx, pācis

pen, stilus, -ī, *m.*

people, populus, -ī, *m.*

pitch, pōnō, -ere, posuī, positum

place, locus, -ī, *m.*

place (*verb*), collocō, -āre, -āvī, -ātum ; pōnō, -ere, posuī, positum

plain, campus, -ī, *m.*

plan, cōnsilium, -iī, *n.*

play, lūdō, -ere, lūsī, lūsum

poet, poēta, -ae, *m.*
poison, venēnum, -ī, *n.*
Pompey, Pompēius, -iī, *m.*
poor, pauper, -is
power, imperium, -iī, *n.*
praise, laus, -dis, *f.*
praise (*verb*), laudō, -āre, -āvī,
  -ātum
prepare, parō, -āre, -āvī, -ātum
prepared, ready, parātus, -a, -um
presently, mox
Priam, Priamus, -ī, *m.*
price, pretium, -iī, *n.*
priest, sacerdōs, -dōtis, *m.*
prison, carcer, -is, *m.*
prisoner, captīvus, -ī, *m.*
procure, comparō, -āre, -āvī,
  -ātum
protect, servō, -āre, -āvī, -ātum
province, prōvincia, -ae, *f.*
punished, to be, poenās dăre
pupil, discipulus, -ī, *m.*

Quaestor, quaestor, -ōris, *m.*
quaestorship, quaestūra -ae, *f.*
queen, rēgīna, -ae, *f.*
Quintus, Quīntus, -ī, *m.*

Race, gēns, gentis, *f.*
rains, it rains, pluit
read, legō, -ere, lēgī, lēctum
read aloud, recitō, -āre, -āvī,
  -ātum
reassure, cōnfirmō, -āre, -āvī,
  -ātum
receive, accipiō, -ere, -cēpī, -cep-
  tum
reed, harundō, -inis, *f.*
relate, nārrō, -āre, -āvī, -ātum
remain, maneō, ēre, mānsī, mānsum
report, nūntiō, -āre, -āvī, -ātum
republic, rēs pūblica, reī pūblicae,
  f.

restore, reddō, -ere, -didī, -ditum
return, in return for, prō (*with
  abl.*)
rich, dīves, -itis
right hand, dextra, -ae, *f.*
river, flūmen, -inis, *n.*
road, via, -ae, *f.*
rod, virga, -ae, *f.*
Roman (*noun*), Rōmānus, -ī, *m.*
Roman, (*adj.*), Rōmānus, -a, -um
Rome, Rōma, -ae, *f.*
rose, rosa, -ae, *f.*
rostra, rōstra, -ōrum, *n. pl.*
round (*prep.*), circum (*with acc.*)
ruin, ruīna, -ae, *f.*
rule, regō, -ere, rēxī, rēctum

Sacred, sacer, -ra, -rum
sacrifice, sacrificium, -iī, *n.*
sad, trīstis, -is, -e
sail, nāvigō, -āre, -āvī, -ātum
sailor, nauta, -ae, *m.*
salute, salūtō, -āre, -āvī, -ātum
save, servō, -āre, -āvī, -ātum
say, dīcō, -ere, dīxī, dictum
says he, she, it, inquit
scarcity, inopia, -ae, *f.*
Scipio, Scīpiō, -iōnis, *m.*
school, lūdus, -ī, *m.*
schoolmaster, lūdī magister, -trī,
  m.
sea, mare, maris, *n.*
seat, sella, -ae, *f.*
second, secundus, -a, -um
secret, occultus, -a, -um
see, videō, -ēre, vīdī, vīsum
see !, ecce !
seize, occupō, -āre, -āvī, -ātum
self, ipse, -a, -um
senate, senātus, -ūs, *m.*
senate house, cūria, -ae, *f.*
senator, senātor, -ōris, *m.*
senators, patrēs, -um, *m. pl.*
send, mittō, -ere, mīsī, missum

send forward, praemittō, -ere, -mīsī, -missum
set free, līberō, -āre, -āvī, -ātum
seven, septem (*indeclinable*)
seventh, septimus, -a, -um
Sextus, Sextus, -ī, *m.*
she-wolf, lupa, -ae, *f.*
shepherd, pāstor, -ōris, *m.*
ship, nāvis, -is, *f.*
shoe, calceus, -ī, *m.*
shop, taberna, -ae, *f.*
short, brevis, -is, -e
shout, clāmor, -ōris, *m.*
signal, signum, -ī, *n.*
silver, argentum, -ī, *n.*
sit, sedeō, -ēre, sēdī, sessum
slain, the slain, necātī, -ōrum, *m. pl.*
slave, servus, -ī, *m.*
slowness, tarditās, -ātis, *f.*
small, parvus, -a, -um
smile, rīsus, -ūs, *m.*
so, ita, sīc
soldier, mīles, -itis, *m.*
son, fīlius, -iī, *m.*
soon, mox
spear, hasta, -ae, *f.*
spirited, ācer, ācris, ācre
Spurinna, Spūrinna, -ae, *m.*
stand, stō, stāre, stetī, stātum
standard, signum, -ī, *n.*
state, rēs pūblica, reī pūblicae, *f.*
story, fābula, -ae, *f.*
story, to cut a long story short, quid multa ?
stratagem, cōnsilium, -iī, *n.*
street, vīcus, -ī, *m.*
strength, vīrēs, -ium, *f. pl.*
stretch out, tendō, -ere, tetendī, tentum (-sum)
sun, sōl, sōlis, *m.*
sustain (disaster), clādem accipere
swift, celer, celeris, celere

sword, gladius, -iī, *m.*
Syrus, Syrus, -ī, *m.*

Table, mēnsa, -ae, *f.*
tablets, cērae, -ārum, *f.*
take, lead, dūcō, -ere, dūxī, ductum
take, capiō, -ere, cēpī, captum
talk, sermō, -ōnis, *m.*
teach, doceō, -ēre, -uī, doctum
tear, lacrima, -ae, *f.*
tell, nārrō, -āre, -āvī, -ātum
temple, templum, -ī, *n.*
terrify, terreō, -ēre, -uī, -itum
thank, grātiās agere
that, is, ea, id ; ille, illa, illud
themselves (*reflexive*), sē
then, tum
therefore, igitur (*second word in clause*)
thing, rēs, reī, *f.*
three, trēs, trēs, tria
three hundred, trecentī, -ae, -a
through, per (*with acc.*)
throughout, per (*with acc.*)
throw away, abiciō, -ere, -iēcī, -iectum
thrust, iniciō, -ere, -iēcī, -iectum
thus, ita, sīc
Tiber, Tiberis, -is, *m.*
time, tempus, -oris, *n.*
tired, dēfessus, -a, -um
Titus, Titus, -ī, *m.*
to, towards, ad (*with acc.*)
to-day, hodiē
toga, toga, -ae, *f.*
toga-clad, togātus, -a, -um
to-morrow, crās
town, oppidum, -ī, *n.*
train, exerceō, -ēre, -uī, -itum
Trojan (*noun*), Trōiānus, -ī, *m.*
Trojan (*adj.*), Trōiānus, -a, -um
troubled, sollicitus, -a, -um
Troy, Trōia, -ae, *f.*

Tullius, Tullius, -iī, *m.*
tunic, tunica, -ae, *f.*
turn, vertō, -ere, verti, versum
turn away, āvertere
two, duo, duae, duo

Unhappy, miser, misera, miserum
unheard of, inaudītus, -a, -um
unless, nisi
upon my word, mehercule ; edepol
useful ūtilis, -is, -e

Valerius, Valerius, -iī, *m.*
valour virtūs, -ūtis, *f.*
Vesta, Vesta, -ae, *f.*
victory, victōria, -ae, *f.*
violence, vīs, vim, vī, *f.*
voice, vōx, vōcis, *f.*

Wage (war), gerō, -ere, gessī, gestum
wait for, exspectō, -āre,-āvi, -ātum
walk, ambulō, -āre, -āvī, -ātum
wall, mūrus, -ī, *m.*
walls, city walls, moenia, -ium,
  n. pl.
wander, errō, -āre, -āvi, -ātum
war, bellum, -ī, *n.*
warn, moneō, -ēre, -uī, -itum
warship, nāvis longa, *f.*
waste, lay waste, vāstō, -āre,
  -āvī, ātum
water, aqua, -ae, *f.*
way, via, -ae, *f.*
weapon, tēlum, -ī, *n.*
weart, fessus, -a, -um ; dēfessus,
  -a, -um
well, bene
West, sōl occidēns
what ?, quid ?
what—!, what a—!, quam—!
what news ?, quid novī ?
when, ubi
when ?, quandō ?

where ?, ubi ?
where to ? quō ?
where from ? unde ?
white, albus, -a, -um
whither ? quō ?
who ?, quis ?
whom ? quem ?
why ?, cūr ?
wicked, scelestus, -a, -um
wide, lātus, -a, -um
wife, uxor, -ōris, *f.*
wing (of army), cornū, -ūs, *n.*
with, cum (*with abl.*)
within, intrā (*with acc.*)
withstand, sustineō, -ēre, -uī
  -tentum
woe is me ! Ō mē miserum !
woe to you, vae tibi !
woman, fēmina, ae, *f.*
wood, silva, ae, *f.*
wooden, ligneus, -a, -um
work, labor, -ōris, *m.*
work, to, labōrō, -āre, -āvī, -ātun
world, orbis terrārum, *m.*
wound, vulnerō, -āre, -āvī, -ātum
wound (*noun*), vulnus, -eris, *n.*
wrap, obvolvō, -ere, -volvi, -volū
  tum
wretched, miser, misera, miserun
write, scrībō, -ere, scrīpsī, scrip
  tum
writing tablets, cērae, -ārum, *f, pl*

Year, annus, -ī, *m.*
yes, yes indeed, ita vērō
yesterday, herī
you, tū, tuī ; vōs, vestrum (vestrī
young man iuvenis, -is, *m.*
yours, tuus, -a, -um ; vester, -tra
  -trum
yourself (*reflexive*), tē
yourselves (*reflexive*), vōs
youth, iuvenis, -is, *m.*